PLACES I REMEMBER

Liverpool FC European Adventures as told by the Fans.

Commemorating the 50th Anniversary of Liverpool F.C. in Europe
Dave Hewitson, Dave Hardman.

This book is dedicated to the memory of the 96 fans who never got to see these places, the 39 who did not return home from Heysel and of Bobby Wilcox, a true legend.

A massive Thanks to each and everyone who contributed their European tales of supporting the best Club in the World. Liverpool FC - You'll Never Walk Alone.
Thanks to Simon Hughes for helping sort the foreword.
And not forgetting Mark Platt, for the contacts, editorial assistance and continued support throughout the project.

1st PUBLISHED; August 2014
COPYRIGHT; Dave Hewitson, Dave Hardman and all Contributors.
DESIGN; Dave Hewitson and Dominic Foster.
All Rights Reserved. No part of this publication may be reproduced without prior permission in writing from the publisher.

Contents

80/81 OULUN PALLOSEURA, ABERDEEN [70], CSKA SOFIA, BAYERN MUNICH [71], REAL MADRID [71]

81/82 OULUN PALLOSEURA, AZ67 ALKMAAR [74], CSKA SOFIA

82/83 DUNDALK [78], HELSINKI JK, WIDZEW LODZ

83/84 OB ODENSE, ATHLETIC BILBAO, BENFICA, DINAMO BUCHAREST [81], AS ROMA [82]

84/85 KKS LECH POZNAN [87], BENFICA, FK AUSTRIA VIENNA [90], PANATHINAIKOS, JUVENTUS [93], JUVENTUS [SUPER CUP] [88]

91/92 KUUSYSI LAHTI, AJ AUXERRE, SWAROVSKI TIROL [95], GENOA [95]

92/93 APOLLON LIMASSOL. SPARTAK MOSCOW

95/96 SPARTAK-ALANIA VLADIKAVKAZ [99], BRONDBY IF

96/97 MYLLYKOSKEN PALLO-47, FC SION [103], SK BRANN [104], PARIS ST-GERMAIN [105]

97/98 CELTIC [107], RS STRASBOURG

98/99 1FC KOSICE [111], VALENCIA CF, RC CELTA VIGO

2000/01 RAPID BUCHAREST, SLOVAN LIBEREC [115], OLYMPIAKOS, AS ROMA, FC PORTO, BARCELONA, DEPORTIVO ALAVES [121]

2001/02 FC HAKA, BOAVISTA, BORUSSIA DORTMUND, DYNAMO KYIV, BARCELONA, AS ROMA, GALATASARAY, BAYERN LEVERKUSEN [126], BAYERN MUNICH [SUPER CUP]

02/03 VALENCIA CF, SPARTAK MOSCOW [129], FC BASLE [133], VITESSE ARNHEM [136], AJ AUXERRE, CELTIC [136]

03/04 NK OLIMPIJA LJUBLJABA [139], STEAUA BUCHAREST, PFC LEVSKI SOFIA, OLYMPIQUE MARSEILLE

04/05 GRAZER AK [153], AS MONACO, OLYMPIAKOS, DEPORTIVO LA CORUNA [158], BAYER LEVERKUSEN [160],

JUVENTUS, CHELSEA, AC MILAN [161]

05/06 TOTAL NETWORK SOLUTIONS, FBK KAUNAS [175], CSKA SOFIA, REAL BETIS [175], CHELSEA, RSC ANDERLECHT [183], BENFICA [187], CSKA MOSCOW [SUPER CUP]

06/07 MACCABI HAIFA, PSV EINDHOVEN, GIRONDINS DE BORDEAUX [190], GALATASARAY [190], BARCELONA [193], PSV EINDHOVEN, CHELSEA, AC MILAN [196]

07/08 TOULOUSE, FC PORTO, OLYMPIQUE MARSEILLE, BESIKTAS JK, INTERNAZIONALE [201], ARSENAL, CHELSEA

08/09 STANDARD LIEGE, OLYMPIQUE MARSEILLE, PSV EINDHOVEN [204], ATLETICO MADRID, REAL MADRID, CHELSEA

09/10 DEBRECENI VSC [206], ACF FIORENTINA, OLYMPIQUE LYONNAIS, UNIREA URZICENI [213], LILLE OSC, BENFICA, ATLETICO MADRID

10/11 FK RABOTNIKI, TRABZONSPUR [217], FC UTRECHT [222], STEAUA BUCHAREST [223], SSC NAPOLI, AC SPARTA PRAGUE, SC BRAGA

12/13 FC GOMEL, HEART OF MIDLOTHIAN, BSC YOUNG BOYS [229], UDINESE, ANZI MAKHACHKALA [231], ZENIT ST PETERSBURG [235]

Foreword

I think about winning the Champions League most days. Someone always reminds me of it, whether I'm walking down the road, in a shop or at home. My son, James, is just as obsessed about football as me.

If I talk about Istanbul for long enough, it gives me goose pimples. I don't think there will ever be another final like it.

Three-nil down at half time to one of the, if not the best teams I've ever faced - we looked dead and buried. As we walked into the dressing room, I felt embarrassed and was just concerned about keeping the score down. I felt sorry for all the Liverpool supporters inside the stadium and at home.

From this desperate point, I don't think any other club than Liverpool could have rescued the situation. Everybody played a role: the players, the manager, the coaching staff and especially the fans.

We were not the best team in Europe that season. If you look at the other teams in the competition and compared the odds, we'd have been way down the list. But we had something the other sides did not probably have and that was the collective – the bond between players and supporters.

As soon as I exited the dressing room, down the long dark tunnel I could hear the fans singing You'll Never Walk Alone. It certainly gave me a lift. I think it surprised AC Milan, even with all of their experience. Everybody knows what happened next. I don't think it would have been possible without the passion and courage of the supporters lifting our morale when it was on the floor.

When I look back at that amazing run, the positive reaction of the fans shouldn't have surprised me. All the way through, they'd been with us. Games at Anfield against Olympiacos, Juventus and Chelsea stick in the mind. When I think about the semi-final particularly, I don't think of Luis Garcia's goal or Eidur Gudjohnsen's narrow miss in injury time. My mind is filled with noise. Anfield has never been so loud. It helped us get the result across the line.

Of course, supporting Liverpool isn't just about the big games. Wherever I've played in Europe, the fans have been there. I remember being in remote parts of Russia and Turkey and asking myself how people made it. The sacrifices people make, just to be there, always amazes me.

As a player, I've always wondered what it is like travelling away with Liverpool to a European game. Now I'm retired, it should give me that opportunity. I can't wait for this season to start.

JAMIE CARRAGHER

Introduction

On the 17 August 1964 Liverpool FC embarked on a love affair with Europe. They set off on a journey to Reykjavik in Iceland for their first ever game in a European competition. Accompanying them on that adventure 50 years ago were a gang of scousers who had never set foot on a plane in their life nor ventured further than North Wales.

Over the course of the next half Century thousands more fans and supporters of the most successful British club in European club football history would venture to foreign lands. The team have played in close to 40 countries out of a total of 54 attached to UEFA in 2014 and at every game in each and everyone of those countries a band of merry men can be heard having travelled by whatever means possible to see their team. Those fans all returned home with many a tale to tell. Many tales were obviously joyous with the number of trophies won whilst others did not turn out as expected.

What we have attempted to do here is deliver some of those adventures in this very book, dating back to that first game in Reykjavik right through to the Zenit St. Petersburg game of 2013. I'm sure most of you will feel an affinity with some of the tales herewith whether its a Toppings coach breaking down, bunking a train or plane, missing a game for one reason or another etc etc

My own tale started in the early 70s. I was allowed to go to the European home games. Maybe it was easier to get tickets to sit as we always ended up in the main stand. An Alun Evans hat trick against Bayern Munich in the 1971 Fairs Cup isn't going to be forgotten even though I was only 8 years old. Momentous nights seemed an inevitability on these great evenings. Who can forget the 1973 UEFA Cup Final. An abandoned first leg at Anfield, due to a waterlogged pitch, with a replay of the game on the following day. We didn't have tickets for either game due to my sister being in Alder Hey but on the night of the replayed game I pleaded with my dad to take me, as it was only 10p to get in. He hadn't heard of that and thought it was a ploy to go, so we had to visit the hospital. On returning home in the car I was again pleading. It's amazing how annoying a 10 year old can be until he gets his way. So we dropped off my mother and other siblings before heading to the ground.

We arrived at the ground just before half time and were able to get into the Kop through the Half-Time gate for a remarkably cheap 5p each. My first time ever on the Kop and it's a European Final. We stood at the very back and I remember being on his shoulders at one point but the noise and atmosphere became overwhelming/terrifying and I asked to be lowered. We won the game 3-0 due to some tactical intuition by the great man that is Bill Shankly. A 0-2 defeat in Germany wasn't enough for us to lose a grip on the trophy and a Victory Parade through the streets of Liverpool soon followed. The following year we beat Stromsgodset and I remember some young kids asking us the score on the way home. '11-0' my dad said, 'Piss off Mister' came the response. It really was 11-0 though and nine different players scored.

Other glory nights included seeing Neeskens and Cruyff playing for Barcelona. We drew 1-1 but would progress to the Final with a 1-0 win in Spain. These were world class players you would only usually see on TV during World Cup tournaments.

Then there was the Bruges, UEFA Cup Final of '76. 0-2 down at Half Time and a Belgium brass band in the Paddock blaring away until three second half goals silenced their clamorous tones.

My first European Away trip was to the Eternal City for the 1977 European Cup Final. A two-day journey on one of the Special trains commissioned to take some of the 26000+ supporters who would be making the expedition. My Raleigh Chopper was sold to fund the trip but a broken collar bone meant me sitting up-right all the way there and back whilst others slept in luggage racks or across seats and floors. A 3-1 triumph meant this was to be the greatest day ever in Liverpool's history. We returned home, this time taking almost three days as we arrived back on the Saturday having missed Tommy Smith's Testimonial the previous evening, but it mattered not. Of those who made that arduous trip over land and sea, many would do the same again in the coming years.

Maybe it's in our blood, many of our forefathers went to sea in the 50s and 60s, joining the Merchant Navy or the Cunard Liners. My Dad was in the 'Merch' and travelled all over. He now regales us with tales of picking up vinyl records in the U.S. and Australia which were unavailable here, plus he saw the Marlon Brando film 'The Wild One' in Buenos Aires. It was banned in the UK for fourteen years. After the film Louis Armstrong played live in the same Theatre. Only recently we found out that my Great Great Grandfather had sailed on the Cunard Lines RMS Aquitania in 1918 and through the 1920s. He was one of the original Cunard Yanks.

That sense of adventure has certainly been passed down and I like many others count the European away trips like a footballer would tally up his appearances.

DAVE HEWITSON

I was coming back on the ferry from Piraeus to Ancona the day after Athens. The boat had a fair few Milan fans on board who were working their way through the extortionately priced Peroni at a rate of knots. One of them looked at me, shrugged his shoulders and said, 'You lucky two years ago, we lucky last night'.

There was no disputing his argument and we raised a glass in acknowledgement. Pretty soon I was sitting with a group of Rossaneri discussing the finer points of football, well as much we could discuss it with my minimal Italian and their minimal drinking capacity. One lad, whose unkempt appearance suggested that Gattuso was his hero, said, 'My uncle was at Anfield in 1965 with Gazzeta Dello Sport. He said that he has never seen a football ground like that. We want to go there so much. When we saw your games against Olympiakos and Chelsea and the ground going mad, we promised ourselves that we would go there one day. We have been all around Europe, but never to Anfield. We want to go. For us going to Anfield is what European football is about.'

'Anfield is what European football is about'. What a great sentiment. He's not far wrong.

Play a European tie at Anfield, and see the away fans in town, their hands full of bags from the souvenir shop, or watch them in the Anfield Road End, everyone of them filming as 'You'll Never Walk Alone' echoes around the ground. You know that these fans will be returning home only too happy to bend their mates' ears about their time in Liverpool.

European football has always held an almost mythical status with Liverpool fans. We have seen the great teams and players of European history parade their skills at Anfield. Internationale, Juventus, Celtic, Ajax, Ferencvaros, Bayern Munich, Red Star Belgrade, Barcelona, St Etienne, Borussia, Benfica, Tiblisi, Roma and Real Madrid are names that conjure up memories of Anfield nights. Mazzola, Cruyff, McNeil, Florian Albert, Beckenbauer, Muller, Hoeness, Neeskens, Rocheteau, Vogts, Totti and a myriad of stars have plied their trade under the Anfield floodlights to leave us with a host of memories. Seeing these names at Anfield was only part of the fun, soon fans wanted to go and see these teams away from home as well and we took to European travel like Father Ted to drink.

Liverpool's love affair with Europe may also stem from the fact that this is not a ste-reo-typical English city. The cosmopolitan nature of the make up of the city has led to an all embracing love of foreign travel and an effort to integrate where-ever we go. We have never been great ones to go looking for egg and chips and a pint of John Smiths. Set us in any bar abroad and we are ordering the local grog and pointing out weird and wonderful meals from menus.

Sit a few of us down with a pint in our hands and the stories of our travels across the world abound. Possibly it stems from the days when every family had somebody in the Merchant Navy and when they had returned to their home port they would regale their family and friends with tales of the bodegas in Valparaiso and the glamorous foods ate in Kowloon and Murmansk.

Nowadays the stories are about glorious victories, over-zealous gendarmerie, drinking kens of dubious reputation and the public transport excursion that went unpaid for. Everyone has a story to tell from the innocence of the Sixties through to the glory of the Seventies and Eighties, the horror of Heysel and the exclusion that followed, the re-turn to European competition with the glory of Dortmund and the Miracle of Istanbul. Everyone has a story from the truly great games to meaningless pre-season friendlies. These stories are your stories – This is truly the stuff of legend.

DAVE HARDMAN

1964/65 EUROPEAN CUP

17 August 1964 Preliminary round
KR Reykjavík   0-5   Liverpool FC

14 September 1964 Preliminary round
Liverpool FC   6-1   KR Reykjavík
Aggregate: 11-1

25 November 1964 First round
Liverpool FC   3-0   RSC Anderlecht

16 December 1964 First round
RSC Anderlecht   0-1   Liverpool FC
Aggregate: 0-4

10 February 1965 Quarter-finals
FC Köln 0-0   Liverpool FC

17 March 1965 Quarter-finals
Liverpool FC   0-0   1. FC Köln
Aggregate: 0-0

24 March 1965 Quarter-finals - Replay
Liverpool FC   2-2   1. FC Köln
Liverpool win on toss of coin

4 May 1965 Semi-finals
Liverpool FC   3-1   FC Internazionale Milano

12 May 1965 Semi-finals
FC Internazionale Milano 3-0   Liverpool FC
Aggregate: 4-3

EUROPEAN CUP. 1ST ROUND, 1ST LEG.
17th AUGUST 1964
LAUGARDALSVOLLUR [10268].
REYKJAVIK. ICELAND
KR REYKJAVIK 0 LIVERPOOL 5

A few of us went. We had to go up to Scotland and catch a flight from Prestwick. It was only a small plane. None of us had ever flown before and we didn't really know what to expect. It's laughable now but we thought the place would be full of Eskimos. However, when we got there it reminded me of a small fishing village and the people were just like us, we couldn't believe it! It was such a long time ago that it's hard to remember all the details now but there was a group of us that used to go everywhere back then. Each time it was like embarking on an exciting new adventure, taking a step into the unknown. Sadly some of those lads are no longer with us, we're all in our 70s or older now, but they were great days. Saying that it doesn't seem like 50 years ago since that first trip to Reykjavik to be honest. To think what this club has achieved since then is amazing. We've had so many fantastic times in Europe and I'm proud to say I was there at the start.
ALAN BROWN

EUROPEAN CUP. 2ND ROUND, 2ND LEG.
16th DECEMBER 1964
HEYSEL STADION [47998].
BRUSSELS. BELGIUM
ANDERLECHT 0 LIVERPOOL 1

After the landslide victory over Reykjavik, this was considered to be Liverpool's first real test in Europe. The Anderlecht team contained a number of players who had starred for Belgium in a recent international at Wembley, but an impressive 3-0 win in the first leg (the game in which we wore all-red for the first time) ensured our passage into the next round was virtually assured. This was a much tighter game though, settled by a Roger Hunt goal in the last minute.
Our Joseph was a long-distance lorry driver out of Warrington and he did a few continental runs, I jokingly asked him if he'd give us a lift to Belgium for the Anderlecht game and I was shocked when he said yes it wouldn't be a problem. We set out on the Tuesday morning, there was me, Tommy Browne and Geoff Airey. This was in the days before containerisation so our kid just moved the crates around in the back of the wagon to make a hole for us to sit down in and off we went. It was a long drive then because the motorway system was not what it is today and it took almost 18 hours to get down to Dover. We got through customs without a hitch, I don't suppose that you could do it now but in those days the customs were quite lax, there was no terrorism or

drugs to worry about then.

We got to Brussels in the early afternoon, and we were made up to get out and stretch our legs. Our kid said that he had to go and unload, then load his wagon and he would meet us in this café where he dropped us at six o'clock to go to the game. We decided to go and get some scran and were made up when we found a chip shop. We couldn't speak Belgian or French but we all managed to order a portion of chips each. The owner was offering us salt and vinegar and offered us another container, Tommy said 'yes please' so the café owner covered his chips in what we thought was Salad Cream but turned out to be mayonnaise, we'd never seen it before, certainly not down Lodge Lane, but it wasn't bad to be honest. There was a bar next to the chippy so we all trooped in. We were wary of drinking foreign beer but the feller standing next to me was drinking what looked like a pint of mild so we ordered three of those, and we had a good few of them, the problem was that we didn't realise how strong this Belgian ale was, so by the time our kid came to pick us all up we were paralytic. I don't remember anything about the match at all except that our kid had a 'gob on' with us all because we were bevvied and acting the goat, and as soon as the match was over we set off back home. The problem was that we were now packed in the back of the lorry, and some of the cases stank of fish, so what with the smell, the lorry rocking from side to side and all the ale that we had supped, Geoff was sick all over the show. Well the smell was that bad that soon both me and Tommy had followed suit so when we stopped for a break our Gerard went off his head with us, the back of the wagon was in a terrible state and we weren't much better. It got even worse when Gerard slung a bucket of cold water over each of us to sober and clean us up. By the time we got on the ferry we were freezing from the drenching and badly hung over. We were reduced to draping our clothing over boiler pipes to dry them out, as the three of us stood there in our skids, socks and Chelsea boots. It was a good few weeks before me and our kid spoke again.

FRANCIS McDONAGH

EUROPEAN CUP. QUARTER FINAL, 1ST LEG.
10th FEBRUARY 1965
MUNGERSDORFER STADION [39139].
KOLN. WEST GERMANY
F.C. KOLN 0 LIVERPOOL 0

This may seem odd to you but I was never that big a Liverpool fan! I'd joined the army when I was 18 was and was stationed in Monchengladbach in the BAOR. Anyway, there was a Major there who was a wee bit eccentric and football mad. One day the Sergeant told me to report to the major's office.
'Right, McCabe, you're from Liverpool aren't you, and you can drive can't you?'
'Yes sir'

'Excellent, your local team are playing in Cologne tomorrow, and you're driving me up there'

'Yes Sir'

I'd never been that bothered over football to be honest. I'd kicked a ball around with me mates and been to the odd game but I was nowhere near as passionate as our kid or our mates, but I wasn't complaining - two days out of barracks wasn't to be sneezed at.

We left the next morning. It only took an hour or so and I was surprised that we were staying in a hotel but ours was not to reason why. I haven't been to Cologne since but it wasn't half bad. There was still the odd bomby but most of the town was rebuilt or getting re-built.

There were a load of squaddies at the game and there was a nasty Germany v England edge to it. There were a lot of MP's also there but they were turning a blind eye to most of the things that were going on. The Major had a nice stand seat and left me on the terraces. I wasn't complaining as he'd weighed me in with a couple of bob. I don't remember much about the game except Liverpool weren't that good. Afterwards we drove back to town and I dropped him off at a brass house before I went off for a pint. The next day I went back for him.

ALBERT McCABE

EUROPEAN CUP. QUARTER FINAL, PLAY-OFF.
24th MARCH 1965
FEYENOORD STADION [47862].
ROTTERDAM. NETHERLANDS
F.C. KOLN 2 LIVERPOOL 2

It was a month later that I was told to report again to the Major's office.

'McCabe, do you know what happened at Anfield the other night?'

'Liverpool and Cologne drew 0-0, Sir'

'Excellent, good chap, and tomorrow they are replaying in Rotterdam. You will be driving again'.

So the next morning we set off again. Yet again we travelled in civvies and stayed in a normal hotel. I got quite excited at the game with Liverpool winning on the toss of a coin after being pegged back from being 2-0 up. The Major must have enjoyed it because he invited me back to the brass house with him. I refused, not because I was shy, but because he was a Major and bevvied, and it may have led to trouble when we got back to camp. So the next day we went back to Monchengladbach. I've been to the odd game since I've come back home but it isn't quite the same anymore.

ALBERT McCABE

EUROPEAN CUP. SEMI FINAL, 2ND LEG.
12th MAY 1965
STADIO SAN SIRO [76601]. MILAN. ITALY
INTERNAZIONALE 3 LIVERPOOL 0

I was the lucky fella who won a competition in the Daily Post & Echo for an all expenses paid trip for two to the return match with Inter Milan at the San Siro in 1965. As my wife was also an avid Liverpool supporter she came with me and it was an unbelievable experience for us both.

My first impression when entering the stadium was the sheer size of the place – I'd never seen anything like it. Anfield and the other grounds in England were much smaller by comparison and seemed a lot more antiquated.

We had seats in the lower tier and were sat among the other travelling Liverpudlians. I distinctly remember two of them having these massive red flags and they went to the upper tier and ran around with them in front of the Italians, just to let them know LFC had arrived!

There was a long line of Italian police stood in front of us and it made me think that they were maybe expecting trouble but there were no real problems until near end when the home fans started setting fire to cushions and throwing them down in our direction. There was also a group who were spitting at us but it wasn't a big deal and we remained in good spirits despite the obvious disappointment of the result.

Throughout the game the noise was unbelievable and was getting louder and louder until our small group decided to silence them by singing 'You'll Never Walk Alone'. That was amazing too because it was like we were on a stage. All the Italians just stopped and watched. It was one of those 'hairs on the back of your neck' type of moments and, fair play, they allowed us to finish before continuing with their own songs.

Afterwards the Italians were understandably in celebratory mood and crowded around us as we made our way towards the coach. Some were shouting and blowing air horns, while others just wanted to shake our hands and wish us well.

It was a great trip and to cap it all we flew home on the same plane as Mr Shankly and the players. Soon after take-off they all kindly signed my match programme. Shanks was the last one and the first thing he asked was how it had been for us at the game. I told him all about it and will never ever forget what he then said. "Aye son, the bloody Italians are alright on their own ground but we'll meet them again one day."

It was the perfect end to what was the most amazing trip, the only shame being that we couldn't hold onto our first leg lead and become the first British team to reach the European Cup final.

TONY JUDGE

1965/66 EUROPEAN CUP WINNERS CUP

29 September 1965 First round
Juventus 1-0   Liverpool FC

13 October 1965 First round
Liverpool FC   2-0   Juventus
Aggregate: 2-1

1 December 1965 Second round
Liverpool FC   3-1   Standard Liege

15 December 1965 Second round
Standard Liege   1-2   Liverpool FC
Aggregate: 2-5

1 March 1966 Quarter-finals
Honved 0-0   Liverpool FC

8 March 1966 Quarter-finals
Liverpool FC   2-0   Honved
Aggregate: 2-0

14 April 1966 Semi-finals
Celtic   1-0   Liverpool FC

19 April 1966 Semi-finals
Liverpool   2-0   Celtic
Aggregate: 2-1

5 May 1966 Final
Borussia Dortmund   2-1   Liverpool FC
After Extra Time

EUROPEAN CUP WINNERS CUP 2ND ROUND, 2ND LEG.
15th DECEMBER 1965
STADE DE SCLESSIN [29534]. LIEGE. BELGIUM
STANDARD LIEGE 1 LIVERPOOL 2

Not a lot to report. I went with two mates, one of whom was a Gillingham fan! We stayed at his folks house in Kent before getting the ferry to Ostend. The third guy was a Rugby player who came along for the crack!
We hitched to and from Ostend in Belgium and got tickets outside the ground, which was easy to do back then.
As I recall we had a hard job getting back from London to Uni at Cardiff because we had to hitchhike as we had run out of money. We got to the Western edges of the Tube without paying and that was it.
All worthwhile though because we won. (2-1, I think that was the score). It was a good night in Liege as I recall too.
Not many visiting fans in those days!
LONGTIME RED.

EUROPEAN CUP WINNERS CUP SEMI FINAL, 1ST LEG.
14th APRIL 1966
CELTIC PARK [76446]. GLASGOW. SCOTLAND
CELTIC 1 LIVERPOOL 0

Celtic was my first European away game. It was the semi-final of the Cup Winners Cup and was the easiest fixture to which we could get to. There was a 'Wow' factor about the tie as we'd never witnessed a crowd so big. We had obviously by then had some magnificent ties at Anfield with the Kop bursting at the seams for the visits of Juventus, Koln and Inter Milan but there must have been about a 90000 crowd that night in Glasgow and they were nearly all standing.
I always remember the crush barriers behind the goal, they looked like railway sleepers and they just broke under the sheer weight of numbers from the Liverpool fans behind the goal.
At that time Celtic were a pretty good team and I'd say they had about 80% of the game but they only won 1-0. We won the return leg at Anfield 2-0 so that put us in the Final. The game at Anfield was probably best remembered for the Celtic fans in the Anfield Road trying to get the game abandoned by throwing bottles onto the pitch near the end of the match.
We were now into the Final which was back in Glasgow at Hampden Park.
PETER HUGHES

EUROPEAN CUP WINNERS CUP FINAL.
5th MAY 1966
HAMPDEN PARK [41657]. GLASGOW. SCOTLAND
BORUSSIA DORTMUND 2 LIVERPOOL 1 AET

My first European final was at Hampden Park. I went by charabanc from the Farmer's Arms in Huyton. We left there at ten in the morning and got to Glasgow around about eight hours later. Everyone on board had a crate of brown or a crate of pale ale, you couldn't move on board for all the bottles. As there were no toilets on the coaches in those days we had to stop every half an hour to water the fields. I'm surprised that it only took eight hours!
The ground was nearly half empty. We had about 18,000 fans there but none of the jocks showed up, they were probably still chokka as we had beaten Celtic in the semis, and it was really lashing down with rain. Only seven lads had tickets the rest of us bunked into a game that we should have won. On the way back we had a flat tyre and didn't get back till eight o'clock in the morning.
ERNIE ASHLEY

I was working in Plessey's in Edge Lane. There were two of us who wanted to go but we were not allowed any time off so we had to work till twelve and then we drove up to Glasgow on the day of the game. The roads weren't that well sign posted then, so we got a wee bit lost after Gretna, and the only reason that we got to the ground was that we followed this convoy of German cars up to Hampden Park. It was only when we got into the ground that we realised how hungry we were, but the problem was that the only money we had were the new English five pound notes, which the Scots treated with great suspicion, probably because of our accent and they refused to take them. Luckily we were able to borrow some odds to get something to eat, which was all we had before getting back to Liverpool and going straight to work at 8.00am the next day.
BRIAN NEWCOMBE

1966/67 EUROPEAN CUP

28 September 1966 First round
Liverpool FC   2-0   FC Petrolul Ploieşti

12 October 1966 First round
FC Petrolul Ploiesti   3-1   Liverpool FC
Aggregate: 3-3

19 October 1966 First round - Replay
Liverpool FC   2-0   FC Petrolul Ploiesti

7 December 1966 Second round
AFC Ajax   5-1   Liverpool FC

14 December 1966 Second round
Liverpool FC   2-2   AFC Ajax
Aggregate: 3-7

EUROPEAN CUP. 2ND ROUND, 1ST LEG.
7th DECEMBER 1966
OLYMPISCH STADION [55722]. AMSTERDAM. NETHERLANDS
AJAX 5 LIVERPOOL 1

We had won the League the previous season so we were in the European Cup. In the December we had an away game against Ajax in Amsterdam and at the time I was working in Rotterdam, so on the day of the game I got a train up to Amsterdam. I didn't have a ticket for the match so I went up to the Stadium. Ajax only had a tiny Stadium so it wasn't played there, it had been switched to the Olympic Stadium in Amsterdam which held sixty odd Thousand. Anyway the game was sold out but as I was walking away disappointed at not getting a ticket this bloke came running after me and asked if I needed a ticket. Of course I said 'Yes'.

It turned out to be on the front row on the half way line behind were Shankly and the Liverpool bench were sitting. I was over the moon, I couldn't have got a better seat.

That day the fog had started rolling in and by Kick Off I could just about see both goals with being on the half way line but those in the ground behind the goals wouldn't have been able to see the opposite goals.

The fog got thicker and thicker, I don't think the game would have been played nowadays.

Liverpool were a bit unfortunate that Johann Cruyff played because he was out of this world. He was like a whippet around the pitch and kept disappearing into the fog. Most of the time the ball was in the net before you knew what had happened. We got beat 5-1 that day and I felt devastated. The Mighty Reds had been taken to the cleaners.

When the match finished Shankly stood up and he was facing the crowd shouting 'You hid in the fog, the conditions were all for you' and he was shouting loudly at the crowd and they were responding with 'Shankly, Ha, Ha, Ha,'

I can always remember it and Shankly was addressing the whole crowd, shouting at them and I was totally taken in by what he was saying and I though we're going to batter these in the home leg. You know what, they were lucky, there's no way they'll get away with this, the conditions seemed better for them. So I was totally taken in by Shanklys rhetoric, shall we say. I was convinced we were going to win as I think the Liverpool crowd were.

There were 54000 for the return leg and I think everyone had been convinced they were a lucky team, but they weren't as it turned out. That game was 2-2 and Ajax went through 7-3 on aggregate.

At the start of the 70s the basis of that Ajax team won the European Cup three times on the run.
PETER HUGHES

1967/68 EUROPEAN INTER CITY FAIRS CUP

19 September 1967 First round
Malmo FF   0-2   Liverpool FC

4 October 1967 First round
Liverpool FC   2-1   Malmo FF
Aggregate: 4-1

7 November 1967 Second round
Liverpool FC   8-0   TSV Munich 1860

14 November 1967 Second round
TSV Munich 1860   2-1   Liverpool FC
Aggregate: 2-9

28 November 1967 Third round
Ferencvaros   1-0   Liverpool FC

9 January 1968 Third round
Liverpool FC   0-1   Ferencvaros
Aggregate: 0-2

1968/69 EUROPEAN INTER CITY FAIRS CUP

18 September 1968 First round
Athletic Bilbao   2-1   Liverpool FC

2 October 1968 First round
Liverpool FC   2-1   Athletic Bilbao
Aggregate: 3-3 AET
Athletic Bilbao win on toss of coin

1969/70 EUROPEAN INTER CITY FAIRS CUP

16 September 1969 First round
Liverpool FC   10-0   Dundalk

30 September 1969 First round
Dundalk 0-4   Liverpool FC
Aggregate: 14-0

12 November 1969 Second round
Vitoria Setubal   1-0   Liverpool FC

26 November 1969 Second round
Liverpool FC   3-2   Vitoria Setubal
Aggregate: 3-3
Vitoria Setubal win on away goals

EUROPEAN INTER CITY FAIRS CUP. 2ND ROUND 1ST LEG
12th NOVEMBER 1969
ESTADIO DO BONFIM [16000]. SETUBAL. PORTUGAL
VITORIA SETUBAL 1 LIVERPOOL 0

Back in the 60's, it was a lot more complicated getting to European aways, but it was a challenge we always relished. So with that in mind there was no hesitation in wanting to go to Portugal to watch the Reds in their European Fairs Cup (or whatever it's called nowadays) 2nd round 1st leg meeting with Setubal, a team many people won't recognise in this day and age.

Back then you just didn't have the type of coverage which is available nowadays and we didn't have a clue who played for them, what their style of play was etc. This, however, made the trip especially intriguing for us.

What also made this trip stand out more than some of the others was the fact that one member of the travelling party (my brother-in-law) skipped jury service so he could go and watch the game over in Portugal. It was even reported in the Liverpool Echo and to this day I still don't know how he got away with it!

Upon arriving at our hotel we discovered that the entire Liverpool team were staying in the same place which was a lovely little bonus and access to them was a lot easier than what I can imagine it to be now!

With their ground not having any floodlights, the game kicked off mid-afternoon 15.15pm which would also be difficult to comprehend in this day and age when it comes to European competition. But as with many a trip, the match itself left a lot to be desired and we succumbed to a 1-0 defeat with the majority of the 90 minutes long forgotten about. Not only was it a non-event but the overall performance of the team left a bad taste in the mouth.

In contrast the second leg at Anfield was a lot more entertaining despite us going 2-0 down to Setubal before a late rally saw us win 3-2 with 'Sir' Roger getting the winner. But with the away goals rule only just coming into play the crowd and players were expecting extra time, so we waited around before an announcement came over the tannoy that we had been knocked out.

FRANK SLATER

1970/71 EUROPEAN INTER CITY FAIRS CUP

15 September 1970 First round
Liverpool FC   1-0   Ferencvaros

29 September 1970 First round
Ferencvaros   1-1   Liverpool FC
Aggregate: 1-2

21 October 1970 Second round
Liverpool FC   3-0   Dinamo Bucharest

4 November 1970 Second round
Dinamo Bucharest   1-1   Liverpool FC
Aggregate: 1-4

9 December 1970 Third round
Hibernian   0-1   Liverpool FC

22 December 1970 Third round
Liverpool FC   2-0   Hibernian
Aggregate: 3-0

10 March 1971 Quarter-finals
Liverpool FC   3-0   Bayern Munich

24 March 1971 Quarter-finals
Bayern Munich   1-1   Liverpool FC
Aggregate: 4-1

14 April 1971 Semi-finals
Liverpool FC   0-1   Leeds United

28 April 1971 Semi-finals
Leeds United   0-0   Liverpool FC
Aggregate: 1-0

EUROPEAN INTER CITY FAIRS CUP. SEMI-FINAL 2ND LEG
28TH APRIL 1971
ELLAND ROAD [40462]. LEEDS. ENGLAND
LEEDS UNITED 0 LIVERPOOL 0

Before the first leg at Anfield, Leeds were considered the favourites for the tie after finishing the previous season runners up in both the League and FA Cup. Liverpool were still undergoing a transitional period under Shanks with new signings. After a humiliating 1-0 defeat to Watford, in the 1970 FA Cup quarter-final, Shankly ripped the heart out of the side and brought in new burgeoning stars. Out went St John, Hunt, Yeats and Lawrence, in came Clemence, Lloyd, Toshack, Hall and Heighway. Liverpool would have seven trophy-less years as this re-building took place.

This was a massive game for us, we'd beaten Bayern Munich in the quarter finals and even though we'd lost 1-0 at home to a Billy Bremner goal the fans were confident of getting a result as we had a decent record against Leeds in those days.

I had my own car then so I drove down with my mate Alan Rotherham. The drive was a bit of a nightmare as there was no M62 in those days, so we had to take the cross country route and we didn't get there till very late. The Liverpool fans were all in the Cowshed End and the gates were locked. We had no other option but to try and bunk in, which we eventually did into the Main Stand. We ended up sitting in the aisle. It was a bad tempered game which ended 0-0, therefore Leeds progressed to the Final were they would defeat Juventus over two legs on the away goals rule.

Afterwards the tension could be cut with a knife and trouble was aplenty as both sets of fans set about each other.

KEN WILLIAMS

1971/72 EUROPEAN CUP WINNERS CUP

15 September 1971 First round
Servette 2-1   Liverpool FC

29 September 1971 First round
Liverpool FC   2-0   Servette
Aggregate: 3-2

20 October 1971 Second round
Liverpool FC   0-0   Bayern Munich

3 November 1971 Second round
Bayern Munich   3-1   Liverpool FC
Aggregate: 3-1

1972/73 UEFA CUP

12 September 1972 First round
Liverpool FC   2-0   Eintracht Frankfurt

26 September 1972 First round
Eintracht Frankfurt   0-0   Liverpool FC
Aggregate: 0-2

24 October 1972 Second round
Liverpool FC   3-0   AEK Athens FC

7 November 1972 Second round
AEK Athens FC   1-3   Liverpool FC
Aggregate: 1-6

29 November 1972 Third round
Berliner FC Dynamo   0-0   Liverpool FC

13 December 1972 Third round
Liverpool FC   3-1   Berliner FC Dynamo
Aggregate: 3-1

7 March 1973 Quarter-finals
Liverpool FC   2-0   1. FC Dynamo Dresden

21 March 1973 Quarter-finals
FC Dynamo Dresden   0-1   Liverpool FC
Aggregate: 0-3

10 April 1973 Semi-finals
Liverpool FC   1-0   Tottenham Hotspur FC

25 April 1973 Semi-finals
Tottenham Hotspur FC   2-1   Liverpool FC   1
Aggregate: 2-2
Liverpool win on away goals

10 May 1973 Final
Liverpool FC   3-0   VfL Borussia Mönchengladbach

23 May 1973 Final
VfL Borussia Mönchengladbach   2-0   Liverpool FC
Aggregate: 2-3

UEFA CUP 1ST ROUND 2ND LEG
26TH SEPTEMBER 1972
WALD STADION [18000]
FRANKFURT. WEST GERMANY
EINTRACHT FRANKFURT 0 LIVERPOOL 0

I joined British Rail in July, 1971. I have never hidden the truth that I joined because of the generous travel concessions an employee was entitled to … at both home and abroad. I knew this would considerably reduce my match-day expenses. After a year of service I was entitled to a European travel card to use, as well as my domestic travel card. During the 1971-72 season I got to know a lot of other Liverpool supporters who regularly travelled to watch the team play, many of them also Railway men like myself and in some cases seasoned European veterans. As Summer turned into Autumn in 1972, I was ready to make my own European debut for a competitive match, to Frankfurt for our UEFA Cup game in the September.

There was a European Travel Office for Railway staff near Victoria Station in London, where staff could book tickets, sleepers, couchettes, etc, but for my early trips I tended to rely on my new friends who already knew what to do and where to go. The match in Frankfurt was played on a Tuesday evening. I was one of a small group of four or five who travelled overnight from London on the Monday evening … train down to the coast, ferry across the Channel, then another train from the French or Belgian port. We had to change trains once. I remember the train going past Frankfurt Airport at about three in the morning. We got to the city-centre shortly afterwards. On arrival you just familiarize yourself with the surroundings and then, as the city wakes up, if you arrive at the time we did, work out how to get to the stadium, where you can get something to eat and drink and book a hotel if you need one. My friends decided to stay overnight after the match but I had already decided to travel back to England the same night. I hadn't told anyone at work where I was going. I had just booked two days holiday, so in theory, I was supposed to be back at work on the Wednesday morning.

We got a bus out to the stadium and were able to buy match-tickets easily enough. Then we went back into town and returned to the stadium in the afternoon. The ground was one of several in West Germany that were being modernized for the 1974 World Cup. We joined in an impromptu game of football in a park near the stadium. As the crowd started to build up, I remember noticing a lot of British soldiers around. There was still a significant military presence in Germany in 1972 and it was quite common to see U.K. troops at matches involving British clubs in countries like Holland and Germany. Holding a two-goal lead from the first leg, I was confident but not complacent. I knew that Eintracht had a good pedigree, mainly from their appearance in a famous European cup final against Real Madrid in 1960. Their team contained a few German internationals including Jürgen Grabowski, the man who had tormented England at the 1970 World Cup and a man who spent his whole career with Eintracht.

I was standing on a huge open terrace behind one of the goals. I was impressed by the

Waldstadion, we had an excellent view and there was never a hint of any trouble from the locals who knew we were visiting supporters. My nerves disappeared as the match wore on and the hosts struggled to make a breakthrough. They had a goal disallowed for offside right in front of us midway through the second half. After that, I knew we would go through. We didn't hang around after the match. It was straight back into town by bus. My friends headed for their hotel and I headed straight for the railway-station and the train that would take me back to the coast. Another overnight ferry and a train up into central London and I was back sitting at my desk by mid-morning. I was absolutely shattered after spending two consecutive nights travelling but for me it was mission accomplished and I was looking forward to the next trip already.

CHRIS WOOD

UEFA CUP 2ND ROUND 2ND LEG
6TH NOVEMBER 1972
NIKOS GOUMAS STADIUM [25000]
ATHENS. GREECE
A.E.K. ATHENS 1 LIVERPOOL 3

My second European away. The first being Eintracht Frankfurt in the previous round. It was also my 20th birthday. A well-organised trip arranged by Jet Set Travel who had a shop in St. John's Precinct in Liverpool city centre. I think we paid about £35 (it certainly wasn't more than £40). For that we got a return flight to Athens, all transfers and two nights at a very pleasant hotel in Vouliagmeni. A seaside resort about a dozen miles South of the Capital.
There was plenty of time to go sightseeing on the morning of the match before we were bussed to the stadium (it was an afternoon kick-off). Emlyn Hughes scored two brilliant first-half goals into the goal behind which we were sitting.
We also got to see most of the 2nd leg of Olympiakos v Tottenham the next afternoon. We had to leave a few minutes before the end to get a taxi back to the airport.
A brilliant trip and a wonderful memory forty years on.

CHRIS WOOD

UEFA CUP SEMI-FINAL 2ND LEG
25TH APRIL 1973
WHITE HART LANE [46919]
LONDON. ENGLAND
TOTTENHAM HOTSPUR 2 LIVERPOOL 1

Tottenham were the reigning UEFA Cup holders, having beaten Wolves over two legs the previous season. That game being the first ever UEFA Cup final after the competition changed names – and this was to be my first European away game.

I was off school on the Easter holidays, so my dad said I could go down with him and his mates who all worked at Cammell Lairds with him. We got 'The Special' down there and it was the first time that I was properly on the ale (I was only 13) and after two cans of McEwans Export I was bladdered.

We'd won the first leg 1-0 and were very confident of going through. Spurs battered us though and we managed to scrape through thanks to Heighway's away goal and some great goal-keeping from Clemence.

After the game we were going back to the train, which went from Tottenham Hale, when we came under attack from some angry Spurs fans. My dad and his mates produced lump hammer's from under their donkey jackets and laid into anything not wearing a red scarf. He had to pay me a tenner not to grass him up to me mam.

ROBBIE HUGHES

UEFA CUP FINAL 2ND LEG
23RD MAY 1973
BOKELBERG STADION [34905]
MONCHENGLADBACH. WEST GERMANY
BORUSSIA MONCHENGLADBACH 2 LIVERPOOL 0

I knew months before that the date of the second leg of the final clashed with an important examination I was due to take. As the team progressed through the early rounds of the UEFA Cup, I knew I might have a tricky decision to make if the club reached the Final. In the end it wasn't tricky at all. I just wasn't prepared to miss the chance of watching Liverpool F.C. win its first European trophy.

I had seen a friendly match at Borussia's Bökelberg stadium the previous Summer, so I knew how to get there from the town-centre but I did not know how difficult it might be to get into a Cup Final there. None of us who had travelled overnight on the ferry from Harwich had a match-ticket in our possession. Everyone I travelled with (members of the London Branch of the Supporters' Club like myself) just wanted to be there. Even if we didn't get in, we still wanted to be there.

To my great surprise when we arrived at the stadium on the morning of the Final, there was a booth open selling tickets, so of course we joined the queue. To get sorted so early in the day was a massive relief and meant that we could enjoy the build-up to the match without the worry of wondering where the hell we might get a ticket.

Liverpool supporters continued to arrive in Mönchengladbach all afternoon, including many British soldiers who were based in West Germany, so many that our own Military Police were also present. Not that there was any trouble but the average squaddie never needed much of an excuse to wind up the locals. Once we got inside the stadium there was the most enormous thunderstorm. It was so bad that a friend turned to me and said, "I think this might get called off". Luckily, the rain eased enough to allow the match to start but we were blown away in the first half. I think Bill Shankly later said that he sensed the Germans had given too much in that first half. They were never the same force after the break. We held on and defended in numbers, not always comfortably, until I remember Alec Lindsay whacking the ball up field and the referee's final whistle blowing at the same moment. Hundreds of our supporters climbed the fences to run onto the sodden pitch and celebrate with the players. I looked at some friends and we just nodded and followed suit. I can't condone a pitch invasion unless it is for safety reasons but it just seemed the right thing to do at the time. The Trophy presentation was a complete farce but down at pitch-level we caught a glimpse of some shiny silver being waved in the air and that was a wonderful sight. A lap of honour was impossible with so many supporters on the pitch but I remember running alongside Emlyn Hughes for a few seconds as he did a very passable impersonation of a Crazy Horse cantering along with a beaming smile that stretched from ear to ear.

We were out most of the night moving from bar to bar until we found a little place that was run by a couple of guys from North Wales. There were almost no German supporters in any of those bars. As we continued to celebrate on the ferry heading back to England, I remember a Dutchman joining our group and informing us "Next week you will see who the real champions of Europe are". He was right in that Ajax would, the following week, win the European Champions' Cup for the third year running. It was a gentle reminder that more important challenges lay ahead for Liverpool Football Club, challenges that would make more dreams come true. But right then we didn't really care what this Dutchman thought. Liverpool had its name engraved on a European trophy and that was the best feeling in the world at that moment. And I never did take that exam!

CHRIS WOOD

We went over here full of confidence after we'd beaten them 3-0 at Anfield but this was a side that contained the nucleus of the West German side that would win the World Cup the next year. I'd bunked all the way there, apart from having to pay on the ferry at Dover, in those days I never knew what a ticket looked like.

Got to Monchengladbach early that morning. We left our gear in our mate's hotel and went off into town.

I met this charming fraulein and we beguiled away the hours in a coffee shop until it was time to go the match. Like the '66 Hampden Park Final it was absolutely lashing down and when we went 2-0 down, we feared the worst but we battled on, defended like Lions and won 3-2 on aggregate.

There was a moat surrounding the pitch and armed police but that didn't stop me getting onto the pitch to salute the players and the manager, the great Bill Shankly. What a team and what a night.

ERNIE ASHLEY

1973/74 EUROPEAN CUP

19 September 1973 First round
AS Jeunesse Esch 1-1   Liverpool FC

3 October 1973 First round
Liverpool FC   2-0   AS Jeunesse Esch
Aggregate: 3-1

24 October 1973 Second round
FK Crvena Zvezda   2-1   Liverpool FC

6 November 1973 Second round
Liverpool FC   1-2   FK Crvena Zvezda
Aggregate: 2-4

EUROPEAN CUP 1ST ROUND 1ST LEG
19TH SEPTEMBER 1973
STADE DE LA FRONTIERE [7000]
ESCH. LUXEMBOURG
JEUNESSE ESCH 1 LIVERPOOL 1

The prospect of watching Liverpool play in a new country appealed to me and as soon as the draw was made I started to look at ways of getting to Luxembourg. As was so often the case, it involved travelling by train to a channel port, across the Channel by ferry (in this case to Ostend) and then on again by train. In the early-1970s you just did what you would do for a domestic match … travel. You didn't have to belong to some travel club. Nobody advised you not to travel without a match-ticket. You just went and worked it all out when you reached your destination. But abroad you had the additional worry of getting inside a stadium without any problems. If you were really stuck, it was quite likely that someone from the club would find a complimentary ticket for you from somewhere. So it was another overnight journey for myself and one friend. We changed trains in Brussels and arrived in Luxembourg about mid-morning. We already knew that the match would not be played in the city of Luxembourg but in the small mining-town of Esch a few miles south of the capital. Getting there might be a problem and getting a match-ticket might be a problem but neither problem was insurmountable because we still had several hours to spare.

We walked for ages and eventually found the hotel, a Holiday Inn, where the club's official party was staying. In the lobby, either about to set off for training or returning from it was Bill Shankly. He noticed us, wandered over and greeted us warmly and also assured us that if we had still not found match-tickets by the time the team's coach arrived at the stadium that we would be 'looked after'. That was a big reassurance for us because we knew by now that the stadium had a tiny capacity. Back in the city-centre in the afternoon, we bumped into a couple of English guys who were working over there. They kindly offered to drive us down to Esch and said match-tickets would be waiting for us there. All it needed was a phone call, which they made on our behalf. They looked after us very well and a couple of years later I bumped into one of them outside Anfield and he remembered meeting me in Luxembourg. We all watched the match together after having a few drinks with them in a bar near the stadium. They wanted to continue boozing after the match but I just wanted to get home, especially as I was furious about the last-minute equaliser we had conceded. Well, they got us back to Luxembourg railway-station but we had hours to wait there until the next train to Brussels. We tried to get some sleep in the waiting room but were disturbed many times by Police wanting to see our passports and travel documents. Once we got out of Luxembourg heading for Belgium, everything went fine and we had a trouble-free journey back to England. The result … failing to beat a team of part-timers … was seen as very embarrassing. I still remember the headline on an English paper I bought during the journey home. "The Terrors Of Toytown" (in, I think, the Daily Mirror) was

27

the paper's view of a David almost slaying a Goliath. But we just couldn't put away our chances on the night and didn't either at Anfield in the second leg. 3-1 on aggregate does not sound comfortable or convincing but the reality is that we were bigger, better and stronger. Having said that, far tougher tests lay ahead if the team wanted to win the European cup.

CHRIS WOOD

1974/75 EUROPEAN CUP WINNERS CUP

17 September 1974 First round
Liverpool FC   11-0   Stromsgodset IF

1 October 1974 First round
Stromsgodset IF   0-1   Liverpool FC
Aggregate: 0-12

23 October 1974 Second round
Liverpool FC   1-1   Ferencvaros

6 November 1974 Second round
Ferencvaros   0-0   Liverpool FC
Aggregate: 1-1
Ferencvaros win on away goal

EUROPEAN CUP WINNERS CUP 1ST ROUND 2ND LEG
1ST OCTOBER 1974
ULLEVAAL STADION [16775]. OSLO. NORWAY
STROMSGODSET I.F. 0 LIVERPOOL 1

Liverpool's 11-0 win in the first leg remains our record victory but despite this game being nothing but a mere formality in terms of our progress Bob Paisley refused to entertain the idea of wholesale squad rotation for the return. He made just two changes to the starting eleven and although another goal-fest failed to materialise, the Reds ran out 1-0 winners thanks to a Ray Kennedy strike in the 17th minute.

I was one of only six supporters who travelled from England to see our Cup Winners' Cup match in Oslo in 1974. Had there been more, I am sure we would have bumped into them at some stage of our trip.

What we did see though was hundreds of Norwegians wearing our colours and the first indication I had that the club was so popular in Scandinavia. Jet Set Travel, based in St. John's Precinct, originally planned to charter a plane out to Oslo from the North West but it was cancelled because they couldn't find enough people who wanted to book onto it after the 11-0 first-leg home win in the middle of September.

I had discussed the idea of travelling to Norway with some friends before the first leg took place and we didn't see a good reason to change the plans we had already made just because the tie was effectively over. Other friends thought we were crazy to contemplate an overland trip of this length when there was no longer anything at stake because a place in the next round was already assured. Two of our group travelled across the North Sea to Gothenburg, myself and three others went the long way around by train through Holland, Germany, Denmark and Sweden before eventually arriving in Oslo on the morning of the match some thirty-six hours after we had left London on the Sunday evening. We were away for five nights, four of which were spent on trains or boats with only one being in a small Oslo hotel the night after the match. The journey back was endless and included the roughest crossing of the North Sea I have ever had the misfortune to experience.

I finally got home sometime on the Friday afternoon. The next day Liverpool were playing away at Carlisle. I woke up but stayed in bed. My travelling for that week was definitely over!

CHRIS WOOD

1975/76 UEFA CUP

17 September 1975 First round
Hibernian FC   1-0   Liverpool FC

30 September 1975 First round
Liverpool FC   3-1   Hibernian FC
Aggregate: 3-2

22 October 1975 Second round
Real Sociedad de Fútbol   1-3   Liverpool FC

4 November 1975 Second round
Liverpool FC   6-0   Real Sociedad de Fútbol
Aggregate: 9-1

26 November 1975 Third round
WKS Śląsk Wrocław   1-2   Liverpool FC

10 December 1975 Third round
Liverpool FC   3-0   WKS Śląsk Wrocław
Aggregate: 5-1

3 March 1976 Quarter-finals
FC Dynamo Dresden   0-0   Liverpool FC

17 March 1976 Quarter-finals
Liverpool FC   2-1   1. FC Dynamo Dresden
Aggregate: 2-1

30 March 1976 Semi-finals
FC Barcelona   0-1   Liverpool FC

14 April 1976 Semi-finals
Liverpool FC   1-1   FC Barcelona
Aggregate: 2-1

28 April 1976 Final
Liverpool FC   3-2   Club Brugge KV

19 May 1976 Final
Club Brugge KV   1-1   Liverpool FC
Aggregate: 3-4

UEFA CUP 1ST ROUND 1ST LEG
17TH SEPTEMBER 1975
EASTER ROAD [19219]. EDINBURGH. SCOTLAND
HIBERNIAN 1 LIVERPOOL 0

You have to trawl through the mists of time to remember matches like this away. It's all a bit hazy but here's what I recall of my first European. I was 17, street wise, obsessed with fashion and had probably the biggest cows-lick this side of the Mississippi. It was 1975 so I was probably a 'bootboy'. I don't think the crossover from Doc Martens to trainees and suedies had taken place just yet. I had travelled up to Edinburgh with my mate Eddie Cox, who is no longer with us. I'm not 100% sure

but I would imagine that we would've bunked the train because back in those days that's what you did. It's weird how little things stick in your mind but my abiding memory of being at the match was that it was so dark. The floodlights at Anfield have always made night matches feel special, but up at Easter Road that night it just felt a bit dull, like they were on half power or something. Another thing that creeps into my mental picture of the night is that all the 'jocks' were big and hairy. Big bushy heads and beards and muzzys. Strange recollections really. Scotsmen in a darkened football

ground. We weren't fazed at all though because we were Liverpool and we were at that teenage stage where hardly anything frightens you. The Scottish fans had been marauding down South for England matches and friendly games for about ten years and had got a bit of a rep, but to us they just seemed like big hairy cavemen.

Give them their due though, they did bring more down to Anfield for the return leg than we took up there. We had about 300 to 400 and yet they had about 2,000 in the Anfield Road at our place.

Considering that hooliganism was de-rigeur at the time, surprisingly there was little or none that we saw or heard about. The Anfield match was an altogether different story as the Hibs fans took a hell of a pasting. They came down to conquer, thinking they'd get a walkover and returned home with their tails between their legs. On the football front. Oh yes I forgot about the ol' football there. I remember us being fairly lucky in both legs. The 1st leg we got beat 1-0 but it could've been two or three with Clemence saving a penno. 2nd leg we won 3-1 and again we used up all our luck. Back in Scotland I have vague memories of us getting knocked back from all the bars for being too young and then traipsing a couple of miles out of the city centre to my Auntie Rhona's B&B up by the zoo. I love my Auntie Rhona. She is not my real auntie but a woman my mum met at school when she was evacuated in the war and they stayed mates all their lives. Strangely I was dispatched to live there a year later for six months when I started to go off the rails and it was a brilliant experience. Obviously I couldn't stay there forever because the Reds were marching on Rome and I had to be there. So there you have it. Hibs away. We were lucky, the lights were dim and they were hairy. Back to you in the studio Brian.

JEGSY DODD

UEFA CUP 2ND ROUND 1ST LEG
22ND OCTOBER 1975
CAMPO MUNICIPAL DE ATOCHA [30000]
SOCIEDAD. SPAIN
REAL SOCIEDAD 1 LIVERPOOL 3

One of the best European aways ever and still at a time when very few supporters did them by making their own arrangements rather than booking on organised trips. My own trip started badly. I went to the wrong port (Dover) and had to get a taxi round to the right port (Folkestone) to join the ferry I knew my friends were on. Across the Channel, into and out of Paris and a long overnight journey by train crossing into Spain in the South-Western corner of France. Real Sociedad play in a shiny new Stadium now, but back in 1975 they were using the Atocha Stadium which was right by the railway-station. The locals were absolutely brilliant. They treated us like kings everywhere we went.

A few of us couldn't face that bloody train journey back home, so the morning after the match we shared a taxi to Santander and caught a ferry that was going to Southampton. It was the first time I had travelled through the Bay of Biscay and it was quite wretched. I made a mental note never to use that route again. Well, we got back to land safely and I had a full 24 hours to recover before getting on the move again to watch the weekend's home match against Derby County.

We won the game easily enough by three goals to one. They were a very average side, so average in fact that Phil Thompson managed to score against them, the other goals coming from Heighway and Callaghan. They managed to score a consolation goal just before the end but this made no odds as we beat them 6-0 in the return leg at Anfield.

CHRIS WOOD

UEFA CUP QUARTER FINAL 1ST LEG
3RD MARCH 1976
DYNAMO STADION [32182]
DRESDEN. EAST GERMANY
DYNAMO DRESDEN 0 LIVERPOOL 0

One night whilst having a couple of bevies with my mates, it was suggested that we should consider going to the away game in Dresden in East Germany. Initially, most of them said "Yes, OK, I'm up for it", we eagerly awaited details of the travel arrangements. Once they were available most of them dropped out of the trip, it was an awful lot of money? We ended up with three of us prepared for the journey and an experience of a lifetime.

At that time, I was earning something like £18.00 a week the cost of the travel package to Dresden was around the £100.00 mark. I worked as much (mid-week) overtime as possible, got money for Christmas presents etc and soon managed to collect enough to afford the trip. We were really lucky at that time because one of my other mates brothers, used to travel to the away games by car, this enabled us to still go to most aways on the cheap.

One night my Dad pulled me aside and gave me £50.00 towards the cost for Dresden, he said "Don't tell your Mum or any of the others, I had a good win on the horses and want you to have this." I told him I had already sorted the money side of things out, but he said "Keep it lad, put it towards any of the away games you have planned." Superb, the old fella always helped me out when money for the games was a bit tight.

We booked our plane, match tickets, hotel accommodation etc with Town's Travel in Liverpool City centre. We also had to go to Anfield to let them know we had booked for the game. No computers in them days, and for some reason we had to take a copy of the booking slip from Town's Travel to Liverpool FC.

We were already members of the "Anfield Special" club, as we tried our best to travel to nearly all the League and Cup away games in them days (Southern based mid-week away games were a pain to get too and home from). January and February were terrible months, West Ham away in the FA Cup (2-0 to the Reds), Derby County away in the FA Cup (lost 1-0) and West Ham away in the league (won 4-0). All via the "Anfield Special" Club because our mates older brother "didn't fancy going" to these games? Man United away (car) and Derby County away (coach) were also attended. We only missed a mid-week 1-0 win away at Arsenal. We were gutted.

Travelling to East Germany was a journey into the unknown, we couldn't find anyone who had travelled last time we played there in 1973. We were told that we could only take £25.00 out of the UK and that owing to political reasons, we would not be allowed to take any books, magazines, newspapers etc into Dresden.

Anyhow, we had managed to beg, steal or borrow enough money to sort out the travel costs and we had £25.00 spending money each. Bags packed with new or best clobber, it was time for the off.

We made our way to Anfield for around 8.30 in the morning of Tuesday 2nd March (Shrove Tuesday) boarded our coaches and were taken to Speke Airport. Upon arrival, we were told we might have to go to Manchester as it was too foggy for the plane to land. Most of the 73 Liverpool supporters complained that we didn't want to go via Manchester, but our complaints fell on deaf ears.

Eventually, we boarded the plane and wizzed off from Liverpool to Dresden, our courier was Christa Berthold, and she was a stunner, long blonde hair and a figure to break your heart. As we approached Dresden airport, Christa stood up and asked us to collect all our daily papers and put them in a bin bag, to be deposed of safely, hmm, I thought, hope its not going to be dead strict over there? A couple of lads rolled up their daily newspapers and put them in their socks, under their kecks.

We got off the plane and were greeted by two lines of heavily armed East German soldiers, a couple of the lads made funny remarks to them, and goose-stepped along the airport reception area, not one of the soldiers, or the Liverpool tour officials laughed.

We soon made our way to the checkout desk and were escorted onto coaches by the soldiers. As we travelled through Dresden, it was VERY noticeable that something "Special" was going on. Christa explained that Shrove Tuesday was a huge celebration in East Germany and that it was Carnival time (Rosa Montag), and that the majority of people wore fancy dress costumes to help celebrate the occasion.

We reached the Newa Hotel in the middle of Dresden, booked in and unpacked our gear in a matter of minutes and headed downstairs. (I shared a room with my mate Ian Nunney from Thornton. Ian was one of my best mates (and still is), and he would travel "anywhere" to watch the Reds. Another lad was Lee, he lived in Warbreck Moor in Aintree. Sadly Ian no longer goes to the matches and we lost contact with Lee some years ago.

Anyway, the time in East Germany was two hours ahead of UK time, so it was still afternoon, and we were thirsty? We were told that the only place we could exchange £'s into Deutchmarks was at the hotel reception, so we changed a £5.00 note for about 7 Deutchmarks and headed for the hotel bar.

We were also told NOT to walk about Dresden alone as "things" may occur, and that it would be best if we stayed in the Hotel and enjoyed ourselves. Part of the deal included a sight seeing tour of Dresden, Christa was going around telling everyone to meet up in the hotel lobby as two coaches had been laid on for us. Being in our late teens we decided this was a definite 100% "no-goer" for us. We were soon joined by many others who wanted to stay and sample the refreshments behind the hotel bar. Christa looked across to us, somewhat bemused as we restarted our assault on the bar. Nobody ever knew the name of the other courier, she was a grumpy soul who kept herself to herself.

Refreshed, it was time to rebel and go outside, we left our copies of the Daily Mirror etc at the hotel bar. About eight of us headed out, all decked in red and white, we walked through a huge Square and reached a shopping complex, we looked at the prices of goods in the shop windows (camera's, televisions etc) and were amazed how cheap they were. The square had statues of famous East Germans and of course influential communist figureheads, armed soldiers goose-stepped along each side of the square, we soon joined in and goose-stepped our way in single line to the sanctuary of a Bierkeller. Eventually we found a Bierkeller and it was massive. Apprehensively we walked in and joined a queue, stony faced people dressed in drab clothing looking at us. We waited in line and ordered our lagers, these were served in huge heavy stein glasses. We sat down at one end of a long line of tables and surveyed the situation, one of the lads had ordered some food, a waitress turned up with what looked like sausage and mash, the meal was huge, and the sausage was about 12" long and looked very tasty.

Hunger pains got the better of us pretty soon all of us had one of these sausage and mash mountains in front of us. The sausage really did look superb, very appetising, one bite soon put paid to our preconceived presumptions, they were horrible full of spices and things that I had never tasted before or since that day. One by one the sausages where tasted and then discarded by their hungry and disappointed recipients. The price of the meals and ale was incredibly cheap, something like 8p for a stein of lager and 12p for the meal, but of course in Pfennings.

As the lager flowed, a couple of lads wearing Dresden scarves approached us, we invited them to sit down and ordered some lagers for them. They turned out to be cracking blokes, up for a laugh and joke and not a hint of hostility from them. They spoke quite good English and we had no problem understanding them, we had to repeat ourselves a number of times, they couldn't understand Scouse. The lads sat in awe of us, and we asked why? They explained that not many away supporters from non–communist countries ever visit Dresden and we where the first English club to bring so many supporters with us.

After many many ales, at around 7.00pm that night, the gorgeous Christa suddenly appeared looking a bit flustered and said that we should be back at the hotel as a "Special" meal had been laid on and everyone was waiting for us. Begrudgingly, we agreed to return to the hotel and walked back with our Dresden mates, purposely behind Christa, all of us lusting after Christa's body.

The hotel people had no idea who was who, so we sat the Dresden lads down and we all enjoyed a free meal and a few free ales. It was noticeable that there were more than 73 Liverpool supporters in the hotel now, around 40 Liverpudlians had driven by car to Dresden, I spoke to a number of them, most were from Liverpool, Kirkby, Huyton and Bootle. Most of them looked knackered after such long car journey's, some managed to last until 11.00pm that night, but not many lasted after that.

The Liverpool Supporters Club based in London had also turned up with around 100 fellow Reds, they had booked their own charter plane independently of the Club and booked accommodation in the same hotel. We had a distinct feeling that the Liverpool officials who organised our trip weren't keen for the "independent" supporters to mix with us, so we made sure that we mixed with them. Anyone who had travelled that far for a match was alright in my book.

The London lads were about 33% split between Scousers, exiled Scousers and Southern based supporters, we had a cracking time with them, as most of them also enjoyed a good bevy and a laugh. For years and years afterwards every now and then you would recognise some of them at other matches.

After a quick shower and change of clothes, it was back to the bar for more ale. We had a few bob still left from our seven Deutschmarks. One of the older blokes from London then approached us and whilst we supped with him, he said he had changed his "allowed" £25.00 with a tout outside for around 3 times the going rate. Happy days, quick as a starving fox after a big plumb rabbit, we legged it up to our room, got our £'s and went outside.

Obviously no-one is going to ask 'Are you a tout?' We must have stood out like sore thumb's, because minutes after going outside this bloke says something like "Hello, are you from Liverpool" a quick scan around and retort "Yes mate we are". Very quickly the deal is done, delighted to have exchanged £20.00 for around £ 60.00 in Deutschmarks. Time to pop back into the bar to share our fortunes with the rest of the lads.

Happy days indeed, within minutes, we had told everyone of the bloke outside, soon all the Reds fans had more cash in their pockets than before they left home. As the bevvies flowed so did the songs, soon we had everyone singing their heads off, our East German friends as eager as any mad Liverpudlian.

After a while one of the lads came in with a dirty big grin on his face and said "Come and look at this outside", we eagerly followed him out to be met by around 100 Dresden supporters. What was he laughing his head off for? Word had got out in Dresden that Liverpool Football Club where staying at the hotel and they thought we were Liverpool players. Within minutes we had all signed their autograph books etc, I think I was David Fairclough. It was really humbling to see how much respect "Us" Liverpool players received from the Germans.

Our hotel was one of three buildings, each separated by a public walkway. As I said before it was carnival time in Dresden, our carnival had not really started yet. As the night progressed, groups of Liverpool fans started drifting off to experience the night-life in Dresden. About eight of us agreed to head off in a different direction and soon we found a Bierkeller that was chocka block full of drunken Dresdenites, all togged up in fancy dress costumes.

The ale flowed as we tried our best to reach and in some cases surpass the same level of drunkenness that the locals enjoyed. The East German people we talked to said that they hated living in East Germany because they had no freedom of speech and had few civil liberties. A few of the older ones didn't like the English because Dresden had been heavily bombed during World War 2. What could we say? Just look apologetic and say nowt. It was not the time or place to talk about the War?

One of the main objections was that they had to take an identity pass with them everywhere they went, and could be asked to produce verification of who they were at anytime and by any of the many various Government people. We were told that it was common for people to hear a knock on the front door (day or night-time) and Government officials would demand immediate entrance into their homes, to check the identities of the people in the house.

They couldn't leave any of the Eastern Bloc Countries, until they were 60 and of course had to have "Special" dispensation from the Government. They were allowed to visit other "Communist" Countries such as Bulgaria and Yugoslavia etc, Yugoslavia was the popular Country to visit for family holidays with the East Germans.

Anyway, after much ale we asked the locals about the nightlife in Dresden, surprisingly we were told about a number of nightclubs on the other side of town, just past our hotel. We set off for a look, as usual goose-stepping our way side by side, but none of us ever reached any of the nightclubs.

Whilst marching past our hotel, someone noticed that there was a nightclub under the second hotel complex next to ours, good idea. Not too far to stagger home. The bloke on the door somehow knew we were staying next door and willingly invited us in. We went straight to the bar to get the ale in for our mob, while the rest found two empty tables and loads of chairs for us to pipe what was going on in the club.

The club was near enough full of Dresdenites, all dressed up in fancy dress most of them up on the dance floor giving it loads to English pop songs. A few fellow Reds had also managed to get in, they soon joined in with us, and the real carnival was about to begin?

One of the lads asked a passing waiter "Hey lad, what time does the bar close mate" the best possible reply came from our new found Dresden mate "Very late, maybe four or five in the morning" maybe later…… We all looked at each other in stunned amazement, all with whopping big dirty grins on our faces, we had hit the JACKPOT!

After copious amounts of German ale, it was party time. To begin with a couple of the lads got a couple of German birds up to dance, one by one we got up on the dance floor with local girls, some even got up with women old enough to be their Mums and or even Grans. Our tables were empty apart from hundreds of empty stein glasses and a number of thirst quenchers saved for later. In time we all ended up wearing fancy dress hats, covered in streamers and having the time of our lives.

Stupid things like you would never do at home suddenly became the craze, the conga was amongst one of the funniest things that springs to mind. We had everyone up, and I mean everyone, doormen, waiters, the whole lot, all in one huge line, everyone bouncing up and down having a laugh.

Another cracker was when the DJ put on a song by ABBA, not my cup of tea but the Germans loved it. They all got up to dance and so did we, fortunately the next song was by Status Quo so we kept everyone up on the dance floor, and taught them how to headbang. It was hilarious watching middle aged people giving it loads, tears ran down our faces as we encouraged them to join in.

As time passed the laughs increased as some of our lads somehow managed to find and dress up in fancy dress costumes, "Have you seen Lee, its his round next, yes there he is dressed up as a bloody gorilla"

You could tell it was Lee, because the gorilla had his Liverpool scarf around his neck and had a pair of Gola trainees on..

As the night progressed the slowies got played, I got up with a few birds and incredibly I copped off with a cracking girl in her mid twenties, Anette. We sat down in a quiet section of the room and enjoyed each others company. As time passed I smuggled her into our hotel, and a "Special" bond between East and West was consummated. We exchanged addresses, and once back in Liverpool continued to write to each other for many months afterwards. I never told my girlfriend back in Liverpool about my relationship.

I eventually went to bed at around 4.00am in the morning and was up around 8.00am with a dirty big grin on my face, word soon got out that a coalition had taken place. I said nothing, just grinned, a ladies honour was at stake. (After all these years I think its OK to tell the truth now).

Anyway, after feeding our faces we went for a walk to clear our heads and to have a mosey around. Whilst walking across the huge Square (again) Dave from Speke climbed up a statue of Lenin and put a red and white scarf around Lenin's neck, now he was a true red. Dave and his mate Philly were real nutcases, daft, and up for a laugh. Dave had this three quarter leather coat on, he rolled his kecks up above his knee's, fastened his coat so it looked like he had nothing on underneath. The looks he got from the passing Dresdenites were priceless. On one occasion a party of school children were walking along in a line, and Dave pretended to flash at the teacher, she laughed her head off, once she realised he had clothes on underneath, she quickly composed herself and hurried the kids along out of the way.

As the day progressed, we ended up back at the Bierkeller. The Germans had by now sussed out who was English and soon approached many of us, asking to buy "Wrangler" jeans, and indeed any "Western" clothes. Many "deals" were done that day, I sold my leather jacket for something like £30.00, and it only cost me £18.00.

Ian by this time had decided to join in with a few Liverpool lads for a game of five a-side in the main Square. This very soon turned into a dozen Liverpudlians against a dozen Dresdenites. A crowd of around a hundred people gathered to watch the fiasco, towards the end of the game it was a dozen of our lads against fifty odd Dresdenites. The solders had had enough, they raised their guns and threatened to arrest any of the Dresden people if they didn't move away. They quickly dispersed.

The soldiers rounded up the dozen Liverpool supporters and frog marched them to our hotel, each of the lads were "fined" 7 Deutschmarks and told not to do it again. The Liverpool tour officials were not impressed with us, yet again!

Fancy being frog marched to the hotel and being fined for having a game of football. We followed behind the "criminals" to our hotel and we stood stony faced in "mock seriousness" as the LFC tour organisers expressed their thoughts on this disgraceful behaviour.

All the lads had a whip round for the offenders which was appreciated and was soon exchanged for beer for all. After a few bevies, we decided that because of the attitude of the German authorities we should go out and start another game of football but with more of us. Christa and the LFC tour organisers pleaded with us and eventually persuaded us not to do so, the other courier stood po-faced and was definitely not amused. Someone mentioned a game of rugby would be a good laugh, we left the hotel for a walkabout on the pretence of looking for a rugby ball, but we went for a few more beers and some food.

We returned to the hotel once again and packed our bags etc. looking out of our window all you could see were hundreds and hundreds of Dynamo Dresden supporters all bedecked in yellow and black. Some had dirty big yellow and black flags held very high in the air, it looked superb.

We were asked to vacate our hotel rooms by tea-time, and leave our bags in a secure room in the hotel. In the hotel corridors were fridge's full of mineral water and fruit juices etc, a number of us emptied the fridge's out and passed the bottles to the many German people outside the hotel. Soon hair dryers, towels, soap etc were passed onto our Dresden colleagues. The hotel people didn't have a clue.

We left the hotel and were mobbed yet again by Dresden supporters each wanting our autograph's or to swap scarves (now I knew how Kevin Keegan must have felt like) eventually we managed to scramble onto our coach as the Dresden supporters chanted "LIV-ER-POOL, LIV-ER-POOL" over and over again.

Once inside the ground, we made our way up to the terraces, we were surprised to find that the Liverpool section had a ring of armed guards around us, properly to protect us from more autograph hunters. As usual a fine rendition of "You'll Never Walk Alone" boomed out from the travelling Kopites, with a healthy number of anti – Man U songs thrown in for good measure (not sick ones). This didn't go down too well with the Liverpool tour officials, words were said, they were not amused, so we all kept on with the anti Man U songs for quite some time.

The ground itself was like a bowl, surrounded by trees, everyone was standing apart from a very little stand behind us, which could only hold no more than 1,000 supporters. The attendance that night was 33,000, it didn't seem that big, but that's what is down in the return programme at Anfield.

The game itself was a very tight affair indeed, Dresden where the top team in East Germany and soon had the Tricky Reds on the back foot, as Liverpool soaked up the pressure and tried to silence the home crowd. Ray Kennedy was alleged to have brought down a Dresden player and a penalty was awarded. Up stepped the Dresden number 10 Kotte, he smashed the ball to Ray Clemence's right into the bottom corner. Somehow Clemence managed to get his fingertips to the ball, and saved the penalty. The ground erupted as the German's sighed in disbelief and we went up roaring our heads off. Possibly Ray's best ever save?

A small scuffle broke out in the Dresden section next to us, we were told it was some anti – Government movement trying to disrupt the match. Some armed soldiers moved in amongst them and the mob dispersed. We started singing "Are you United in disguise" pointing at them, the humour was lost on them.

As the final whistle blew, we went ape, a 0.0 draw, a superb result, all set up for a cracking return game at Anfield. The Liverpool players walked right up to us and acknowledged our support, even Bob Paisley stopped and clapped us, we felt dead proud.

We had to wait behind for 10/15 minutes as the soldiers ensured that our departure from the ground was clear and safe. As we boarded our coaches a number of Dresden supporters broke through our armed escort and exchanged scarf's and badges with fellow Reds. I gave a Liverpool pin badge in exchange for a Dresden pin badge. I still have the badge as a memento to a very special time in my life.

After the game, we headed back to our hotel to collect our luggage and to load up the coach. Outside the hotel I met Anette for the very last time, she was wearing the Liverpool scarf I had given her the night before. She gave me a dirty big hug, whispered something "special" in my ear, we kissed then reluctantly left each other.

We passed out most of our Deutchmarks and Pfennings to the Dresden supporters gathered yet again outside our hotel and gave our hosts in the hotel a couple of bob for their fine service in keeping us fed and our throats well lubricated. We didn't need the money but they did.

The coach trip to the Airport seemed to take an age and a half, our coach was not

40

involved in the nudge as mentioned above, our coach driver continued straight to the Airport. We gathered together in the Airport lounge, once the other coach arrived, we all put the last of our Deutchmarks and Pfennings into a kitty and we all had one last beer in Dresden.

The Liverpool players, management and directors arrived soon after, the players were allowed a quick drink with us, before being whisked away. Somewhere I still have two Dresden programmes, one signed by all the Liverpool players and Bob, the other unsigned.

The plane trip home was surprisingly very high spirited, as everyone exchanged stories of the chaos and merriment that we had all contributed too. Christina thanked us for sharing our (in her words) unique sense of humour and zest for life with her. She said she had never experienced "anything" like "us" and said "we would be welcome back with open arms anytime".

We went through the usual booking-in procedures at Speke Airport, met up at the foyer and were told that we had to make our own way home (no coaches to drop us off at Anfield). We said our goodbyes and managed to get a taxi home. We had very little English money on us, and had to stop off at Lee's to borrow some cash from his Dad which was repaid at the next home game.

Next day, the family asked what it was like in Dresden, "Oh a bit quiet, not like around here". My Dad came home from work and asked, I told him it was superb and most of the above story. He saw the glint in my eyes and the grin on my face and I sensed that he had an idea of what we had been up to.

Despite being told not to venture out of our hotel, I can honestly say that the majority of the Dresden people we met were superb, a credit to their city and their football club. Our next game after Dresden away was Middlesborough at Anfield, the following Saturday. We got beat 2-0 and some of the lads moaned on the way home. I didn't, I had the time of my life. A once in a lifetime opportunity that I will never forget.

ROBBIE ASHCROFT

UEFA CUP SEMI FINAL 1ST LEG
30TH MARCH 1976
CAMP NOU [70000]. BARCELONA. SPAIN
BARCELONA 0 LIVERPOOL 1

We got the coach from outside the Empire in Lime Street on the Monday evening heading for the ferry at Dover for the match on the Wednesday. The match was fantastic with Toshack scoring early in the game and the Reds hanging on to record a rare home defeat for Barcelona in a European tie.

Trouble broke out outside the Nou Camp after the game and I am embarrassed to say that, along with another Liverpool lad, I was hauled off to the local nick after trading punches with a group of Barcelona fans who were trying to forced their way onto our coach, to this day I still can't work that one out. They released us a few hours later after the usual finger printing and dropped us on the main route out of town, almost peseta less and being advised by the policeman to head for Santander were we could try to catch the ferry to England (really helpful).

We quickly thumbed a lift to a place called Lleida and then another lift to a service station on the outskirts of Zaragoza were we managed to persuade the cafe owner to give us a cup of coffee and a pastry in exchange for a Liverpool scarf. It was there our luck changed when a guy sitting in the cafe noticed our Liverpool shirts and approached us to find out what had happened. He then offered us a lift in his lorry which by chance was taking a load of tomatoes to Glasgow. He hid us in the cab and smuggled us on the Santander to Plymouth ferry and dropped us off at the top of the East Lancashire road where the other guy, Billy from Widnes, phoned his Dad who picked us up in the early hours of Friday morning.

The funny bit was that I was home before my mates on the coach which went via Dover and I can still remember the look on their faces when I was waiting for them outside of the old Legs of Man as the coach pulled up. We also wrote a song on the ferry going over which I remember to this day and is sung to the tune of Viva Espana……

Oh the Scouse are off to sunny Spain - a viva Bob Paisley
To see the Barcelona game - a viva Bob Paisley
Oh we're going there to win the cup - a viva Bob Paisley
And Johan Cruyff can go to f**k - it's Liverpool for the cup
ALAN PARKINSON

UEFA CUP FINAL 2ND LEG
19TH MAY 1976
OLYMPIA STADIEN [29463]
BRUGES. BELGIUM
CLUB BRUGES KV 1 LIVERPOOL 1

We got the boat over from London on the Sunday and arrived in Bruges in the late afternoon. There was me, Dick Barry, Kevin Crowley, Sue Tweddle and Brida. Our timing was immaculate because as we parked ourselves in this bar in the main square the area filled up with Bruges fans coming back from the game where they had clinched the League title. They were all in fine form and were having a good old sing song. As soon as there was a lull in the singing I decided to enliven the proceedings with a quick burst of 'Oh when the reds go up to lift the UEFA Cup…..'. The immediate response was all the Belgians started singing and buying us ale. After a good few pints the bar manager asked where we were staying, as we hadn't got around to sorting that out yet we said that we didn't know. Not a problem says he, my mate round the corner has a place, so off we went.

The hotel was fine and after packing our gear away we went downstairs for some food and some more ale. There was a group of very well dressed lads in the corner, one of whom seemed quite well known as people kept walking up to him and shaking his hand. After a while he walked over to us.

'You are Liverpool fans yes?'

Well this was a bloody soft question considering we were decked out in red and white and had been singing for about an hour but we politely responded in the affirmative.

'Do you need tickets',

Now none us had tickets but as it was only Sunday we had three free days to sort ourselves out and as this lad was obviously a tout there was no need for us to part with our money just yet. So we told him that we were ok. He looked doubtful and said,

'Ok if you have no luck I'll be here tomorrow' and walked off.

The next morning we headed up to the ground. It was cracking the flags and we were all optimistic of getting our hands on a few spares. When we got there we were giving out badges and spares to all the staff there, girls in the ticket office, the commissionaires, even the hot dog salesmen. Everybody loved us but there was nothing down for us as regards tickets.

We were back sitting in the hotel bar when the lad from the night before walked over, still looking very smart and in a different suit from the night before.

'I hear that you have no tickets, can I help you?'

We went into a huddle and it was decided that we would take him up on his offer if the price was not too extortionate. He said that he would wait outside. So we had a whip round for the tickets and I stuck an empty bottle in my pocket in case things got out of hand. We walked out of the bar and down this alleyway, I was waiting to be jumped any second, this felt so wrong. At the bottom of the alley was this big, flash Mercedes, obviously being a tout paid well, which we got in and he set off.

'Do me a favour, my English friend. Look in the glove compartment and you will find a newspaper, look at the picture on the front page'.

A bit bewildered I did as I was told. On the front page there was a picture of the King of Belgium meeting with the lad sitting next to me – the mayor of Bruges! I roared out laughing and turned round and said,

'Now should I throw that empty bottle away?'

I was still laughing as we got to the ground. He took us into the Supporter's Club, where he called over somebody who looked like an official.

'How many tickets do you need?'

I said about ten and he proceeded to go into his pockets and produce a handful of spares.

'We always keep some back for visiting away fans. If you want anymore please let us know'.

I let my new found friend buy a pint of some Belgian beer, treated the bar to a version of 'Romeo and Juliet' and came back into town with my wedge of tickets.

The next night all the crew started arriving. We were treated to the bizarre sight of Bobby Wilcox (all 20-odd stone of him) riding around the main square on a kid's bike.

Naturally all hands were encouraging him and Bobby was playing up to his audience. Next thing he went straight through a bar's glass window. The owner came out screaming and shouting and the police, who before had been laughing with us, were now looking a bit serious. Bobby rose to the occasion. He organised a whip round, weighed the owner in and still managed to get a couple of quid for the ale. A great trip – and we won the cup!

FRED SEPHTON

1976/77 EUROPEAN CUP

14 September 1976 First round
Liverpool FC   2-0   Crusaders FC

28 September 1976 First round
Crusaders FC   0-5   Liverpool FC
Aggregate: 0-7

20 October 1976 Second round
Trabzonspor AŞ   1-0   Liverpool FC

3 November 1976 Second round
Liverpool FC   3-0   Trabzonspor AŞ
Aggregate: 3-1

2 March 1977 Quarter-finals
AS Saint-Étienne 1-0   Liverpool FC

16 March 1977 Quarter-finals
Liverpool FC   3-1   AS Saint-Étienne
Aggregate: 3-2

6 April 1977 Semi-finals
FC Zürich   1-3   Liverpool FC

20 April 1977 Semi-finals
Liverpool FC   3-0   FC Zürich
Aggregate: 6-1

25 May 1977 Final
Liverpool FC   3-1   VfL Borussia Mönchengladbach

EUROPEAN CUP ROUND ONE 2ND LEG
28TH SEPTEMBER 1976
SEAVIEW STADIUM [10500]
BELFAST. NORTHERN IRELAND
CRUSADERS 0 LIVERPOOL 5

It's a balmy Monday evening in late September 1976, and I'm down at the Pier Head with a group of Annie Road urchins and loyal older Kopites. I'm sporting a black eye, received two days earlier at Newcastle when I got jumped on the way back to Manors railway station, a supposedly safe haven for away supporters travelling to the game on the Special. The rumour was that hundreds of Geordies were waiting to ambush Reds fans at the main-line station, but their mob was so big they could afford to send a platoon to greet us at this branch-line outpost, and I got done in. I was just unlucky.

But hey, let's not allow such trifling inconveniences to detract from the excitement of a boat ride to Belfast during the height of the sectarian troubles. I could sight our ship berthed and ready to sail the high seas in nearby Princes Dock, and after a stewards enquiry with the chaps and much back-slapping for my bravery two days earlier, we eventually charted a North Western course and set sail into the Mersey at 10.30 pm. Being young lads we treated sleep like the impostor it ought to be on these special European trips, and after a few beers it was time to act out scenes reminiscent of Pirates of the Caribbean as a good friend called Tommy Scouser took the brave but unusual decision to clamber along the sides of the ship with a drop of 60ft to the churning black sea a mere slip of the hand away.

He made it to first class...just...and then decided he didn't like the facilities on offer so climbed back to his Kopite mates in 3rd class. We eventually arrived at an overcast and drizzly Belfast at 6.30am, and were met by a couple of Irish lads who invited us to join them at their local watering hole. There was me, two lads from Liverpool, and these two Belfast boys, and we all piled into their little motor. What the heck, we'll have a laugh, I thought. Big mistake! After a tour of the city's finest hot-spots...the Shankhill Road and the headquarters of King Billy's provincial orange order, I slowly began to realise that I was now mates with a couple of foot-soldiers from the UDA. 'Oh shoite', I exclaimed quietly, before vowing not to shout 'hail hail' to anybody all day.

By lunch-time we'd found seats near the bar in a social club on the outskirts of Belfast. The exterior design of the building was creamy white and all purple and orange on the inside. There were pictures of the Queen and King Billy on every wall...even in the toilets...and I began to feel uneasy. Wisely, I kept my mouth shut about Celtic being my second team, and successfully mimed when they started singing 'The Sash My Father Wore' as the ale kicked in.

It gets a bit surreal at this point, because one of the Belfast lads suggested we all go back to his house and meet his family. So we drove through country lanes to a drab looking housing estate where I got to meet his mother and sisters and grandmother, along with five kids with snotty noses. We were offered cups of tea and ham sandwiches, and being starving, I said…' Yeah, go 'ed I will have a sarney, thanks'.

After an hour of forcing bread and sliced ham into my mouth as well as teaching the kids the words to 'You'll Never Walk Alone' we waved goodbye to this lovely family and drove to Crusader's ground near the docks. We stood on the small open terrace to the left of the goal, and guess what? I copped off with what appeared to be the girl from Ipanema…not really, more like King Billy's younger sister. I don't think it was my boyish good looks that impressed her, more likely that she fancied a bit of love action with a Scouser who was a card-carrying fully paid up member of the Kop choir. We went round the back of the small kiosk at the side of the terrace at half-time and had a snog, which was nice.

There weren't that many Reds from Liverpool at the match…just a few hundred…but we were treated like Kop royalty by the Belfast Reds. It did sound a bit strange hearing thousands of Irish supporters singing to the tune of 'Scouser Tommy' in a 'dead on' accent, sounded great though! We won the game in a canter, 5-0, but just before the end of the match I was warned to be on my toes for the short walk back to the docks where our passage back East awaited. Streetwise is as streetwise does, and I followed the crowds along the dock road before turning left and entering the safe haven of the shipyard after a fraught twenty minute walk that had my eyes searching not for football hooligans but paramilitary revolutionaries on a mission to shoot Kopites whose second team is Celtic.

It was a trip fraught with danger and excitement and a world away from the delights and glory that was Rome eight months later, but I wouldn't have missed it for the world.
EDDIE COTTON

EUROPEAN CUP QUARTER-FINAL 1ST LEG
2ND MARCH 1977
STADE GEOFFROY GUICHARD [38000]
SAINT ETIENNE. FRANCE
A.S. SAINT ETIENNE 1 LIVERPOOL 0

A good trip anyway, despite the defeat. The club's first competitive visit to France attracted massive media interest as we prepared to play the current French champions and also the defeated European Cup finalists from the previous season. A flight from Speke to Lyon before being bussed into the city centre and having a couple of hours to ourselves before re-boarding the coach and heading South towards our final destination. Then the coach pulled into a motorway service station, where everyone was held until all the other vehicles had arrived so that we could continue to Saint-Éti-enne in one big convoy. Sadly, there was quite a lot of petty pilfering by some of our supporters from the shops at the service station. It took a while before that could be sorted out but eventually we all arrived at a massive car park close to the stadium. The atmosphere/noise inside the stadium was awesome. We were in the huge covered

terrace behind the goal to the right as the cameras looked. Watching the highlights again I had forgotten just how good Phil Thompson's headed chance was in the first half although I do remember Steve Heighway racing clear and hitting a post in the second. Just when it looked as if we would hold out for a creditable draw, sloppy marking at a corner saw Dominique Bathenay volley past Ray Clemence from about eight yards out. Losing was a huge disappointment. It was very cramped standing on that terrace and many of us were drenched with sweat and also drenched from the urine-filled plastic bottles that had been thrown at us by some dirty French bastards higher up on that terrace. To be honest I was glad to get out of the town and back to Lyon airport. We got back to Liverpool at about two in the morning.
CHRIS WOOD

When I was still at school no-one you knew went to European away games. That was the preserve of proper arl fellas, blokes over thirty who drank fifteen brown bitters a night and who worked at Fords. The odd teenager might have been to Leeds away in the Fairs Cup, but no-one our age ever went anywhere abroad on their own. The tales we'd heard off blokes going to extreme lengths to get somewhere obscure, we'd only heard about in war films, left our heads reeling. In our eyes, an unaccompanied, independently organised week-long foray into Europe was akin to an expedition to the source of the Nile. I say 'independently-organised' but the organisation went no further than a vague plan to "get off the ferry at Calais and ask the first fella in a uniform where Dresden is".

So when our chance came, we jumped at it. 1976-77 saw our most realistic opportunity since 1965 of winning the European Cup. We'd talked of going to Rome for the final but in the quarter-final we drew one of the best teams in Europe, St Etienne. 'Les Verts' had been in the previous year's final, out-playing, but losing 1-0 to Bayern Munich at Hampden. They also had, in Dominique Rocheteau, one of Europe's greatest attacking talents, as well as a murderous Argentinian psycho called Osvaldo Piazza who promised to destroy Keegan and Toshack.

Thinking we'd probably get beaten I decided to go. It was the first game in Europe after the Christmas break. We'd beaten Trabzonspor, which seemed at the time to be as far away as Outer Mongolia, and Crusaders of Belfast (which only looked like it was in Outer Mongolia) before Christmas, and when my birthday came round I asked for just the one present, the fare to France. My mum wasn't too enthusiastic. And with good reason. I'd just broken my leg playing footy thanks to a Terry Darracott look-a-like of a full back with a tackle that was as late as The Old Grey Whistle Test. I was in plaster from my toes to my nuts, and would remain so for five months. To appease her my cousins agreed to come along and steer me safely to the game and home again. To them the excitement of watching a club away game in Europe was heightened by the fact that they were both Evertonians. This was a wildly strange and previously unimagined proposition for them both, but if it meant staying awake for 72 hours drinking Pernod they said they'd be up to the task. And so it proved.

The coach was a wreck, a good decade past it's best days, but still one of Crown Topping's better vehicles. It had no video system, not even a radio. And certainly no toilet. Just as we were about to pull away on the journey someone pointed something out to the driver. There was something, no, someone, on the roof. The driver got out and ordered down some lunatic who'd secured himself to the top of the bus with a knitting needle driven into the roof. His plan had been to hang on, like an Indian commuter on the train in Calcutta, until we'd got to the M62, where his mates would get the driver to pull over at Burtonwood. He'd then slip aboard as we set off again. He never made it to France, alas. Not even to Childwall. He was kicked up the arse and told to go home.

With no music, entertainment was provided by the forty or so of us young lads singing football songs, drinking and reading copies of Escort or whatever other 'gentlemen's entertainment' could be stolen from service stations along the way (It was widely considered the French version of motorway porn was far superior, despite us not being able to read the reader's letters. We were particularly struck by their preference for the more heavily-pubed female, the kind of naked model that looked like she had a Coldstream Guard climbing out of her.

We had left Liverpool at tea-time on the Monday, crossed the Channel the following morning and by mid afternoon were being driven round and round the Paris ringroad by a driver who quite clearly had no idea where he was, having never done a run further than Alton Towers before. The Eiffel Tower kept appearing on the horizon as the afternoon slipped away, on the right, on the left, behind us. We didn't care as we still had some duty-free left.

By now our leaders had emerged. Two nutters a couple of years older than us. One was playing a bugle, the other singing through a loud hailer. One variation when they were bored was to play the bugle through the loud hailer. Late on Tuesday night, after losing many hours orbiting Paris, the coach, by now a foul-smelling fug of flatulence and unwashed teenage feet (think of a submarine full of Camembert, that's been stranded on the sea-bed for a week and that's being crewed by tramps), creaked into Lyon.

It was, by now, too late for us to do anything. There would be no waiters outside Lyonnais pavement cafes brushing crumbs off the tables and gesturing for us to sit down. We'd dreamed of a Europe where Les Pubs were open all night and wine flowed like water. Lyon, however, was shut. Some of those on board had opted for a hotel rooms for an extra twelve quid, but not us. Whilst a few lads broke back into the coach and slept there, about a dozen of us, including the two nutters, stumbled off into the night looking for somewhere to kip. As we headed towards the railway station, we could hear them singing and playing the bugle whilst looking for a doorway for the night.

Lyon railway station is huge, but deserted at 2am. It was perfect for us. Six of us lay down on a marble concourse, stretched a Liverpool flag over us and within seconds were all sound asleep. It was a jolt, when 6 hours later, we awoke with hundreds of commuters milling round, stepping over us, hurrying to work. I think I'd taken a toothbrush and a clean pair of undies and socks. I'd also brought a red and white adidas t-shirt and a silk scarf as my match-day attire. Suitably washed and brushed up we set out to enjoy Lyon and find some breakfast.

Now, at 17 my French was crap, but compared to the rest of the group I was like the French Stephen Fry. More than eloquent and erudite enough to order coffee and cheese butties anyway. And as the day wore on we began to understand that 'beer' was the same and that the waiters understood what 'chips' meant.

Mid afternoon there was a brief stop in a sex shop, where eight of us crammed into a video booth (the littlest of us, Steve Monaghan, was at the front working the buttons and putting the French Francs in) as the manager roared laughing. After this typically continental diversion there was a more Scouse one with some bored, mechanical shop-lifting in a record shop. We then moved onto a leafy square to eek out glasses of Kronenburg and play footy till the coach was due to leave. One lad (no names) was keen to earn some beer money and was trying to sell the shop-lifted goods (a 'Manhattan Transfer' album, I ask you!). Everyone was skint so he gave it to a waiter in exchange for two ciggies.

Come tea-time and we are all assembled back by the river to get the coach the thirty miles to Saint Etienne. The two nutters were there looking bedraggled and bemused. The trumpet player without his shoes, but with a bandage round his head. He'd been playing the bugle on a parapet when he fell off a bridge onto the riverside quay. When he woke up his shoes and trumpet were gone. He said to his mate,

'Didn't you notice something had gone?'

(Pause) 'I noticed it had gone quiet... does that count?', came the reply.

We got to Saint Etienne about an hour before kick-off, just as it was starting to get dark. There were just five or six coaches in the dark cinder car-park behind the away end. All were from Liverpool travel companies. In total there were around three hundred of us there. Apparently around 1000 travelled, but we never saw too many about and the end we were in wasn't segregated. It was a large, old terrace with a low dark roof. Very British looking and in keeping with St Etienne being an mining town. I hobbled down near the front just behind the goal and my cousins hauled me up onto a barrier. The pitch looked intensely green in the floodlights, the stands all dark brown and black, flecked with the green colours of the locals. Sitting next to me was a pretty, young French girl. Around us was about a hundred of the younger Liverpool fans, the older ones having moved up to the back of the stand, presumably to get a better spec and cadge Gauloise ciggies off the locals. St Etienne had brilliant fans, loud and colourful. Just like us.

The only thing I remember singing is 'Can you hear us on the telly over there?', which no-one at home watching on Sportsnight could hear amidst the cacophony. It really reminded me of Anfield.

It was a tight game. Both sides had ambitions in this competition and both were in great form in Europe. For the most part we cancelled each other out. That, of course, delighted us, as a 0-0 draw with the home leg to come, was a textbook Liverpool European display, especially as Kevin Keegan was missing the game through injury. We almost snatched an away goal too, when Steve Heighway broke away in the second-half, racing towards us. Holding off the defender he shot past the keeper but against the post. However, 'Les Verts' didn't have their reputation for nothing and sure enough, Heighway's attack, having jolted them, they snatched a goal with ten minutes to go. It was from a corner down at the far end. We saw the ball deflected across the box, following a mis-kick to Bathenay, who'd also score at Anfield in the second leg, he then poked it home from close-range, past an unusual looking yellow-shirted Ray Clemence. Cue pandemonium all round. I just sat there. The girl next to me must have taken pity on me as she shook my hand, kissed me and then gave me her 'Allez Les Verts' scarf. I gave her my red silk scarf. She smiled. I was about twenty seconds away from falling in love when there was a roar to our left. Heads turned. Some thin, wiry Scouse lads were fronting a massive, blonde French bloke. He slowly took his jacket off and carefully removed his rings in readiness for fisticuffs. He then pointed at the main Scouser as if to indicate this was to be 'man-to-man'. The Scouser nodded. Then as the blonde Frenchman began to take out an ear-ring he was leapt upon by half a dozen Scouse lads, boys really, who all threw a few good digs in each before disappearing into the crowd. As he picked himself up and wiped blood from his nose I was suddenly filled with relief knowing I was wearing his team's colours.

Out in the coach park afterwards there were a few scuffles, but nothing of note. However, as our coaches prepared to leave, engines revving, spewing thick clouds of diesel exhaust into the night air, a few carefully lobbed bricks put the windows in. The resultant night-time journey up through central France towards the Channel was undertaken with a window out near the back. It was freezing but everybody was too knackered to care. After an hour of comparing souvenirs and bragging about being in (or near) scuffles, the coach suddenly fell silent as one-by-one we took the knock, snoring towards Paris. Having a full plaster cast on my leg meant I was given the prime bedtime location, wrapped in a flag lying in the aisle of the coach on a bed of newspapers, cigarette ash and crushed beer cans.

Next thing I knew it was daylight and seagulls.

JOHN MACKIN

EUROPEAN CUP SEMI-FINAL 1ST LEG
6TH APRIL 1977
STADION LETZIGRUND [30000]
ZURICH. SWITZERLAND
F.C. ZURICH 1 LIVERPOOL 3

After being on the dole for the past six months and arriving back from St. Etienne three weeks previous, I thought 'Christ, what am I going to do for Zurich?' I had bunked the train back with a Transalpino ticket so I still had the return half left, as it was valid for two months. I had a brain wave and decided to buy a load of silk L.F.C scarves, which were only 30p each. I bought approximately 36 scarves and sold them for £10.00 each outside of the Zurich ground. I only had one left and Nature Boy sold it for £5.00 but I gave it to him for 30p. I said 'Why did you do that?' he said 'I never had the heart to sell it for £10.00.' I said 'Yeah, you never gave me the other £4.70 back.' Anyway the moral of the story was, I paid one way with Transalpino to Zurich, three nights in a nice hotel, pissed for three days & nights and come back with £10.00 more than I left with. Fellas who were working and never had enough cash to go said 'How the fuck did you do it?' 'Experience does it.' I told them.

PHILIP ASPINALL

Another quick in-and-out trip but the first time I had seen Liverpool play in Switzerland. It was a well-organised trip too, that did not involve an overnight stay but did include the guarantee of a match ticket. The flight was from Speke to Zurich, where coaches were waiting to take us into the city centre. We had a few hours to kill before heading for the stadium. Near the stadium a bar was showing live, the first leg of the other semi final, Dynamo Kiev v Borussia Mönchengladbach. Kiev won 1-0. I wasn't really bothered who our final opponents might be. We had to get there ourselves first.
 I recognised the stadium as a well-known athletics venue but I knew next to nothing about the Zurich team. I just knew that we ought to be able to beat them over two legs. But we had a shock when they scored an early penalty. At that stage I was not too worried because there was a lot of time left. Within a few minutes Phil Neal had equalised and would add a penalty of his own after Steve Heighway had put us ahead with a wonderful individual goal. As Neal's penalty went in, we wildly celebrated the victory that we were confident would take us to Rome, irrespective of what happened in the second leg, which we won easily enough anyway.
The coaches were all lined up outside to take the visiting supporters back to the airport. It was a bit chaotic there with several flights waiting to leave. As my flight was called, a friend who was on the same trip expressed his doubts that we would leave on time because the team's flight had not yet left. Maybe that normally happens but it didn't on this occasion because we boarded our plane without seeing anything of the club's official party even though it too was scheduled to return to England from the same airport. I remember it was a beautiful clear night and it was easy to recognise the layout of London as we flew over it. We got back to Speke in excellent time, so excellent that I only just missed the 00.30 from Lime Street to London (Euston). After hanging around the airport for a while and watching the team come through, I walked to Allerton station to wait for the first morning train to Crewe, where I boarded a fast train to Euston. Despite being present at a match halfway across Europe the previous evening, I walked into my office at about 10.30am, hung my scarf on a peg and placed my bag of duty-free somewhere safe. By this time my colleagues were used to me disappearing for a couple of days at a time. They didn't need to ask why I hadn't been at work the previous day. They knew … and my all-day smile made sure that they didn't forget either.

CHRIS WOOD

EUROPEAN CUP FINAL
25TH MAY 1977
STADIO OLIMPICO [57000] ROME. ITALY.
BORUSSIA MONCHENGLADBACH 1 LIVERPOOL 3

It was an early Saturday morning and my younger brother and I got onto the coaches, at Williamson Square, provided by Toppings Coach Tours. They had certainly seen better days, just your basic coach, usually seen shuttling the pensioners around Liverpool on bingo nights. No air conditioning, no toilet and certainly no reclining seats! Yet these two coaches had to travel down to Wembley for the FA Cup Final, then to Paris, onto Milan and finally to Rome culminating in one of LFC's finest nights in LFC history.

After the FA Cup Final, with a bit of time to spare, we went to McDonalds. There were very few in the UK and they were a novelty. Also it was at a time when MUFC and LFC supporters actually spoke to each other in civil tones! We had been discussing the match with two MUFC supporters. Yes they had Cockney accents even then! All of a sudden two policemen came over to arrest my brother, on suspicion of pick pocketing. When asked 'Why?' the witness with the police said 'Well he was wearing red and white' Coming to my brothers defence I said 'just take a look around' there must have been about 300 people in McDonald's and everyone of them was wearing red and white. Looking rather sheepish the police left and we heaved a sigh of relief, as the coach was due to leave in the next hour or so. Then the real fun began.

The coach was old and we had just about made it off the ferry into France, when about a third of the way to Paris it broke down. As a consequence we arrived in Paris at about 2am, travelling through the 'red light district'. Many on that coach had never set foot outside of our beloved city and to see all these 'Ladies of the night' openly standing on the street selling their wares, had these homespun lads open mouthed and goggle eyed! We left Paris the following day and once again we broke down. This time a hire coach turned up. A state of the art Volvo with air conditioning. To say the folks in the other coach were jealous was an understatement. We even had two local drivers and they got us to Milan in record time. Unfortunately the other coach took a wrong turn and went over the Alps instead of through the tunnel, got hopelessly lost and arrived eight hours behind.

We all eventually arrived in Rome and 'Mr Topping' who by now was close to a nervous breakdown, gave us the match tickets and made a sudden departure. On close inspection we realised we were in the German end of the Stadium. The Italian police were not very friendly, even quite hostile. Strangely though when we went 3-1 up, they became quite friendly.

Our return journey was fairly uneventful until we came to the point where we had picked up the hired coach which was replaced by a school bus. To say it was cramped was an understatement. It got us to the ferry. where we walked on and were met by our transport back to Liverpool from Dover. Another 'bingo' coach which lasted fifty miles before that too broke down. The driver had had enough and got off and hitched a lift

home. Yet another coach came to pick us up and we eventually arrived back in Liverpool in the early hours of Sunday morning.
ROGER ADAMS

It was the sight of Lime Street Station that did it.

I'd stayed on Sunday night at my mate's flat on the Wirral. He hadn't got a ticket, but crossed the water with me anyway, just to see me off. A couple of quick pints of Higsons in the old Carnarvon Castle and down to the station for my train at about 1pm.

What a bloody sight. Reds everywhere, with those chequered flags covering every inch of station wall and the singing, echoing around the concourse.

There were more than 20 trains booked, and I was booked on to No 7. The excitement even then was all-consuming. The FA Cup Final defeat to United, by the most freakish goal to ever win a Cup Final, had vanished from our consciousness. Our Holy Grail lay 1000 miles further south.

We knew the trains were being sent the long way round, through Belgium and Germany, because of a French rail strike. What we didn't know was the condition of the trains nor the sheer length of the journey. Nor that they'd squeeze 20+ train loads into just a handful of trains, though admittedly they were roughly the length of the Chilean coastline.

They were emphatically not the Orient Express. Ours ran out of water by Tuesday lunchtime. Nobody could wash or, worse still, use the toilets. No food or drink was available, so whenever the trains stopped at a station everyone had to jump off, use the toilets and buy what they could at station buffets. With over 1000 people on board, you can see the problem there.

The late Spring heat on the trains was stifling and unrelenting throughout Tuesday, until nightfall brought some relief. With eight people crammed into compartments designed for six, any two at one time had to lie in the overhead luggage nets. That's how football fans were regarded then, like cattle for live export.

Yet nothing could quell the excitement. The Red legions descending upon the Eternal City produced a culture shock. They blocked the traffic, swam in the fountains and were a nuisance to young women. Stripped to the waist in the Spring sunshine, many were noisy and drunk in the cafes, bars and piazzas.

It was the 25th of May, 1977, a magical date for Liverpool supporters, captured in the Kop's version of 'Arrivederci Roma', 'We're on our way to Roma, on the twenty fifth of May'.

There was magic everywhere, in the Stadio Olimpico, in its unsurpassed setting surrounded by trees, in all those red and white chequered flags, in the famous Joey Jones banner, even in the majestic fighting cocks design of the match ticket.It was the day the Reds finally became European champions and you never forget your first time.
CHRIS ROWLAND

54

1977/78 EUROPEAN CUP

19 October 1977 Second round
Liverpool FC   5-1   1. FC Dynamo Dresden

2 November 1977 Second round
FC Dynamo Dresden   2-1   Liverpool FC
Aggregate: 3-6

1 March 1978 Quarter-finals
SL Benfica   1-2   Liverpool FC

15 March 1978 Quarter-finals
Liverpool FC   4-1   SL Benfica
Aggregate: 6-2

29 March 1978 Semi-finals
VFL Borussia Mönchengladbach   2-1   Liverpool FC

12 April 1978 Semi-finals
Liverpool FC   3-0   VfL Borussia Mönchengladbach
Aggregate: 4-2

10 May 1978 Final
Liverpool FC   1-0   Club Brugge KV

EUROPEAN SUPER CUP FINAL 1ST LEG
22ND NOVEMBER 1977
VOLKSPARK STADION [16000].
HAMBURG, WEST GERMANY.
HAMBURG S.V. 1 LIVERPOOL 1

If Rome had marked a watershed on the pitch it also marked one off it. All Summer people talked of the great trek across Europe. Virtually everyone in the city knew of somebody who had gone to the Final and, as always happens in Liverpool, the stories lost nothing with the telling. St Etienne and Rome had given me a taste for European travel and I was looking forward to our next trip. The first snag was that as European Champions (How good does that sound?) we bypassed the first round, the second snag was that we were then drawn against Dynamo Dresden, somewhere in the dull and grey confines of communist East Germany. Clearly this may be a bit of a problem. This just shows how things have changed. Nowadays I would be chomping at the bit to get there, but in those far off times Eastern Europe was viewed with great suspicion and not a place for a young whippersnapper like myself.

Fortunately salvation was at hand. A small paragraph in the Echo announced that Liverpool had agreed to play FC Hamburg over two legs in the Super Cup.

A subsequent 'after work pint' in the Slaughterhouse found me chatting with Stevie Smith who casually announced that his dad worked on the North Sea Ferry that went from Hull to Hamburg and that he could get us there and back for a fiver each.

So a couple of weeks later we found ourselves on the wet and cold Hamburg dockside en route to the Reeperbahn where we touched lucky again. Being from Liverpool we were naturally curious about seeing the Star, Astra and Kaiserkeller bars were the Fab Four plied their trade. The barmaid in our first port of call was a fortyish blonde bombshell, who on hearing our accents, broke into a big mad smile, exclaiming: 'I was working here when all of the Liverpool groups were here, such happy days.'

Being a gentleman I refrained from asking in what capacity she was working, and just let her ramble on and looking at the pictures of her cuddled up to a very young looking George Harrison. She insisted that we stayed in the spare rooms above the bar, cooked us a massive scran and later on in the night we met all of her friends, an event that I will draw a discrete veil over but, suffice to say, we both made thorough pigs of ourselves.

The next morning saw us heading up to the Volkspark Stadion to pick up any souvenirs and see what the ticket situation was. Again our luck was in. As we got to the stadium the Liverpool team coach was arriving. As the team disembarked we saw Peter Robinson getting off.

'Any chance of any spares please Peter?'

Most football club secretaries confronted by two disheveled rag-arses would've run a mile. He just smiled and said: 'Just the two is it lads? Be here an hour before kick-off. Oh by the way, be careful in that Reeperbahn area.'

What a gentleman, somehow I cannot imagine that happening anymore. We were at the ground a hour beforehand to meet him. He was his naturally urbane self, passing over the tickets, asking how we were enjoying our trip and casually asked where we were staying. We muttered something about Ingrid's Bar in Saint Pauli. He tutted, said something about boys being boys, waved away our offers of payment and left us clutching our tickets.

The game was crap, I think. We had made the most of German hospitality before the game and were more than happy to carry on partying until the wee small hours afterwards. The next morning saw two very young, very happy Liverpool fans wending their weary way home. Free digs and tickets, cheap beer and lashings of sex. No more Colwyn Bay for me, it was Europe whenever I could afford it now.

DAVE HARDMAN

EUROPEAN CUP QUARTER FINAL 1ST LEG
1ST MARCH 1978
ESTADIO DA LUZ [80000].
LISBON. PORTUGAL.
BENFICA 1 LIVERPOOL 2

Back in the 70s Benfica were viewed as being European royalty. As kids we'd all watched the '66 World Cup when the nucleus of the great Portuguese side came from Benfica with players such as Eusebio, Torres and Coluna lighting up Goodison Park (well somebody had to!). So when I saw a small advert in the Echo advertising a 3 night stay in Lisbon for £98 then me and Nicky Roughley booked it right away.

The first part of the trip was the first train out of Lime Street down to Euston and the tube to Heathrow. What with the carryout on the train and the Duty free bar we were a happy band of travellers as we took off for Lisbon. Our trip was enlivened by finding Francis Lee, he of Norman Hunter punching, cheating and diving fame, sitting in the seat behind me. Most togger players surrounded by 50 odd drunken Scousers would have been a wee bit taken aback but not our Franner. He gloried in the attention, saying that he didn't mind the Kop calling him a womble as at the time he was on mega-bucks compared to all of us. He also took great delight in telling us how he turned down Bill Shankly so as to sign for Man City from Bolton. Replete with that last statement he sat back with an exceptionally smug expression. One of the older lads took a last slurp of this Duty Free Johnny Walker, belched then said,

'Well lad I suppose it's good thing that you never did sign for us……………….
Because you were fucking shite'.

The back of the plane erupted with hilarity as we touched down in not so sunny Lisbon. Now a word to the wise. This is March 1978, and football fashion is on the march. We are from Liverpool and by God we are cool and trendy, so when I was told by my mother to take something warm 'just in case' I just laughed as only a cocky teenager can because I knew that it was far more important to look smart than to look warm, anyway this was sunny Portugal, red Adidas t-shirts would be fine. The one ever so tiny flaw in this argument was that Portugal was currently undergoing some of the worst storms it had experienced in a quarter of a century. By the time we had got from the plane to the arrivals desk we were drenched. Thankfully the hotel bar was warm and we sat there till the rain abated and our jeans had dried out before we mooched out to discover the delights of Lisbon.

Our hotel was on the top of the Avenua Liberdade so we walked down the hill into the old town towards the docks where we found the Liverpool Bar, the New York Bar and the legendary Texas Bar, which had some of the friendliest customers that you could meet.

It had stopped raining on the day of the match so we headed up to the Stadium of Light. Given that it is one of Europe's most famous grounds it was a wee bit of a let down. Just an empty bowl with little or no facilities, with the hills around the ground studded with what looked like shanty towns.

Next to it was the team's training ground which we then bunked in to, until one of the elder (i.e. in his 30s) members of the crew pointed out that the Benfica manager was John Mortimore, who had played for Chelsea in the 1965 FA Cup semi final and had been torn to shreds by Peter Thompson. When I say he pointed out I mean he shouted it all around the training ground, accompanying it with the 'While on the bus to Villa Park' song. We were escorted out of the training ground and so headed back to our hotel. We just managed to get back inside when the deluge began. It was raining stair-rods and the rumours were flying around,

'The ground's flooded'.

'The game's off'.

'There are no flights home for over a week'.

We finally got told the game was deffo on. We had all changed into our warmest gear, in my case a paper thin Harrington jacket (why didn't I listen to my mam and take my snorkel?) and boarded the coach to the ground. It was pitch black when we got there, with thunder and lightening crashing in the skys and the hills around the ground were lit up by brazier fires in the shanty towns, it looked like a view of Dante's Inferno. Inside the ground was even more bizarre. There were about 500 of us in an upper section to the right of the goal, whilst everybody else in the stadium seemed to be holding an umbrella. Every time that the lightening struck it reflected off the sheen of the umbrellas lighting up the stadium like a strobe.

The match was a farce. The ball wouldn't run on such a water-logged pitch and both teams were reduced to keeping the ball in the air. We went a goal down but equalised from a Jimmy Case free kick that aqua-planed off the pitch past the keeper. Our second goal was even more bizarre, Emlyn Hughes went down to the by-line crossed the ball away from the goal but it was carried over the line by a gust of wind with the goalie wrong-footed.

We got back to the hotel and got changed. I was drenched through to the bone but even worse news was that my Harrington jacket weighed about eighteen stone and held more water than Langton Dock, and I had left my one year cardboard passport in the inside pocket and now it had been reduced to papier-mâché mush.

The next morning the Portuguese equivalent of the yellow pages did not give any details of any British Embassy and with the rain lashing down it didn't give me any incentive to go traipsing around Lisbon, so I spent the last night of the trip enjoying the hedonism of the Texas Bar. To be honest, it was no big deal. When I got to passport control at Lisbon airport I just presented what resembled a piece of Weetabix with my picture attached and to the general amusement of the assembled staff they waved me through. Similarly at Heathrow, I was met with initial bemusement and then with resignation, and I was back home to Blighty.

DAVE HARDMAN

EUROPEAN CUP SEMI-FINAL 1ST LEG
29TH MARCH 1978
RHEIN STADION [67000]
DUSSELDORF. WEST GERMANY
BORUSSIA MONCHENGLADBACH 2 LIVERPOOL 1

In 1978 we travelled to Germany for the European Cup Semi Final. It was £41 on a British Rail Special.

I remember at Five in the morning that we stopped outside Stamford Bridge (on the train) for some peculiar reason.

We got over to Germany, or West Germany as it was known in them days and the bizzies got on the train. I think it was customary in them days that whenever you went through a country that the police would get on to make sure everyone was behaving themselves. Anyway, would you believe it? one of them has his wallet hoisted. That's it, the train wasn't moving 'til he got it back. It eventually duly flew out of a window on to the platform, minus his wedge I presume. We were then able to get on our way.

I can remember being in the ground with Borussia Monchengladbach, 1FC Koln and Fortuna Dusseldorf fans milling about.

We got beat 2-1, Rainer Bonhof putting a free-kick through Clemence's legs.

In the station after the game all of the Germans were fighting each other, they didn't seem concerned about us and we were all done in anyway.

On the boat home I'm sure it got ransacked, I could be wrong but I don't think I've ever been on a boat that hasn't been.

I grant you it's not a riveting read but my memories fading.

STEVE METCALF

1978/79 EUROPEAN CUP

13 September 1978 First round
Nottingham Forest FC   2-0   Liverpool FC

27 September 1978 First round
Liverpool FC   0-0   Nottingham Forest FC
Aggregate: 0-2

EUROPEAN CUP 1ST ROUND 1ST LEG
13TH SEPTEMBER 1978
CITY GROUND [38316] NOTTINGHAM. ENGLAND.
NOTTINGHAM FOREST 2 LIVERPOOL 0

I don't remember exactly why Paul Bromley and I decided to book on Crown Coaches for this one. We must have been skint at the time as travelling by Crown was problematic at best. They could catch fire (Aston Villa), go to the wrong ground (West Ham) or get lost (pick any one of several), so it was with a wee bit of trepidation and a lot of smuggled ale that we set off from St John's Lane.

We started off on the normal route, M62 and then M6 but concern set in when we continued onto to the M1. As usual the driver seemed oblivious to advice as to which direction to take and ploughed on regardless.

It was only as we approached Rugby that he realised that maybe he needed to turn off the motorway. Time was now of the essence as it was only half an hour before kick off so we needed to avoid anymore delays. Of course I shouldn't really need to explain what happened next but the damn coach broke down on the outskirts of Nottingham. I think it was around Beeston.

Some of the lads decided to head off to the ground. The second-half was just about to start but the rest of us just piled into a pub to listen to the game on the radio (No Sky TV in them days folks!).

We lost the game 2-0 and were suitably well pissed off, apart from one lad who had got lucky with a local lass and reckoned he had had his evil way with her in a barn! The lads who had headed up to the ground reckoned that they had bunked into the Trent End and had been sussed but nothing happened.

The replacement coach finally turned up and we eventually we got home at about 3 o'clock in the morning.
ANDY McINDOE

EUROPEAN SUPER CUP FINAL 1ST LEG
4TH DECEMBER 1978
EMILE VERSE STADION [35000]
BRUSSELS. BELGIUM.
ANDERLECHT 3 LIVERPOOL 1

I left the Sportsman pub on the Friday night with 40p in my pocket. Platform 9'ed it down to the smoke as we were playing Arsenal on the Saturday. I'd asked my mate to call at ours and get my passport as he was coming down on the Bright and Early.

Still with only 40p, we bunked into Highbury where we got beat 1-0. After the match there were about two hundred of us who were going to Belgium.

As we came out of Highbury we came under attack on Highbury Hill. We charged up the hill where a mate of mine decked Jenkins causing half of them to flee. We mopped up the rest.

Bunked the train to Dover, then also bunked the ship to Ostend, then bunks (still half canned) to Bruges where I fell asleep between two seats and somehow ended up on the Luxembourg border. It was here that I got legged by some officialdom but managed to evade capture before bunking back to Bruges.

There I met up with a few lads. It had been snowing and as we walked into the town, three or four bikers went passed. We started throwing snowballs at them causing one to come off his bike. They go spare but we just carry on into town.

Twenty minutes later and we're in a bar when about 20/30 bikers roll into town. We hid. They never collared us. A narrow squeak there.

We decide to go and watch Cercle Bruges v Holt in the same Stadium as FC Bruges play in. The place where you bought your souvenirs from only had a King Eddie Cigar box as opposed to a till. As you can imagine that went amongst various other things.

By this time I'm knocking about with three bona fide dippers. They're copping for all kinds and kindly box me off. We end up in a nightclub and I steal a sheepy that's hanging up. We get off and then stupidly go back to the same nightclub. The owner of the coat jumps on me. A brawl ensues (by the way we're all 17/18 years of age). We take a hike.

Fast forward to the next day, Monday. A day on the zap! Copping for birdies an' stuff. We bunk into the ground where the Reds get beat 3-1.

The hard bit for me was trying to re-bunk the boat home. With the aid of a perfectly choreographed fight amongst ourselves I slip through the net. Plain sailing all the way home. Not a great story, but shows what can be done with 40p in them days.

The sheepy by the way turned out to be a camel skin affair. You could tell by the hump in the back. Haha. That's all I heard for the next few weeks.

STEVE METCALF

1979/80 EUROPEAN CUP

19 September 1979 First round
Liverpool FC   2-1   FC Dinamo Tbilisi

3 October 1979 First round
FC Dinamo Tbilisi   3-0   Liverpool FC
Aggregate: 4-2

EUROPEAN CUP 1ST ROUND 2ND LEG
3RD OCTOBER 1979
BORIS PAICHADZE NATIONAL STADIUM [90000]
TBILISI. RUSSIA.
DINAMO TBILISI 3 LIVERPOOL 0

The draw for the 1st round of the European Cup in October 1979 saw Liverpool FC paired against a team from Georgia in the far-flung outpost of Russia. Now it had been 3 years since I started following the Reds in Europe as a 16 year old, FC Bruges being the first game in the Uefa Cup Final in 1976, after that first foray into Europe, I was hooked.

The next season in '77 saw me travel to St Etienne, FC Zurich and the Eternal city itself ROME. Even in the Summer of '77 there was the Amsterdam Tournament, then Hamburg in the Super Cup. What a year1977 was. A young Scouse kid sampling these sinister Cities, don't think I've ever been the same since.

Into 78, Borussia Monchengladbach, Anderlecht, then onto another European Cup Final. These 3 years were the best ever following the Reds. The fashion has been well documented whilst sampling these European cities, those European fashions ended up in Halewood, Scotty Road, Huyton , Kirkby and all over the City.

When the draw was made all the usual suspects who travelled with me got in touch, 'Mono are we going to Russia?' 'Too right we are.' but there was one slight problem about this trip, it wasn't on Transalpino's route. Hmmm… Liverpool had their own Anfield Travel Supporters Club, the price was £160 for a 1-night stay and in 1979 that was a lot of money.

John Gargan, Terry McKenna, Mark Hook and myself booked the trip along with 30 or so young Kopites and Road-Enders, the other 150 seemed to be Well-Off business people.

Before the trip to Georgia we got to see Tbilisi at Anfield in the 1st leg. Strangely there were only 35,000 there that night, even though it had been a year since we were knocked out in the first round against Notts Forest.

On the night, for me, Liverpool were fortunate to come away with a 2-1 win. Goals coming from Davey Johnson and Jimmy Case, but we could see Dinamo were a class act and this tie was far from over, which made the trip to Georgia all the better.

A week before the away leg the Pink Echo ran a double page story about the capital of Georgia. It said that Tbilisi was the Florida of Russia, the people were the friendliest, their doors were always open to strangers and best of all the sun shines daily. Happy days, Florida here we come.

The build up to this game, for me personally, was exceptional. After three years of travelling all over Europe, this was another level, having never been to an 'Iron Curtain' country. The flight to Russia was departing from the old Liverpool airport. There was a bit of snobbiness in the Departure Lounge where the fans with a few quid were just staring at these young lads in their Lois jeans, trainees and adidas cagoules. Once on the plane we got the cards out and started playing chase the ace, to the amusement of our fellow Kopites.

Also in the Echo piece it said a pair of Levis would fetch £100, my holdall consisted of 3 pairs of old jeans, six ham sarnies and a packet of coconut chocolate biscuits [them pink and white ones]. We couldn't exchange any money over here, it had to be done in Russia. Now being on the dole the flight had skint me, so I had a grand total of £3 but with the £300 I was going to make I didn't need anymore.

After a three hour trip we landed in Moscow. As we were descending we all looked out of the windows, fuckinhell la, it looks cold out there. Now most of us have got light Summer gear on and I've got a pair of sandals from Harold Ian. The plane lands, the doors open, now I've never felt a chill like this before. It travels right down the aisle. As we depart the plane, on the tarmac were 100's of Russian soldiers all in big grey overcoats with their fur hats. They started laughing as we ran to the comfort of a warm building. It was there that we had to go through customs. We were fucking freezing to the amusement of the Ruskies.

After being interrogated for a few hours we now had to board another plane for another three hour journey to the Florida of Russia. Under armed escort we board an Aeroflot plane. This is Russia's answer to British Airways. As soon as we take off I could hear things rattling. Fear starts to grip everyone, this is going to be one dodgy flight, so there was no 'chase the ace' on this flight. Also we were all still thawing out from the severe cold snap in Moscow. Sunnier climes await.

We eventually arrive in Tbilisi safe. As we depart the shed of a plane we were greeted by local schoolchildren all neatly dressed in white shirts and red ties. Looks like the Echo was right about the friendliest people.

We board the coach to the hotel and as we drive through Tbilisi we could see it was a drab and miserable place. The buildings were grey with woman brushing the streets with their brooms. The hotel looked decent enough as we all checked in. Then there were words of warnings from the Anfield travel club and our Georgian host. We were told not to venture out on our own and don't change your money on the street, but the rumour of you getting five times as much as the official exchange rate did seem a better option. At least my three quid will go further along with my £300 I'm going to make on my jeans.

Within minutes of us arriving we had a quick swill then about twenty of us escaped from the hotel without any escorts, so we thought? As we walked around Tbilisi seeing the sights, well, statues of Stalin and Lenin, it was a very eerie place and the people seemed very sad. We walked around the city for hours on end and could not see any, lets say 'proper shops'. There were just bits of food in these very sparse buildings, but we had our sights set on selling our jeans. People just stared at us. We were alien to them. They had probably never seen any Westerners before, never mind Scousers. I don't think we'll be bringing any fashion back from here. Not one person approached us for our jeans. We were asking anyone who looked at us, but it was apparent that these were poor people. One thing that did stand out was that everywhere we went we kept seeing these two same fellas. They were deffo the KGB or the UAB,

After our tour of Tbilisi we decided to head up to the ground. By now we had our very own fan club, people were just following us, but this next sight has stayed with me for 30 odd years. As we approached the stadium we could see, and I'm not messing, thousands of people all in one line. Now we're all thinking they must be queuing up for tickets. As we got nearer the people were coming out of this building, not with a match ticket but with loaves of bread. It really hit home, even though we all laughed and made a joke of it, but it was really sad. Communism ehh ?.

Minutes later though we all perked up when the Liverpool team coach passed us. They couldn't believe their eyes when they seen about twenty of Liverpool's finest. Thommo and Sammy Lee both banging on the windows to us, happy days. So back to the hotel with our legion of followers and the two chaperones.

Once in the hotel I remember us getting a bollocking from the stewards for getting off on our own. Anyway we saw more of the city than they did, so back to our room with jeans still intact. On the way to our room we all noticed a lady just sitting on a chair 'fuckin' ell the size of her punk rockers'. Now she was no Elle McPherson, more of a Bella Emburg, but after visiting the sin cities of Amsterdam and Hamburg every port and all that. Being a young baby faced lad I thought she took a shine to me with her smiles. We all thought she was a lady of the night after a bit of chatting to her with my hands, I just wanted her to come to the room but she wouldn't get off her fat arse. Fuckin' ell what kind of midnight is this. John and Terry were calling me, it's time to go the match. Bella I'll see you after the game girl. She gave me a kiss on the cheek, to the amusement of the lads.

We all met in the reception. Now we've had no food all day and didn't fancy sampling the shite that was on offer, so my mams last two ham sarnies bit the dust. We were all excited now and couldn't wait for the match to start. We boarded one of the 3 coaches. As we approached the ground there was thousands of Georgians singing and shouting at us, it was hostile but not in a frightening way. We entered the ground and congregated in the middle of their 'Main Stand'. It was a massive round concrete bowl with very high walls behind both goals. As we were waiting for the game to start, disaster struck, the heavens opened and it absolutely pissed down. We were all soaked to the skin. I had wondered why the locals were all in their overcoats and hats. So much for the Florida of Russia. Later on we were told it was the worst weather in Tblisi in thirty years. Just our luck.

It didn't dampen our spirits though once the reds entered the pitch. The Scouse Red Army belted out YNWA but the 100,000 Georgians made this deafening noise that was so different to any Western crowd we had ever heard. Then they all lit paper torches, it was a sight to behold 'welcome to the iron curtain'.

It was now kick off time. As early as the second minute Jimmy Case had a shot on goal but the keeper Gabeliya produced a fine save. The rest of the first half saw Liverpool being content to defend. Dinamo had most of the ball but to our surprise little penetration. We held on till half time at 0-0. The rain was still poring down but we all knew

Dinamo weren't finished yet. The second-half starts and the Georgians begin to press the Reds and in the 54th minute Dinamo get the goal that they need. Vladimir Gutsaev being the scorer. That goal meant that the Reds would go out on the away goals rule and some locals invaded the pitch. We now need to get forward more and create more chances but as we do Dinamo expose our gaps in the defence and in the 80th minute our hearts sank as Ramaz Shengeliya made it 2-0. Again the fans run onto the pitch to round off a bad night at the office. Chivadze made it three after he converted a penalty. Liverpool were well beaten by a a great Dinamo Tblisi side. In a way they reminded me of the great Red Star Belgrade side that also defeated us in 1973. Now for the second season running, in the European Cup, we have been knocked out in the first round. The end of the game once again saw the 100,000 Dinamo fans light up the Georgian sky with their home made fire flares. It was a sight to behold. Saying that, I don't know how they stayed lit with all this rain. but it was one impressive sight. Obviously there was no segregation so we had to make our own way back to the coaches. We were being goaded by the locals, as I've said, it was a bit moody but not in a frightening way. Not exactly the chicken run at West Ham like. We board the coach soaked to the skin as we stare out at the thousands of joyful Georgians. We take it all in, one final look at the massive concrete bowl, home of Dinamo Tblisi.

On the coach we were told there was going to be a banquet reception in our honor. Happy days. The first thing on my mind was a nice warm shower but once again sitting right outside my room was the one and only 'Bella Emburg'. John and Terry shoot into the room while now I'm trying my hand with 'the lady of the night' but all she did was smile and sit on the chair. I even offered her my 3 quid and a pair of Levis but she was having none of it. What kind of brass are you girl. I need to get ready for this banquet. The warm shower ended up a cold swill. All of my clobber was soaked. The jeans that I brought over were massive on me, so off I went down the apples with only my boxer shorts on. All to the young lads amusement, except the toffs from the Anfield Travel Club. The food was awful. Now I've demolished my sarnies but I remember the chocolate coco biscuits, so that was the banquet done and dusted.

The trip to the Tblisi, The Florida of Russia, was a great experience, having been to most of Liverpool's games in Europe this trip is right up there, It wasn't about the glory on the field this time but the whole experience of the Iron Curtain and communism, being greeted in Moscow by 100s of soldiers, the freezing weather there, the dodgy Aeroflot plane, the hotel, the city of Tblisi with its endless statues. people queuing for their daily bread, the sunshine that didn't happen, the pissing down rain, the two KGB who followed us all day, my three quid, three pairs of jeans and finally 'my lady of the night'. Somewhere in the Kremlin the KGB will have a secret tape of a young Scouse lad,,,,,,
My journey wasn't over yet. After another dodgy six hour flight we landed in the old Speke Airport, the same one the Beatles flew into years earlier. This time there wasn't thousands of people there. Just outside was an 88 bus from Garston to Halewood. That's for me and John while Terry headed back to Litherland. As we get on the bus we give the driver two bob [10p] and we sit at the back just chatting about our mad journey, but

as we get to Hunts Cross a bus inspector gets on. Now we don't want to get the driver in trouble so as he says 'tickets please' we start looking for our imaginary ticket. 'Right you two, where have you been?'

'RUSSIA,,,,' we both replied.

'So we've got a pair of smart arses ehh??'

'No mate, honest, we've been to see Liverpool'

We get our proey and match tickets out and he says 'Fuckin' ell lads, that's the longest trip anyone has ever had on two bob'. He laughs and shakes our hands.

That night john Gargan and myself went out to the Leather Bottle and the Halewood Hotel telling all the lads about the tales of Tblisi. Looking around Halewood the Florida Of Russia didn't seem so bad after all.

STE MONAGHAN

1980/81 EUROPEAN CUP

17 September 1980 First round
AC Oulu   1-1   Liverpool FC

1 October 1980 First round
Liverpool FC   10-1   AC Oulu
Aggregate: 11-2

22 October 1980 Second round
Aberdeen FC   0-1   Liverpool FC

5 November 1980 Second round
Liverpool FC   4-0   Aberdeen FC
Aggregate: 5-0

4 March 1981 Quarter-finals
Liverpool FC   5-1   PFC CSKA Sofia

18 March 1981 Quarter-finals
PFC CSKA Sofia 0-1   Liverpool FC
Aggregate: 1-6

8 April 1981 Semi-finals
Liverpool FC   0-0   FC Bayern München

22 April 1981 Semi-finals
FC Bayern München   1-1   Liverpool FC
Aggregate: 1-1
Liverpool win on away goals

27 May 1981 Final
Liverpool FC   1-0   Real Madrid CF

EUROPEAN CUP 2ND ROUND 1ST LEG
22ND OCTOBER 1980
PITTODRIE STADIUM [24000]
ABERDEEN. SCOTLAND.
ABERDEEN 0 LIVERPOOL 1

Having squeezed past the Finns of Oulu Palloseura in round one courtesy of a 10-1 win at Anfield, it was Aberdeen up next. The Dons' new all-seater stadium was definitely one to tick off.

We didn't know much about them to be honest. We knew they'd broken the Old Firm's domestic dominance by winning the Scottish League, and they had a promising up-and-coming manager called Alex Ferguson. Oh, and their centre back pairing of Willie Miller and Alex McLeish had somehow kept Alan Hansen out of the Scotland team. They also had Doug Rougvie, Mark McGhee and two more who ended up at Old Trafford, Jim Leighton and Gordon Strachan.

Liverpool's ticket allocation was a paltry 900. You had to book the special transport to get one. We booked the train for an early start from Lime Street, with plenty of packed food and a few cans smuggled aboard despite the supposed curfew. We were far from alone in this respect.

The first surprise was just how far past Glasgow Aberdeen is. As we drew into Aberdeen station around teatime, it was already dark and very cold and icy. Although only late October, the snow-pocked countryside suggested we were back in Finland like the previous round.

In the 70s and 80s away matches were not generally regarded as an opportunity to meet other fans and chat about football in a cosy social environment. They were hostile enemy territory, to be treated as an SAS raid – get in there, do it and get out. Any lingering doubts otherwise would have been dispelled the second we jumped off the train, by the very first Scot we saw. An old hag straight from the opening scene of Macbeth (except Shakespeare's witches weren't pulling a shopping trolley as I recall). greeted us with a growled 'fuck off yae English bastards.' Or perhaps it was 'welcome to Bonnie Scotland'. After a quick couple of pints and some fish and chips, we made our way towards a rather excitable Pittodrie. With a 24,000 full house, our 900 felt the need to make up for our lack of numbers by standing and singing constantly throughout the 90 minutes. It also helped us keep warm. We started the game with a useful trio of Scots of our own – Hansen, Souness and Dalglish - but it was an Englishman, Terry McDermott, who scored the game's only goal after just five minutes. With an away goal in the bank, we were never really threatened after that.

We grabbed some carry-out on the way back to the station for the endless journey back to Liverpool. Mission accomplished, for team and fans alike. It was approaching dawn when we got back to Limey.

The return leg at Anfield was a comfortable 4-0 win, cementing Liverpool's place in the Quarter-Finals and our special place in Ferguson's 'heart'. CSKA Sofia next, then Bayern

in the semi-final and Real Madrid in Paris, Barney Rubble sealing our number three.
CHRIS ROWLAND

EUROPEAN CUP SEMI-FINAL 2ND LEG
22ND APRIL 1981
OLYMPIA STADION [75000]
MUNICH. WEST GERMANY
BAYERN MUNICH 1 LIVERPOOL 1

I was in the Woodpecker pub in Kirkby on the Easter Monday when the manager, Dave Brookes asked me if I fancied going to Munich for the semi final. I said 'OK', went home, got some kip and remembered my birth certificate for the one-year passport. We got the 'Bright and Early' to London the next day, arriving in Munich via a great train journey down the Rhine.

In Munich we met up with all the other lads and we all went to see Phil Thommo who had tickets for them. Phil was injured and was giving out tickets for the game. The lads all got their tickets and then at the end Thommo said to me 'What's wrong with your kipper?', I said 'I haven't got a ticket.' so he said 'Why didn't you say?'. I told him I only came at the last minute and it wouldn't be fair. So he said 'I'll take you to the players hotel and see if I can get you one.'So we headed off to the hotel reception and on getting there he said to me 'Don't move.' Next thing he came walking back with Bob Paisley and Bob says to me 'Are you the lad without the ticket?' I said 'Yes Mr Paisley'. He then said 'Here's one, I don't want any money but don't travel to Europe without a ticket again.'

Irish radio had listened in to our conversation and asked me for an interview which me Ma heard back home. I then went and had a drink to calm down before then realising 'How am I going to get to the game?' The Irish lads seen me and said 'Just get on the press bus.' So I got on and only one person questioned me, Stuart Hall. The Irish lads said to sit down by them.

We got to the ground and witnessed a magnificent night for the Reds and I got myself on T.V. after we scored.
KEIRON MORGAN

EUROPEAN CUP FINAL
27TH MAY 1981
PARC DE PRINCES [48360]. PARIS. FRANCE.
REAL MADRID 0 LIVERPOOL 1

Travelling the day before to Paris, to see the 'Mighty Reds' playing the 'Mighty' Real Madrid in the Final of the 1981 European Cup, was a dream come true for me on a personal basis. Real Madrid, the most successful side in the competition, and we were playing them. Although, it was Real Madrid, my confidence was high, especially after seeing our wonderful supporters in vociferous happy mood, on the streets of Paris. Every Liverpool supporter looked forward with great anticipation to what would be our third European Cup win. I travelled overland with two University friends, Tommy (Wiggy) Wignall and James Thompson. When we arrived that night, we were starving as I recall. The first restaurant we had seen after booking into our hotel was an Italian Bistro. I don't know exactly where it was, but it looked good.

So, starving and very tired after travelling all day, we walked into the Italian Bistro. The lads knew I spoke Italian, so they asked me to order in Italian! I looked towards a waiter in all black with slicked back black hair and called him over. We knew what we wanted, so in my finest Italian, I proceeded to order! Feeling smug with myself, in what was my finest hour in Paris, the slick black haired waiter, politely bent down and said in his finest Dublin accent;" I didn't understand a word you said, could you repeat it in English please." The lads fell about, and I went as 'Red' as our team's shirt!

Twenty four hours later, we were in the Parc de Princes, celebrating LFC's magnificent win, through Alan Kennedy's wondrous winning goal to lift the European Cup for the third time in our illustrious history!

FRANK CARLYLE

1981/82 EUROPEAN CUP

16 September 1981 First round
AC Oulu   0-1   Liverpool FC

30 September 1981 First round
Liverpool FC   7-0   AC Oulu
Aggregate: 8-0

21 October 1981 Second round
AZ Alkmaar   2-2   Liverpool FC

4 November 1981 Second round
Liverpool FC   3-2   AZ Alkmaar
Aggregate: 5-4

3 March 1982 Quarter-finals
Liverpool FC   1-0   PFC CSKA Sofia

17 March 1982 Quarter-finals
PFC CSKA Sofia 2-0   Liverpool FC
Aggregate: 2-1
CSKA Sofia win after extra time

EUROPEAN CUP 2ND ROUND 1ST LEG
21ST OCTOBER 1981
OLYMPISCH STADIUM [12000]
AMSTERDAM. NETHERLANDS.
AZ67 ALKMAAR 2 LIVERPOOL 2

1981, The year Casual culture went continental in Liverpool and probably the year the rest of the country started to take note.

The Reds had played in Munich in April, Paris in May and had a pre-season tour of Switzerland in the Summer. The thieving that went on across Europe that year was unprecedented. Stores had no alarm systems, trainers were left out in pairs, security guards did not seem to exist. Careers must have been forged on the back of Liverpool F.C. conquering Europe. Even the mode of European transport, Transalpino, could be used on the cheap by altering the destination. The 'Rub-Out' as it affectionately became known.

Myself and Eric had done two of those three jaunts. Picking up trainers and sportswear en-route. We had even bunked the train down to Switzerland after the Paris Final just to pick up some exclusive adidas trainers which we couldn't find in France.

You should all know the story of how Liverpool fans started a clothing revolution on the streets of the UK and how that revolution changed the face of the High Street forever. Witness sports shops on every corner and sportswear as every-day wear, none of which was apparent in the 70s. This European tale takes in some of the shenanigans from a late 70s/early 80s European game.

The game had been switched to the capital, Amsterdam, as Alkmaar's ground was considered too small for a match of epic proportions as the visiting Liverpool FC.

Only 12000 attended the game but this was still more than the 8900 capacity of Alkmaars own Alkmaardehout Stadium.

Our plan was to do the trip as cheap as possible. We must have been the only ones to have paid full fare on Transalpino in the last few years and obviously with working I was always in fear of losing my job should I be caught stealing. So for this trip we thought, lets at least save some money on the train journey. Transalpino was booked to the Hook of Holland and as Amsterdam was only half an hour away, we wouldn't even do the 'Rub-Out'. We'd just chance it.

Bit of a mistake that. How were we to know ticket inspectors would get on the train. We were both escorted off and placed in a holding cell in one of the stations before being released with what was a piece of documentation and an insistence that we pay the 'Fine' at our local Post Office otherwise we could never enter Holland again. 'Yes, sure, we'll pay it when we get home'. I still have the document somewhere in the loft.

We arrive in the Dam later that morning. Part two of our money saving adventure included 'cheap digs'. It was here that we meet Marty, a seasoned traveller to all away games, who says we can kip in his hotel room. Our luck is changing.

After throwing the bags in, we head off for some Dutch lager. Oranjeboom, if memory serves me right. We talk often of the influence that a foreign culture has on us, even something like the lagers we drink abroad suddenly turn up back home weeks later. The Harrington in town started selling Oranjeboom a few weeks later. I even remember Keiths Wine Bar on Lark Lane selling Effes a week or so after the Istanbul Final.

Now with some 'Dutch courage' we head off looking for some Fila or any other cool sportswear unavailable back home. We head to 'De Bijenkorf', known as the 'Harrods of Amsterdam'. If anywhere sold 'high-end' goods it will be this place. Sure enough the third floor has an array of designer labels including some nice thick Fila ski jumpers. It was rather chilly outside, so these would come in handy for the forthcoming Winter. No assistants were to be seen, so it's into the changing rooms, jumper on, Jacket over the top. Not the most intricate way of relieving a store of its goods but we were amateurs.

This soon became apparent as on approaching the exit I see a big! security guard standing there and next to him are those alarm posts. Crap, I didn't even check the Jumper for an alarm. This must be the only store in Europe with fecking alarms and security guards.

Suddenly the shop has turned into a sauna. Its warm in there anyway, but I've got my own jumper on, a bloody thick Fila ski jumper and a Winter jacket. Sweat is pissing down my forehead and running down my nose. A couple of options are running through my head.

1; Carry on to the exit and leg it as fast as I can,

or the more thoughtful

2; Go to the bogs and check the jumper for alarms and if it is alarmed leave it there.

I go for the obvious number 2 option as being caught by some burly bouncer and held in a headlock until police arrive has little appeal.

I shoot up the escalator and enter the toilets only to realise that I had just walked through some alarm posts. This actually means there's no alarm on the jumper, either that or the heat being generated from my body is masking the alarm. I pat myself down and can't feel any alarms on the jumper. I've come this far so I decide 'nothing ventured, nothing gained'.

Ten minutes later and I've met Eric outside, both warm as toast in the Winter chill. It's here we see three or four regular travellers with their customary empty Head bags. We brag of our exploits and they head off to the third floor of said Department Store. The next time we see them is on the boat heading home selling Fila Ski Jumpers to would-be fashionistas. They had brazenly put the full rack of twenty or so jumpers into their empty Head bags and just walked out. I think I'll leave that thieving lark to the professionals.

The game was an exciting affair in more ways than one. The Reds reversed a two goal deficit to draw 2-2 but Eric had disappeared during the second-half to go fighting some Ajax Skinheads who had turned up in the opposite end.

We had arranged to meet up later at the bar around the corner from our hotel. I got there first and counted my remaining slummy which was enough for a couple of pints.

Eric was late but as I was preparing to leave he turns up with a tale of being arrested for fighting in the ground, taken to a police station before being released in the middle of nowhere.

'Anyway, less of the chat. How much slummy have you got?' Theres enough for a bevy each as we count it on the bar in front of a disconsolate barmaid who seems to have had enough of being paid with copper. After our final bevy, which should have been it for the night, a guy walks in with a 'brass' in a fur coat on his arm. He hears our accents and makes light conversation about being from Liverpool but living in Amsterdam. He gets the ale in for us, seeing as we're skint. The barmaid has a stern look on her face. She knows we can't get him a bevy back and we assume she thinks we're taking the piss out of the guy. The conversation continues with our guest. We joke of how much he must be enjoying the 'delights' of Amsterdam. Then, bizarrely, we discover this guy is a distant cousin of Eric. Suddenly he's getting the champagne in, toasting the fact that we are Scousers in a foreign land. The barmaid tries to tell him we're taking the piss and have no money but this guy loves us. Either that or he doesn't want us to mention the girl on his arm to anyone. Maybe he's married and wants us to keep 'stum'. Anyway we leave at about 4.00am bladdered and promising not to say a word.

DAVE HEWITSON

1982/83 EUROPEAN CUP

14 September 1982 First round
Dundalk FC   1-4   Liverpool FC

28 September 1982 First round
Liverpool FC   1-0   Dundalk FC
Aggregate: 5-1

19 October 1982 Second round
HJK Helsinki   1-0   Liverpool FC

2 November 1982 Second round
Liverpool FC   5-0   HJK Helsinki
Aggregate: 5-1

2 March 1983 Quarter-finals
RTS Widzew Łódź   2-0   Liverpool FC

16 March 1983 Quarter-finals
Liverpool FC   3-2   RTS Widzew Łódź
Aggregate: 3-4

EUROPEAN CUP 1ST ROUND 1ST LEG
14TH SEPTEMBER 1982
ORIEL PARK [16500]. DUNDALK. IRELAND.
DUNDALK 1 LIVERPOOL 4

The combination of Thatcherite economics and the troubles over the water saw a relatively poor turn-out for this game. Very few people showed any interest in making their way over. The perceived wisdom was that that the security would be more lax going via Dublin than by going via Belfast, so we decided that the night boat would be the answer. Perhaps me and Paul Mac had drunk too much in the Dominion or perhaps the Dock police were more efficient than usual but we were collared right away and forced to pay £2.50 as 'walk on' passengers.

This had made a severe dent in our finances but luckily Paul had his magic 50p piece and had soon emptied the fruit machine in the bar which more than made up for us having to travel legitimately and paid for a few pints of Guinness.

We got to North Wall at about seven in the morning, had a wonderful Irish brekkie and got a coach up to Dundalk. Given the then current state of Liverpool we were gobsmacked going through North Dublin at how impoverished the place was. It seemed to be mile after mile of Gerrard Gardens style tenements and we were made up to be out of Dublin's fair city.

Dundalk seemed to be relatively picturesque when we arrived, we went to to the chippy and then decided to go for a pint. This was when things started to go a wee bit strange. The pub we went to seemed normal enough from the outside but once we went inside we were in a different world. All conversation stopped as we walked in and ordered a coupe of pints, the barman looked at us with something approaching awe and asked what we were doing there. In my naivety I assumed that he was asking about our presence in the city as opposed to this particular pub and we replied that we were here for the match, he nodded sagely and disappeared into the back bar.

We were soon joined at the bar by a well dressed, middle-aged chap who was only too happy to chat to us about everything under the sun i.e. Where we were from, where we worked (as if?), how long we had supported Liverpool, how much we knew about the club. Even in my Guinness befuddled state I realised that we were being interrogated, so to divert our friend's attention I pointed to the TV behind the bar that had a big hole in the screen and several wires hanging out,

'What happened there?' I asked.

He smiled and said,

'One of the boys was here, on holiday from Belfast. He was watching the racing and when his horse lost he shot up the telly'.

We left our drinks on the bar and fled.

Further down the road was another pub. It seemed full of Irish Liverpool fans and we finally relaxed. We mentioned our experience to the girl behind the bar,

'Jaysuz, you've been to the Armalite Arms and survived, youse wil be famous round here now'.

We now added Jameson's to our rounds of Guinness and consequently the match passed in a blur. All that I can remember is that we won 4-1, it was chokker and David Hodgson missed an open goal for 6 yards out. We got a lift back down to Dublin and got a free ride on the ferry back home, so much for the security!

DAVE HARDMAN

1983/84 EUROPEAN CUP

14 September 1983 First round
Odense BK   0-1   Liverpool FC

28 September 1983 First round
Liverpool FC   5-0   Odense BK
Aggregate: 6-0

19 October 1983 Second round
Liverpool FC   0-0   Athletic Club

2 November 1983 Second round
Athletic Club   0-1   Liverpool FC
Aggregate: 0-1

7 March 1984 Quarter-finals
Liverpool FC   1-0   SL Benfica

21 March 1984 Quarter-finals
SL Benfica   1-4   Liverpool FC
Aggregate: 1-5

11 April 1984 Semi-finals
Liverpool FC   1-0   FC Dinamo București

25 April 1984 Semi-finals
FC Dinamo București   1-2   Liverpool FC
Aggregate: 1-3

30 May 1984 Final
AS Roma   1-1   Liverpool FC
Liverpool win 4-2 on penalties

EUROPEAN CUP SEMI FINAL 2ND LEG
25TH APRIL 1984
STADIO NUL [60000]. BUCHAREST. ROMANIA.
DINAMO BUCHAREST 1 LIVERPOOL 2

This was our first non-organised trip behind the Iron Curtain. We flew to Bucharest from Manchester on the day before the game, a place of brutally grey Stalinist buildings (Bucharest not Manchester!). Our hotel was nothing much to write home about so we went off on a pub crawl around Bucharest. We soon realised that this place was hardly New Orleans at Mardi Gras time, so we sloped off to the player's hotel for a pint with some of the other lads.

As usual we over-indulged ourselves in the local ale and on getting back to our hotel one of our lads kicked in the door of this empty room next to ours. The next morning, bleary-eyed and farting, we were awoken by the local gendarmerie who piled into the room complete with an irate hotel manager, kicking us out of bed and waving guns around. As they couldn't speak English and our Romanian wasn't that good a Mexican stand-off ensued until an interpreter arrived. She told us that they required our passports until we paid up for the damages. We refused point-blank knowing that if we gave them up we could end up in all types of problems.

Eventually we were herded out of the hotel, put onto buses up to the ground then after match were taken straight to the airport and put on the plane which, all things considered, what pretty decent of them.

BRIAN

After winning the first leg at Anfield 1-0 we set off for Bucharest determined to see us win through to another European Cup Final in Rome. We left Liverpool airport at around midday the day before the game, on Tamron Airways – Romanian Air Transport. The plane was very basis with female stewardesses who were quite frightening. The only drink we were offered was wine. We arrived into Bucharest Airport which was full of Romanian Air-force planes. As we were preparing to go through customs we noticed the official team place arriving, even though it had left Liverpool nearly two hours after us. We were thoroughly searched going through customs and made well aware how Dinamo would win this second leg. After eventually clearing customs we were loaded on to some very old coach's, accompanied by a police escort and each with a leather coated local police officer on board.

We were taken to our hotel – Hotel Bucuresti – booked into our rooms and told a meal would shortly be ready for us. We all went down to the dining room where the meal was very slowly served and it seemed part of a plan to ensure we stayed in the hotel for night. We eventually got fed-up waiting and decided to go outside and find somewhere to have a drink. There were people waiting outside the hotel asking for cigarettes, chewing gum and toiletries. We ended up in a club and spent an hour or two enjoying some very cheap drinks. On returning to the hotel the people who had stayed were still waiting for their food! The next morning we decided to have a look around the city and were surprised at some of the primitive sights – horse-drawn carts, women cleaning the roads and plenty of empty shops.

Wherever we went people wanted to sell us their currency, offering five times the normal exchange rate. We did not want or need any more money but to get rid of a man who kept bothering us we decided to exchange £10. On handing it over he gave me a bundle of notes and proceeded to run as fast as he could. On opening the bundle we found out why – the notes were just a load of scrunched up newspaper!

On returning to the hotel we were informed that there had been some trouble. Three rooms, we were told, had been trashed and the Romanians wanted more money from us otherwise we would not be taken to the match. After much haggling, an agreement was eventually reached. Money was reluctantly exchanged and we were on our way. Tickets were only given out when we reached the ground and because the police did not want anyone hanging around outside we were forced to go in early. Once inside the locals were very vociferous, with a lot of vitriol aimed in the direction of Graeme Souness who had been involved with an incident during the first leg which resulted in a Dinamo player suffering a broken jaw.   There was no roof on the stadium and with the match being played in heavy rain we were all soaked through but a 2-1 win, giving us a 3-1 aggregate victory and securing our place in a fourth European Cup Final, meant that didn't matter at all. On the coach journey back to the airport, again with a full police escort, many Romanians sportingly lined the streets to wave us off.   Once back at the airport we prepared to celebrate but, to our horror, quickly discovered that everything for sale was in US dollars. Thankfully we came across a friendly waiter in the cafe who was more than happy to supply us with bottles of wine in exchange for our Romanian currency. The team then arrived and the celebrations commenced, with some of the players getting the beers in for the supporters. The plane journey home was another long one but it had been well worthwhile.

KEITH STANTON

EUROPEAN CUP FINAL
27TH MAY 1984
STADIO OLIMPICO [69693]. ROME. ITALY.
AS ROMA 1 LIVERPOOL 1 (2-4 Pens)

My journey to the Enternal City of Rome started two weeks before the final.
Still living in Basel, Switzerland in them years I boarded a train with the destination 'Liverpool', a journey that used to take twenty two hours each way. It was a journey I made over two hundred times for hundreds of Liverpool home and away matches in the very late 70s and 80s.
A nine hour train to Calais, board a ferry to Dover followed by a train to Victoria

station, tube to Euston and finally the train to Lime Street. Those were the days before Easyjet and Ryanair.

They were fantastic years, mysterious adventures years and if I could turn the clock back now I would do it all over again.

So on 12th May 1984 I found myself at Meadow Lane, Notts County. A dire 0-0 but did we care? Nope not a toss, we were CHAMPIONS AGAIN!

I booked into the usual place, the YMCA on Mount Pleasant, they were the days I hardly knew anyone up here in Liverpool, a city I moved to in 1989 because of the love for our magic club and I've been here ever since.

Three days later we played our last league game, another draw this time at Anfield v Norwich (1-1 Rush) and after the game the Liverpool ticket manageress Maggie sorted me with a European Cup Final ticket. I didn't really know Maggie back then and little did I know that two years later I would find myself in the Liverpool Echo with Maggie, the paper reporting on me being the first ever foreign based Liverpool season ticket holder.

The day after the Norwich game I tackled the return journey back to Basel, somewhere along that journey I LOST THAT ROME TICKET!!!! I was devastated, absolutely gutted and horrified, it was as if someone punched me in my stomach, no way JUST NO WAY, how could I lose that ticket??

I remember four days before the 30th of may I put a announcement on Radio Basel asking listeners if anyone had a spare ticket for the European cup final…. Looking back I have to say "WTF was I thinking of?"

Why would anyone in BASEL of all places have a spare ticket for Liverpool v AS ROMA European Cup Final? Just how stupid and naive was I? Surprise surprise no-one replied.

My mind was made up though, I was still going to Rome without a ticket. So I was walking around Basel on the Monday morning, 28th May and noticed two Liverpool fans. I approached them and in my broken and crap English explained to them that I was looking for a ticket and then my jaw dropped to the floor when they said "We've got a spare one"

Ok, them two must have seen me coming from a billion miles away because they charged me £50, or was it 50 Swiss francs just can't remember. A big amount of money anyhow thirty years ago. Ha ha! I have to laugh about it now, cheeky Scouse bastards. So the three of us boarded the train from Basel to Milan then onto Rome.

Sadly I cannot remember their names, I would love to find them again and maybe someone reading this story can help. I did see the two lads the season after Rome in the Kop v WBA though.

So we arrived in beautiful Roma, what a fantastic place that is, history written on every corner of the city. Magical!!

I told the two Scousers that I will book into a hotel, all I remember is that it was a cheap gaff and I paid for two nights there, then the three of us went about to bars for bevvies and laughs. We had a brilliant time, then late into the night I had this brainstorm and said "I will bunk you two into my room!!"

So, pissed, we sneaked past the Italian Hotel receptionist and voila! In my room we were!!! Easy as cake!!!

One on the couch one on the floor and the king himself in the bed of course.

BANG BANG BANG!!!!!! "OPEN THE DOOR" was the shout.

There was the fella from reception going bananas "WTF" I thought!!!

"OUT!! ALL OF YOU OUT!!!"

So much for my great idea!!

He give me my passport back and booted the three of us onto the street, the cheeky bastard refused to give me the money back I paid for the two night stay!!!

So what now? Termini train station it was.....in the grass for two nights. We laughed, we drank, we ate and sang the whole of Tuesday. Ditto on the Wednesday also.

Approaching the Olimpico it was fantastic being part of it all, entering the arena, more like a giant COLOSSEUM with 60000 mad Italians smelling blood. It was out of this world.

The Roma end packed ready to burst five or six hours before kick-off. Flares, noise, songs, drums, smoke, bounce, fuck me they were up for this.

A big banner said "NO PASSA IL STRANIERO!!" (the foreigner will not pass!)

The Liverpool squad walked onto the running track about a hour before kick off to soak up the atmosphere while there was a pre game being played. For my life I can't remember who the two sides were and an almighty whistling concert rolled towards our end, coming from Roma end, ear piercing stuff.

kick off was now approaching as the two teams walk onto the pitch, the Roma noise was madness. We gave as much as we had, players like Nicol had faces like rabbits caught in the headlights, fear written all over them but not the emperor himself Souness! He just trotted onto the pitch, looked around and thought "Is this fucking it??" I just loved the man, he was and is my all time favourite Liverpool player. We all know he messed up good style with the S*n interview but take that away...fuck me what a player what a colossus!!!

So here we were, in the lions' den and the plan for all Romans supporting AS was.....we were gonna get it that night, according to them we were just there to get slaughtered!!!

The game was tense Phil Neal 1-0, Pruzzo 1-1, extra time tension, unreal....penalties, Nicol missed first and we all feared the worst. Queue spaghetti legged legend Bruce, haha unbelievable, Conti and Graziani must have thought "WTF is this fella doing??" and it worked!!! Neal, Rush, Souness all scored, now it was up to Barney Rubble to make us European Champions   again......GEEEEEEEEEET IN!!!!!

Buried under a pile of people, strangers hugging and kissing me. We done it again!!!!

Against all the odds in Roma's colosseum in Roma's own backyard we killed the lion!!!
FANTASTIC

Souness does his trot, sticks his chest out and lifts that glorious looking trophy into the dark Roma sky BOOOOOOOOOOM

We walked out of the ground and saw some bad scuffles but the five of us (we had befriended an Austrian and German lad) just walked away from it all.

I heard all the stories of how bad it was, how the Italians attacked anything that spoke English or wore a Liverpool top.

Actually we walked along some massive road, this Italian approached us and asked us for help, his FIAT 500 Topolino had broken down in the middle of the road....the five of us just lifted the tiny car up and dragged it to the side of the street.

At the end of the day we were EUROPEAN CHAMPIONS and we could have moved mountains.

Six Months later I travelled on my own to Tokyo for the Intercontinental Cup clash v Independiente Buenos Aires.....but that's another story

MARCO CATENA

1984/85 EUROPEAN CUP

19 September 1984 First round
KKS Lech Poznań 0-1   Liverpool FC

3 October 1984 First round
Liverpool FC   4-0   KKS Lech Poznań
Aggregate: 5-0

24 October 1984 Second round
Liverpool FC   3-1   SL Benfica

7 November 1984 Second round
SL Benfica   1-0   Liverpool FC
Aggregate: 2-3

6 March 1985 Quarter-finals
FK Austria Wien 1-1   Liverpool FC

20 March 1985 Quarter-finals
Liverpool FC   4-1   FK Austria Wien
Aggregate: 5-2

10 April 1985 Semi-finals
Liverpool FC   4-0   Panathinaikos FC

24 April 1985 Semi-finals
Panathinaikos FC 0-1   Liverpool FC
Aggregate: 0-5

29 May 1985 Final
Juventus 1-0   Liverpool FC

EUROPEAN CUP 1ST ROUND 1ST LEG
19TH SEPTEMBER 1984
STADION LECHA [35000]. POZNAN. POLAND
K.K.S. LECH POZNAN 0 LIVERPOOL 1

Going to Poland at the height of Ronnie Reagan's Cold War seemed like a really weird idea, so me and Quinny booked with Ross Travel and off we went. Mike Ross had been doing cheap European trips for 10 years and always provided value for money. We flew to West Berlin, which in those pre-Glasnost days was a really wild place, most of its occupants had this attitude of 'live for today, tomorrow we're getting invaded'. After two nights of unremitting hedonism comprising of 18 hour
benders, Chinese brothels on the Unter und Linden, and accidentally trespassing into the Russian Zone, we set off for the dubious delights of Eastern Europe. If Berlin was the bright lights of Europe then Poland was the prison spotlights of Europe. We waited for over an hour in East Berlin Hauptbahnhof for our train. When it finally arrived we were herded into a metal, seatless carriage that looked that it had been used to ferry Panzer Korps troops to the Battle of Leningrad. After a journey of interminable delays we finally arrived in Poznan. Nowadays Poznan is an Easyjet destination but my impression then was one of unremitting greyness. All the buildings were grey, the hotel was grey and the grass on the pitch seemed to have a grey tinge. The match was only notable for a mini-riot that ensued before kick off. A group of Poznan fans held up a large 'SOLIDARNOSC' flag, which prompted the local riot police to charge into the crowd. The crowd opened up to let them through before converging and engulfing the police, who appeared back on the pitch minutes later, looking battered and bruised. The game was won with a solitary John Wark goal, who was having his most productive season with the Reds. It was a typical Liverpool European performance with the team dominating most of the play. The Poznan coach had stated before the game that he would resign should his team not make the last four. He, in fact, lasted until the last day of the year.
Back at our hotel, tastefully decorated in Poznan grey, the production of a $10 note sent the local population into a frenzy of attentiveness, the bar staff dispensed Vodka with abandon whilst the local female population of the bar (All trainee nuns obviously) viewed us as their ticket out of Poland and did amazing things with Colgate Ultra. It may have been grey but it was a great trip.
DAVE HARDMAN

EUROPEAN SUPER CUP FINAL
16TH JANUARY 1985
STADIA COMUNALE [60000]. TURIN. ITALY.
JUVENTUS 2 LIVERPOOL 0

I think this game has largely been forgotten coming as it did in between 'The Glory that was Rome (Part II)' in May 1984 and Heysel in May 1985. There had been difficulty finding dates for the usual two-legged Final and a compromise was reached to play it as a one-off tie at Juventus' home ground, the Stadio Communale in Turin. Like the World Club Championship, I don't think Liverpool took the Super Cup too seriously back then and treated the games like nothing but a glorified friendly. Just a case of play the game, don't get beat by too many, avoid injury and pocket the cash.

Owing to severe Winter weather all over Europe this game was in doubt in the days leading up to it and Liverpool only took off late the day before after confirmation from Turin that the pitch had been cleared of snow. Even then there still remained a risk it wouldn't go ahead if there was a further deterioration in the weather. Liverpool's game the previous Saturday was off, their last game being a 3-0 FA Cup win over Aston Villa at Anfield on 5 January.

Fueled by a few pints of Golden a couple of weeks earlier I vaguely remembered saying I'd be up for a trip there, if we could arrange something at a realistic cost but having heard nothing and with the weather implications I thought nothing more of it, until a phone call on the Sunday night. Turns out I'd agreed to go by car with three mates and as much as I didn't really fancy it the trip was on and it would hit their costs if I pulled out. A car had been hired, the hire company was told we were going on a golfing trip to the Scottish Highlands to explain the high mileage but avoid the extra charges for taking it outside of the UK. I lived in East Kilbride, near Glasgow, back then and needed to get myself down to Liverpool to meet two of the lads, Ian (Kendo) & John (Bury), who were picking up the car then driving to Bristol to pick up another lad, Pete Matthews, an exiled Scouser who organised coaches up to Anfield for every home game. In the end the easiest way was to get an overnight train to Bristol on the Monday and the lads picked me up at Bristol Parkway early on the Tuesday morning.

The car, an old Austin Morris, looked a bit of a banger but was very comfortable inside with plenty of room. The roads weren't too bad at first and we made it down to Portsmouth in plenty of time for the ferry to Le Havre in France. Pete had good contacts up at Anfield and before we boarded the ferry he phoned the Development office to check that the official club party had actually set out.

The ferry crossing wasn't too bad and we arrived in Le Havre late Tuesday evening. The weather forecast didn't look too good so we decided to just get right on with the 500-mile trip down through France and over the Alps into Turin. No real problems through France, other than tiredness, but the section over the Alps was a nightmare with snow and ice and not being helped by the fact that the engine packed in three or four times, partly owing to the freezing weather and partly owing to the state of the old banger. If it wasn't for Kendo we would never have made it. Each time we broke down he had the problem sorted within a short space of time with some running repairs although at the time it seemed an eternity in the freezing cold until the heaters came back on.

We eventually trundled into Turin early afternoon and sorted ourselves out with a cheap Pensione hotel. Our original intention had been to set out on the return journey straight after the match but we were all in need of some sleep so we reckoned it was best to get a few hours kip after the game albeit that we would have to be on the road by 5am to get back to Le Havre for our booked ferry. As we parked up by a school some kids saw the UK number plates and started off with the 'Juve' chants while bombarding us with snowballs which we just laughed off but it was a sign of things to come.

After dumping our bags we headed for the hotel in the city centre, where the official club party was staying, as Pete had arranged to get us match tickets off Jim Kennefick from the Development, who looked after the supporters who travelled with the club party on European trips. With the tickets obtained and paid for, Jim said we were welcome to travel to the Stadium on the coach carrying the twenty or so supporters who'd travelled with the club plus the Press lads. Sorted, so we got a few beers in and in truth, it was just a few with exhaustion rapidly setting in.

The journey to the Stadio Communale didn't take long and we were dropped off right by our entrance. The snow was piled high all over the city and even at the stadium it was was piled several feet high all around the pitch. It soon became clear that the pitch was barely playable and I doubt if it would have went ahead if it hadn't been for the money coming from the live TV coverage in Italy. Such was the attraction of Liverpool though that despite the state of the pitch, the freezing conditions and live TV coverage, a crowd of 60,000 turned out to see Juventus win 2-0 against a pedantic Liverpool with a goal in each half from their Polish winger Zibi Boniek.

Throughout the match the small group of Liverpool fans were subjected to being bombarded by snowballs and lumps of ice, with any attempt to 'return fire' being met with a swift reaction from the Carabinieri. The atmosphere became increasingly hostile despite Juventus cantering to a win and as the coach, which we had got the lift on to the stadium, was going directly back to the airport we had to make our own way back to the hotel. Despite not wearing any colours, we were sussed out before we had left the stadium vicinity and it looked pretty hairy for a bit but it was Kendo to the rescue again as he virtually commandeered a passing taxi that was heading for the VIP entrance and ordered the driver to get us away pronto!

The rest of the trip was pretty uneventful. Straight back to the hotel for a few hours kip then a drive back over the Alps and up through France. No more car problems and we made it back to Le Havre just in time for the overnight ferry on the Thursday. Peter agreed to do the driving when we got off the ferry so the other three of us got tore into a couple of cases of French lager. We stayed over in Bristol on the Friday night then drove on to Liverpool first thing on the Saturday where the real Liverpool team turned up to notch a 4-0 League win over Norwich City. Last act of the trip was for the hero of the hour Kendo to return the cleaned-up car and confirm that we'd had a great few days' golfing in Scotland!

JIM GARDINER

EUROPEAN CUP QUARTER-FINAL 1ST LEG
6TH MARCH 1985
GERHARD HANAPPI STADION [20000]. VIENNA. AUSTRIA.
FK AUSTRIA WIEN 1 LIVERPOOL 1

One of my favourite Euro trips was Liverpool v Austria Memphis or Vienna in some record books. My first, you could say modern, Euro away trip. I had been on previous pre-season tours, Euro games, two Euro finals (three if you count Wembley) by trains, ferries and coaches. Only time I'd flew was by Swissair when I got a free flight after a few free nights of accommodation all provided by their friendly neutral Government. We had previously beaten Lech Poznan and Benfica and were drawn against the Austrian champions on our way to the final in Brussels.

My mates lived and worked allegedly in London at the time. He rang, "Fancy a trip to Vienna flying to Munich a few days earlier for our next adventure?" "Sounds great to me. Fuckin' ell, all those Bier Kellers! Hope they're like them ones in town with the strippers on before the game!" Remember that you old bastards?

So I got the train to Euston on my own. The whole of Skem had emigrated to the Smoke at the time. Was it all the work or all that money the government still provided us with? Both I thinks. Anyway, I arrived at Euston to be greeted by the pals. Alright lads, three of us with flight tickets and a late arrival. "I'll just get a ticket at the airport when I get there lads." We travelled to Heathrow. Bumped into a few lads at the airport from that other famous new town not far from Skem, soon to be very popular with Tesco's and some blue noses. 'Alright lads going the game?' Yes! Fuckin' ell they've got the same travel advisors itinerary as us! All on the same wavelength. Methinks this could be fun. They have the same problem, one lad who looks like he's just come straight off the building site is looking for a flight ticket as well. So we go around a few booths trying to purchase said tickets with no luck. Passed from one booth to another. It was getting late. Decisions had to be made.

'Alright lads were coming with yer. We'll 'ave to bunk the plane.'

So we go through all of the security into the duty free area. Grab a few scoops in duty free. Do a bit of shopping, Now I was used to shopping for myself on these trips but fuckin' 'ell these lads were on a different planet to me! One smooth brother would be chatting the assistants up. The other brother, the rougher one (only messin') and pal would just empty shelves of perfume, ciggies, ale, anything to make money for this, next and future trips. Yes these lads followed the Reds everywhere for a living. A full rack of stylish leathers were gone, just because "me bird will like that."

Anyway, on to the flight. It was as easy as bunking the last stagecoach to Skem after the game on a Saturday. Munich was again an eye opener with these lads. Loads of beer, loads of smoke and a new sport introduced. These were the famous dippers! Even had a go meself but only with some daft German who'd been following us on our pub crawl all day. Fuckin 'ell that German ales alright innit? Big glasses and dead strong! Few days in Munich. Loads of those Kellers visited. No strippers in them though and we decided to get the night train through to Vienna the night before the game.

We decided to find a sleeper on the train. Sloped into one of those with about 3 beds on each side. Only one person in it. Fuckin 'ell, later on we found it was a fraulein! Would have been done for rape, stalking or anything these days. A guard must have seen me entering as a little later he opened the door, hit me over the head with a cosh and left again. Instant fascist justice! Certainly helped me sleep. A day in ahhhhhh Vienna. You can sing that bit. In one shop I was a bit slow, it must be the hangover or the cosh to the head and I was asked kindly to visit a room with the helpful assistants who told me that I was incorrect in thinking everything was free in Austria. They let me go a few hours later and I had a nice photo taken outside the shop named 'KLEPTOS' - very appropriate!

Anyway, to the game. Yes, we were here to see the mighty ones. 1-1, Rush scored one, Rush scored.........no, just one I think. [that lager must have been stronger, it was Nicol who grabbed our goal – ED]. Deffo beat that shite at Anfield and on to the Semis. The dippers had different sport in mind now, dipping. Onto trams I think or trains or buses or all. They just told me make a nuisance of yourself, push, shove, sing, shout abusives, anything for a distraction. Fuckin' ell I'm dead good at that I can tell you. I've done it every Sunday morning for years.

Back to the hotel. We found one where the official trips were staying and were kindly invited to a few floors in Reds lads' rooms. Some wannabe pop star had been in Vienna that night so we took the piss out of him and his fans in the bar all night. The legendary Nik Kershaw if my memory serves me. It usually doesn't.

So a trip back to Munich and another load of ale and then our flight home. Ohhhhh-hhhhh shit! Yes, two lads still ticketless. No way were we buying tickets! This bunking planes was easy. As you can imagine, German security, efficiency was better than British Airways so these boys were on the ball and on to us.

'Just stick together lads. Giz all your boarding passes and we'll be OK', said the Kirkby lad.

Fuck me, I've just handed me ticket over and we're hustling through. About three checks on boarding passes and we are walking to the plane with staff massed at the bottom of the stairs. We are fucked! Anyway, as we get to the stairs there's a damsel in front pushing a pram. Well you know Scousers when ladies need a hand. We're all carrying her pram up the steps to the plane with bemused security trying to stop us as we've all got a hand on the pram and one lad showing our passes. Thank god, empty seats. Quick as a flash little Macca's safely under the seats. The lad straight off the building site, about six foot, is under them but the steelies he's had on all week are sticking out. After a great week together we don't want anyone making their own way home from Germany.

It would probably take them two days on their own. So there's another boarding pass check by security, names, passes etc. and still no one has spotted the bunkers. Now we are pissing ourselves laughing. The Germans are scratching their heads. 'There was deffo more.'

The pilot informs them we've go to go now or miss our slot so they reluctantly leave the plane. The take off was unbelievable. Shouts, whoops of delight. We opened our free bottles of duty free champagne and as the heads were popping from under the seats it was a feeling which surely cannot be beaten..

Anyway we won the home game 4-1. I Didn't go the semi because of work. Our new found friends certainly did! I still see them in strange airports and cities all over the place and laugh about this one. Final against Juve stopped us winning it FIVE times but Brussels etc…..well that's another story.

NEIL [SKEM]

EUROPEAN CUP FINAL
29TH MAY 1985
HEYSEL STADION [50000]. BRUSSELS. BELGIUM
JUVENTUS 1 LIVERPOOL 0

In Memoria e Amicizia.
In Memory and Friendship.

Rocco Acerra
Bruno Balli
Alfons Bos
Giancarlo Bruschera
Andrea Casula
Giovanni Casula
Nino Cerullo
Willy Chielens
Giuseppina Conti
Dirk Daenecky
Dionisio Fabbro
Jacques François
Eugenio Gagliano
Francesco Galli
Giancarlo Gonnelli
Alberto Guarini
Giovacchino Landini
Roberto Lorentini
Barbara Lusci
Franco Martelli

Loris Messore
Gianni Mastrolaco
Sergio Bastino Mazzino
Luciano Rocco Papaluca
Luigi Pidone
Bento Pistolato
Patrick Radcliffe
Domenico Ragazzi
Antonio Ragnanese
Claude Robert
Mario Ronchi
Domenico Russo
Tarcisio Salvi
Gianfranco Sarto
Giuseppe Spalaore
Mario Spanu
Tarcisio Venturin
Jean Michel Walla
Claudio Zavaroni

1991/92 UEFA CUP

18 September 1991 First round
Liverpool FC   6-1   FC Lahti

2 October 1991 First round
FC Lahti 1-0   Liverpool FC
Aggregate: 2-6

23 October 1991 Second round
AJ Auxerre   2-0   Liverpool FC

6 November 1991 Second round
Liverpool FC   3-0   AJ Auxerre
Aggregate: 3-2

27 November 1991 Third round
FC Wacker Innsbruck   0-2   Liverpool FC

11 December 1991 Third round
Liverpool FC   4-0   FC Wacker Innsbruck
Aggregate: 6-0

4 March 1992 Quarter-finals
Genoa CFC   2-0   Liverpool FC

18 March 1992 Quarter-finals
Liverpool FC   1-2   Genoa CFC
Aggregate: 1-4

UEFA CUP 3RD ROUND 1ST LEG
27TH NOVEMBER 1991
TIVOLI STADIUM [12500]. INNSBRUCK, AUSTRIA
F.C. SWAROVSKI TYROL 0 LIVERPOOL 2

We went to Swarovski Tyrol (Innsbruck) in November 1991. There was myself and my mate Mike, who is 80 next year.
In those days the UEFA cup was on a Tuesday, so with money being a bit tight, we thought that instead of flying it would be a good idea to go on a coach with Selwyns.
We arrived at Anfield on the Monday morning with loads of booze ready for the three day trip and carried it all onto the bus. Great stuff, start of a three day party, we thought, but just as we were about to set off a load of coppers arrived.
'Stop the bus'. New UEFA rules, no drinking on official trips.
We had to get all of the ale off the bus. It must have stretched five hundred yards down one of the side streets.
We got to Innsbruck on the Tuesday afternoon absolutely knackered. I think we had about four hours free time before the game. Innsbruck was a fantastic place with the big ski jump overlooking the ground. The Reds won 2-0 with Dean Saunders grabbing a brace.
After the game we had about an hour before the coaches left, so we grabbed a couple of bevies in a local bar.
As we come out of the bar, my mate turned the wrong way. We couldn't find him anywhere. Then just as our bus was about to go, after waiting an extra half hour, he turns up.
The journey home was a nightmare, best remembered for powdered chicken soup and Billy Connelly DVD's. Every time you woke up you hoped you were on the M6 but each time the only sign you could see was AUSFAHRT, which obviously meant we were still in Austria or Germany.
Finally we got home, I think it was early Wednesday afternoon. We swore we'd never again go by coach. Which we never did until we played Standard Liege a couple of years ago but that's another story..
PHIL ROOSE

UEFA CUP QUARTER-FINAL 1ST LEG
4TH MARCH 1992
STADIO LUIGI FERRARIS [40000].
GENOA. ITALY.
GENOA 2 LIVERPOOL 0

This was Liverpool's first competitive game against an Italian club post-Heysel and perhaps not surprisingly there were all sorts of hoops to jump through before the club would release tickets to fans making their own way. We didn't fancy staying in Genoa itself with all the restrictions that was likely to involve, so I suggested to the boss, the one and only Bobby Wilcox, that we head for the seaside resort of Rapallo, about sixty miles outside Genoa. The Scotland team had been based there during the 1990 World Cup in Italy and I knew lads from the Tartan Army that had based themselves there too and had a great time.

So seven of us, led as always by Bobby, flew from Manchester to Milan first thing on the Monday, then hired a twelve seater self-drive minibus for the drive to Rapallo, which took no more than a couple of hours even allowing for my slow, very slow, driving on the steep, hilly, scary descent into Rapallo itself. We didn't have a hotel booked but there was no shortage of small hotels in the resort and after parking up the minibus just behind the main promenade and greatly helped by one of the lads, Stevie Crockett, being able to speak good Italian, we were soon sorted out with a decent, cheap billet for three nights.

Although it was out of season for the seaside resort there were still plenty of small bars open and we faced none of the animosity or refusal to serve that had been predicted for Genoa in the Press. The only thing we faced was the amusement of the well wrapped-up locals who couldn't understand us walking around in t-shirts in the Spring sunshine as to them it was still like winter compared to the temperatures they get there in the Summer months. Actually, there was one problem. Back home on domestic away trips Alan 'Cabaret' always took control of the beer kitty for the Wilcox crew but he wasn't on this trip so I was landed with the duty. It seemed like every bar we were in they would only have six big glasses & no matter how hard I tried I always seemed to be stuck with the small glass with seven in the round.

We ventured into Genoa the day before the game, a thirty minute train ride from Rapallo, to suss out the lay of the land. No problems encountered and we had no problem getting served in bars. Funny incident occurred when we were sitting having a quiet beer outside a café in the city centre. Most of the Liverpool players, accompanied by manager Graeme Souness and coach Phil Boersma, came strolling past on an after-lunch walk from their hotel which turned out to be close by. I remember a young Steve McManaman addressing Bobby as 'Mr Wilcox' much to our amusement but then Stevie Nicol topped it off in responding to Souness's question as to whether any of the players fancied a coffee by saying "I'll have what they're having", pointing to the tray of large beers being delivered to our table by the waiter! Souness' look at Stevie was priceless! And by the way, as had become the norm, the tray contained six large beers and one small one, the curse of the six glasses had struck again!

On the way back to the station we bumped into a group of Reds who were struggling to get anywhere to stay in Genoa so we took them back to Rapallo with us and Stevie Crocket's interpreter skills got them sorted out with a hotel in no time.

There was a very high police presence in Genoa on the day of the game and to avoid the drinking ban in force we just travelled up there later in the day. The Stadio Luigi Ferrari was filled to its 40,000 capacity and considering the stadium had been rebuilt for the

96

World Cup just two years earlier it was disappointing that the only way you could get a decent view of the pitch, from the low-set away end, was by standing on your seat. Genoa led by just the one first half goal until a second goal a couple of minutes from time put them very much in control for the second leg at Anfield which we lost, 1-2, in any case.

The rest of the trip passed off without incident. The only happening of any note was when we went back to pick up the minibus which we hadn't been near for three days. Just as we were getting ready to drive off a little, old guy with a peaked cap and an ancient ticket machine appeared from nowhere and demanded that we pay for parking. There didn't appear to be any parking notices about so we were all set to argue until we realised the sum being demanded was under £10 for the three days, so we paid up out of the money left over in the kitty, seeing as we could only ever seem to get six big beers at a time rather than seven…..!!!

JIM GARDINER

1992/93 EUROPEAN CUP WINNERS CUP

16 September 1992 First round
Liverpool FC   6-1   Apollon Limassol

29 September 1992 First round
Apollon Limassol 1-2   Liverpool FC
Aggregate: 2-8

22 October 1992 Second round
Spartak Moscow   4-2   Liverpool FC

4 November 1992 Second round
Liverpool FC   0-2   Spartak Moscow
Aggregate: 2-61995/96 UEFA CUP

12 September 1995 First round
FC Alania Vladikavkaz   1-2   Liverpool FC

26 September 1995 First round
Liverpool FC   0-0   FC Alania Vladikavkaz
Aggregate: 2-1

17 October 1995 Second round
Brøndby IF   0-0   Liverpool FC

31 October 1995 Second round
Liverpool FC   0-1   Brøndby IF
Aggregate: 0-1

UEFA CUP 1ST ROUND 1ST LEG
12TH SEPTEMBER 1995
SPARTAK STADIUM [33500].
VLADIKAVKAZ. RUSSIA
SPARTAK-ALANIA VLADIKAVKAZ 1 LIVERPOOL 2

In these enlightened days of the internet and numerous budget airlines, booking independent travel is relatively easy but back in 1995 it was a whole different ballgame and as soon as the draw was made you knew this was going to be a hard one to get to. Vladikavkaz is the capital of North Ossetia, a semi-independent Russian Republic some 1,100 miles south of Moscow and bordered by Georgia and Chechnya in the shadow of the Caucasas Mountains. Getting to Moscow was do-able but getting from there to Vladikavkaz was proving to be a nightmare. Aeroflot internal flights or the train were considered but both cost and time effectively ruled those alternatives out.

Me and a good mate, Phil (Antrobus) who I'd met on a pre-season tour a couple of years earlier were still up for the trip. Having travelled with the club a couple of times, when getting off work was tight, so necessitating a quick in and out, I checked to see what the plans were for the team. Their usual schedule was to travel out on the day before a game and fly back straight after. It was an expensive way of doing things but handy for getting to a game with minimum time off work, especially for the more difficult places to get to. The club was struggling themselves though. Insurance costs for a plane from their usual source at that time, Aer Lingus, was proving prohibitive owing to the proximity of the Chechnyan border to Vladikavkaz, with the Russians involved in an increasingly violent struggle with Chechnya seeking independence. Other carriers were also reluctant to fly so close to a war zone and the club had started making plans to fly by scheduled airline to Moscow then onward to Vladikavkaz. No places for fans if that happened so it looked increasingly like being a non-starter.

Then, around a week before the tie I got a call off the club to say that if we could get down to Anfield next morning with the documents and details needed for a Russian visa, plus the little matter of £500, then a few places were available for supporters, on a first come first served basis, to travel on a plane chartered to carry the team and press. It was a lot to pay out for a one night stay but with no other way of getting there we went for it. Now if we'd have known at that stage that the plane had been chartered off Aeroflot, the only carrier that would fly so close to the war zone, we might have had second thoughts. I certainly would have, I'm a bad flyer at the best of times, but you live and learn.

The look of disbelief on the players and press lads faces when they saw the Areoflot charter plane had to be seen to be believed. It had definitely seen better days and I'm pretty sure I wasn't the only one bricking it before take-off. No safety talk, some seats missing safety belts and no overhead lockers, just an open shelf. To be fair though, it was a fairly smooth flight and the flight staff were more than generous with the in-flight drinks and the forty five or so supporters were fairly merry by the end of the five hour flight. There wasn't much warning that we were coming in to land, just one minute the plane was descending past mountains, the next we were landing bumpily with the surreal sight of cows grazing on the unfenced grass area next to the runway and even more surreal was the sight of several massive helicopter gunships parked close to the ramshackle terminal building.

After going through the usual seemingly never ending Russian immigration process we were loaded on to a couple of ancient coaches for the twenty minute ride into the city centre. On board was a lad from the British Consulate giving us a list of 'do's and don'ts' on personal safety and he turned out to be a Red from Bootle originally. He also introduced a Russian who was to be our contact if there were any safety issues. His appearance and demeanor alone suggested he was not a lad to be messed with and the bulge under his jacket wasn't his wallet. Police cars stopped the traffic, not that there was much, at every junction and after negotiating the numerous potholes we arrived at our hotel. Now the one benefit in travelling with the official party used to be that you stayed in the best of hotels but this one was a dump. To be fair though, I think it was maybe the only 'suitable' hotel in the city as the players, directors and press were also billeted there.

There wasn't exactly a lot in the way of bars and we'd been warned not to wander too far from the hotel for our own safety but like most of the other Reds we ended up in the one bar come club we could find. The vodka was ridiculously cheap but the only beer consisted of cans of German and Turkish lager, many of which were past their sell by date. It turned into not a bad night though with the usual sing-song as the drink took effect and we only decided to leave once they ran out of beer. Being a club it was a case of getting a bill at the end which can often be a cue for a rip-off but when the bill arrived it seemed not too bad at all, albeit that they were charging more than what had been listed in the 'menu' which I'd pocketed earlier as a souvenir, so we paid up and walked the short distance back to the hotel and went to the bar there.

We'd been back there a short while when there was a bit of a commotion and the lads who had been on the next table to us in the club came in pursued by a couple of the bar staff from the club. The lads were saying their bill was for far more than they'd drunk and they refused to pay for any more than what they claimed to have had. It looked like turning ugly and the police getting involved but when I got a look at their bill it soon clicked, our bill had been so cheap because we'd been given theirs by mistake and they'd subsequently been handed ours. We tried to get this across to the bar staff from the club and were trying to say that we were good for the additional money but they were just shouting and very threatening and the situation wasn't helped by the plod from Merseyside Police travelling with the club assuming we'd been at it and making his own threats. Enter the big Russian lad we'd been introduced to on the bus from the airport as being in charge of security. A few sharp words from him to the club bar staff and things calmed down. He asked me to explain what had happened and I told him, making it clear that although the bar bills were well 'over the top' based on the price list in the club, it was all relative, and we were good for the money. He had another word with the club staff and said they were claiming that the prices were correct. At that stage I remembered the menu I'd taken as a souvenir earlier and showed him. He took the bar staff aside and gave them some money out of a roll of cash he produced and although they didn't exactly seem overjoyed they soon went on their way with what seemed like a lecture from him and as I said earlier he didn't look like the sort of person to mess with. He refused to take any money off us for the bill saying that the club staff had indeed been trying a rip-off on the prices and that it was now taken care of as we were guests in his country. Result!

Once again, the usual sing-song started up as the evening wore on and the Liverpool club doctor came down to explain that although the players' rooms were on the top floor they could hear the noise coming from the bar and he asked if it could be toned down a bit to let the players get a decent night's sleep before the next day's game. One Red just carried on singing though, the Doc was about to say something a bit stronger until he noticed the 'culprit' was none other than club chairman, David Moores, who had clearly made the most of the hospitality at the official reception!

The next day saw Liverpool go a goal behind in the first half but Steve McManaman equalised before the break and Jamie Redknapp grabbed the winner early in the second half, the 2-1 win taking us through after the return leg at Anfield a couple of weeks later finished 0-0. Our Russian hosts put the small band of Reds in the 'Presidential Box' which was really just an elevated section at the back of the stand and the only downside was Liverpool director Noel White taking the huff at the Reds fans having access to a bar under the stand and demanding that we be herded back into our 'Box' which sadly we were.

After the game it was straight back to the airport for our return flight to Liverpool. A couple of the big Russian helicopter gunships took off in advance of us boarding and our big Russian mate did nothing to settle the flying nerves by calmly explaining that they were taking precautionary measures to avoid a potential rocket attack on our plane by rebels from neighbouring Chechnya. I'm glad to say though that the flight home passed off without incident, the beer flowed and with the two hour time difference now in our favour we landed back at Speke in the early hours of the morning. Well, I say without incident, but there was a bit of a kick-off as we got off the plane when Neil Ruddock decked Robbie Fowler apparently over some 'prank' that had went wrong on the trip. I vaguely remember reading something later about Robbie cutting up a pair of Ruddock's trainers in retaliation for Ruddock having a crap in his trainers in the hotel. Boys will be boys! I wonder what Noel White had to say about that one………..

JIM GARDINER

1996/97 EUROPEAN CUP WINNERS CUP

12 September 1996 First round
Myllykosken Pallo-47   0-1   Liverpool FC

26 September 1996 First round
Liverpool FC   3-1   Myllykosken Pallo-47
Aggregate: 4-1

17 October 1996 Second round
FC Sion 1-2   Liverpool FC

31 October 1996 Second round
Liverpool FC   6-3   FC Sion
Aggregate: 8-4

6 March 1997 Quarter Final
SK Brann   1-1   Liverpool FC

20 March 1997 Quarter Final
Liverpool FC   3-0   SK Brann
Aggregate: 4-1

10 April 1997 Semi Final
Paris St-Germain 3-0   Liverpool FC

24 April 1997 Semi Final
Liverpool FC   2-0   Paris St-Germain
Aggregate: 2-3

EUROPEAN CUP WINNERS CUP 2ND ROUND 1ST LEG
17TH OCTOBER 1996
STADE DE TOUBILLON [16500]
SION. SWITZERLAND
F.C. SION 1 LIVERPOOL 2

This appealed to me as soon as the draw was made. Even though it had been several years since I had been to a European away, I always preferred the smaller, provincial towns to the big cities, partly because in many cases I had already visited those cities on non-football trips. I booked a two-night trip with the first night being in Montreux and the second night in Sion itself. The flight to Geneva was uneventful, as was the coach journey from the airport to the picturesque town of Montreux, which was where the problems started. Situated on the eastern side of Lake Geneva, Montreux is an idyllic location and well known for its nightlife as well as its Jazz Festival. There were numerous bars and restaurants within walking distance of our hotel. On the trip with me was a friend from Northern Ireland (Jim) and a Norwegian I knew as Benny who earlier in the 1990s had spent a whole season on Merseyside so that he could go to as many Liverpool matches as possible. Not far from the bar where the three of us were enjoying a quiet drink, a fire broke out in a waste-bin and Benny wandered up the road to take a look. With arsonists being known to often hang around to see the results of their handiwork, Benny's interest attracted the interest of the Police when they arrived, along with the fire brigade. Jim and I watched as Benny was put in a car and driven off. We knew not where. We tried to find out where our Norwegian friend had been taken, at which point the Police decided to put me in a car as well and drive me off in that, leaving one confused Irishman standing on the pavement. Jim eventually found the police station where Benny and I had been taken and after being questioned they were satisfied that we had not been involved in starting the fire and allowed us to return to our hotel for a good nights kip.

 Overnight some items went missing from a glass cabinet in the hotel. This theft was discovered the next morning so more police were called while the tour representative tried to get the matter resolved. But we were told that we were not going anywhere until the missing items were returned. Obviously the English overnight guests were the prime suspects. We were free to walk around the streets but we could not leave the town. Despite that warning, I wandered up to the railway station to check the times of trains from Montreux to Sion. It was possible to get there but by the time I returned to the hotel everything had been resolved and the police allowed (maybe encouraged) our party to leave for Sion.

 We got to Sion maybe three hours before the match, checked into our second hotel and the match-tickets were distributed there. We were not allowed inside the stadium until the coaches from Liverpool had arrived so that we could all be kept together. Expecting some supporters to travel without tickets (as they always did), some tickets were being sold from a table near the away turnstiles. So I think everyone who travelled did get in ok. We were firm favourites for the game but conceded the first goal before recovering to win the match 2-1. There was a good rapport between the supporters with both sets of fans chanting the other club's name at the end (this happened at Anfield as well), even though the locals were confused at our mispronunciation of Sion (which came out as Sigh-on not See-on as it should have been). It was a pleasant town and we got a good reception when we went into a bar for a post-match drink. The next morning we were bussed back to Geneva airport and got a quite fantastic view of the Alps as we took off. When I added the match-details to my personal records book on returning home, I realised to my surprise that it had been my first European away since the 1981 final in Paris. But I was glad I went on this trip to Switzerland. It re-kindled a lot of memories of trips in the 1970s and, the Swiss Police presence apart, was a most enjoyable couple of days.

CHRIS WOOD

EUROPEAN CUP WINNERS CUP QUARTER FINAL 1ST LEG
6TH MARCH 1997
BRANN STADION [12700]
BERGEN. NORWAY
S.K. BRANN 1 LIVERPOOL 1

I was only about 13 at the time and travelled with my dad, uncle and my uncle's mate. It was my first European away and I think it was with Global Travel that we went with. I just remember getting to our hotel where just me and my dad were booked in to.

We had to get a water ferry over to my uncle's hotel and the driver of taxi was getting tortured because he looked like Jimmy Tarbuck.

Once we got to my uncles hotel, we met up with him and went out for the night. As we were walking around we saw loads of girls outside a hotel. This hotel was posh, like the Ritz. When we got closer we saw it was the Liverpool team. We got up to the front door and then my dad's mate said to the fella on the door that we were with the team and that he was the pasta chef. So the concierge keys us in.

All I remember that night was Roy Evans having a meal with Peter Robinson, Stan Collymore standing by the reception and players just going constantly up and down in the lift. I remember going to the toilet and Ronnie Moran coming in, pissed, telling me I should be in school. He was sound. Then I remember my uncle saying to Rob Jones or Carragher, "How do you know if you're in the side? Does Roy Evans come in and tickle your balls and say 'You're in the side'"

Anyway, the next day comes and we take a look around Bergen. It was a boss place. We got a coach up to the ground. The travel company didn't seem to have enough tickets for everyone but we made sure we got ours and started to walk down a hill to get into the ground.

The ground was small and compact with just like tarmac to stand on. Fowler scored a

great goal and David James gave his gloves to some Norwegian kid.
My first Euro away had finished and I loved every minute of it
BILLY CARNEY

EUROPEAN CUP WINNERS CUP SEMI FINAL 1ST LEG
10TH APRIL 1997
PARC DE PRINCES [35142]
PARIS. FRANCE
PARIS SAINT-GERMAIN 3 LIVERPOOL 0

There were about twelve of us having a ball in Paris. When it was time to go to the match we got the Metro to the ground. As we walked out into the road we were slap bang in the middle of hundreds of PSG skins and we stood out like sore thumbs. I had a bright coloured Lacoste shirt on while all of the skins had those green bombers on and that!!

Some little prick popped up at the side of me and tried to smash a glass on my head, he couldn't get near my head because I was about six foot taller than the little runt.

The whole road seemed to be coming towards us and surrounding us. I kicked the little prick up the arse and he ran back into the crowd. Digs started to rain down on us and we all ended up in our own little battles but we were outnumbered badly. One lad, Bucko, got his leg broken badly, another got a glass smashed in his face. I ended up surrounded by between eight and ten skinheads.

I was bladdered and felt like I was dreaming. In a split second I thought to myself 'Say something in French you learnt at school'. I was shit at French and hated it but one saying always stuck in my head was 'Ou est les plage?' I started shouting it at them and throwing my arms around. 'Ou est les plage?' 'Ou est les plage?' They all stopped and looked at me as if I was a bad crank. In that split second I legged it and they seemed to leave me alone. 'Ou est les plage?' means 'Where's the beach??'

In the middle of downtown Paris some six foot Scouse grock is in a life and death situation demanding directions for a fuckin' beach. I escaped with a bit of a cut on my head, others weren't so lucky.

The return at Anfield wasn't the nicest of experiences for the same gang of vile shithouse skins though!!!....

The result? Well Liverpool and in particular David James were unbelievably crap and we lost 3-0.

Although we won the return game 2-0, it just wasn't enough to go through to the Final in Rotterdam against Barcelona.
KEV MORLAND

1997/98 UEFA CUP

16 September 1997 First round
Celtic FC   2-2   Liverpool FC

30 September 1997 First round
Liverpool FC   0-0   Celtic FC
Aggregate: 2-2
Liverpool win on away goals

21 October 1997 Second round
RC Strasbourg   3-0   Liverpool FC

4 November 1997 Second round
Liverpool FC   2-0   RC Strasbourg
Aggregate: 2-3

UEFA CUP 1ST ROUND, 1ST LEG.
16TH SEPTEMBER 1997
CELTIC PARK [48526]. GLASGOW. SCOTLAND.
CELTIC 2 LIVERPOOL 2

As soon as the draw was made you knew you just had to be there. It wouldn't be easy getting tickets, but it didn't get much bigger than this, Liverpool versus Celtic at Parkhead in the first round first leg of the UEFA Cup. It was a tie that really captured the imagination.

Not just for us Reds either, the game was straight away tagged, typically, the 'Battle of Britain' and I remember the interest in the match around the country was such that it was to be shown live on a special Match of the Day special, which back in them days was unusual.

Of course for us Liverpudlians it would be the first time we'd played Celtic since they had been our first opponents after the Hillsborough disaster. It was game of huge significance, we had a bond with Celtic, we shared an anthem, now we would play them in a competitive match for the first time since 1966.

Like us, Celtic were not enjoying the best of times domestically and had been clearly cast in the shadow of the 'nine-in-a-row' Rangers side. Leading up to the game Liverpool were clear favourites but I don't think any of us thought it was going to be easy, especially in the away leg up there.

The same went for the task of getting tickets for the game. Everyone it seemed was going to be in Glasgow for this one and, tickets or not, three of us decided we weren't going to miss it.

The game was on a Wednesday which meant a day off work to travel, but I'd just started a new job so I had to throw a sickie to go. Not normally behaviour I'd condone, but when Liverpool is your life and they've got a big game, nothing gets in your way.

We travelled up on a coach organised by Liverpool's Development Association, the reason being that it came with a guaranteed match ticket. The only downside to this, of course, was that it was deemed an 'official' trip. This has never been viewed as the coolest method of getting to a Euro away but at least it saved the hassle of trying to find tickets up there. It also meant that the bus would be 'dry', or at least that was the idea.

The coach went from outside the Arkles on Anfield Road and I still remember it being pretty cold and grey as we stood outside there, waiting for it to arrive. It was an early morning dart so the Arkles was closed and we stood cluching our bags of sarnies and sausage rolls. Unbeknown to the jobsworth stewards though these were heavy sausage rolls disguised as contraband, cans of lager. Hardly the crime of the century, but he who dared definitely won.

The drive North was fairly uneventful, the calm before the storm you could say. We did manage to bag the back seat for this trip and happily drank our cans without challenge in the end. Only downside to that being we drank them too quick and had ran out by the time we reached Carlisle. Such bad planning that would usually see you heavily criticised. Fortunately Glasgow isn't one of Scotland's far outposts and we were soon there. The singing always increases when you drive into opposition territory and this trip was no different, we were here, but this was different, better, special. We might have gone on a coach and it might have taken less than three hours, but this was a European away day, we were playing Celtic, at a ground you always wanted to go to, and history was being made.

We were dropped off at a pub called the Horseshoe Bar in the centre of Glasgow. The Horseshoe is one of Glasgow's most famous pubs, because of the rivalries in the city they didn't normally allow football shirts being worn, or football songs being sung, but today the Horseshoe was a Liverpool pub.

The atmosphere built throughout the afternoon, the drinking gathered pace, and so too did the eagerness for the game. The songs always become more intense and pointed as Kick Off approaches and it was no different on this day. The Glaswegians were perfect hosts, forget arguments that Scottish football is no good, this city knows big football matches, they happen every week and the way we were welcomed by the Horseshoe's regulars ensured a good humoured and warm atmosphere as the afternoon wore on. Through the haze we almost forgot there was a match to go to. It's a regular occurrence when you're following Liverpool on the road. The coach was to pick us back up and take us to the ground. When that time came it felt, as always, like the match was interrupting a good bevy but we were all looking forward to getting to the ground and the afternoon sesh in The Horseshoe had served only to increase the atmosphere of both the volume of our singing and eagerness to get in there.

The atmosphere inside Celtic Park didn't disappoint. It was phenomenal, it doesn't disappoint. The crowd was nearly 50,000 capacity, but the noise was of twice that many. Make no mistake, Celtic were relishing this as much as us and they were making themselves heard. To be honest this is what you came to see, the Liverpool fans contributed in their usual magnificent way, but the tone and intensity of the home crowd was just as revered. The singing of You'll Never Walk Alone before kick off was everything you'd hoped it would be, both sets of fans in unison singing the same song, but definitely trying to outdo each other. The result was breathtaking and the stage was set. What an occasion.

We found ourselves 2-1 behind in the 74th minute when James brought down Larsson and Donnelly stepped up to convert the resultant spot kick. James was booked and a miserable journey home appeared alarmingly on the horizon. Thoughts turned to, could we get any ale for the coach home!

It wouldn't be the end of the world losing this game. It was only the first leg and we had an away goal, but to lose such a big game, to lose any game for Liverpool was hard to take.

Just when it seemed we would endure an arduous journey home up stepped Steve McManaman to score a 90th minute equaliser that would be go down as the defining memory of this match. Stevie was in our half when he picked the ball up, he sauntered past one man and then continued forward, it seemed in a flash of an eye and he was on the edge of their box, he then curled a brilliant shot past Gould and into net. We'd got out of jail and the away end reacted like they had.

There was time for another blast of You'll Never Walk Alone before the final whistle, only this time it was us Reds who were delivering the most passion. McManaman's goal proved decisive because the home leg was 0-0 and we went through on away goals. The journey home from Glasgow was joyous, we had no cans and we no longer had the back seat either, but a last minute goal feels like a win and so it proved because following a goalless draw in the second leg that was the goal that took us through.

LEE BROWN

1998/99 UEFA CUP

15 September 1998 First round
MFK Košice   0-3   Liverpool FC

29 September 1998 First round
Liverpool FC   5-0   MFK Košice
Aggregate: 8-0

20 October 1998 Second round
Liverpool FC   0-0   Valencia CF

3 November 1998 Second round
Valencia CF   2-2   Liverpool FC
Aggregate: 2-2
Liverpool win on away goals

24 November 1998 Third round
RC Celta de Vigo 3-1   Liverpool FC

8 December 1998 Third round
Liverpool FC   0-1   RC Celta de Vigo
Aggregate: 1-4

UEFA CUP 1ST ROUND, 1ST LEG.
15TH SEPTEMBER 1998
LOKOMOTIVA STADION [4500]. KOSICE. SLOVAKIA.
KOSICE 0 LIVERPOOL 3

Kosice away was always going to be a bit of a mission, and so it proved. Just before the advent of cheap flights, we were forced to fly from Manchester to Brussels to Zurich to Budapest and then on by train to this isolated Slovakian outpost. We were meeting Ally and Jimmy who'd gone direct from London to Hungary, but the thought of driving to Gatwick and all the arsing around that that entails was a no-no. So a day of flight hopping with the great bar room philosopher Danny Giles was the only way forward.

A night on the razz in the Hungarian capital and an early start to board one of the few trains that ventured over the border through Kosice was the aim. A welcome sight in the form of about thirty like minded die-hard fans greeted us at the station for the last leg of the journey. God knows how they got here but they did.

My abiding memory of the pre-match bevvy was buying a round of drinks for ten of us and it coming to the equivalent of £2.20. Not each pint, but for the lot. 22p a pint eh! We should come here more often.

The match itself was a non-event as the Redmen outclassed the Slovaks 3-0 without getting out of first gear. Incidentally the crowd was one of the smallest I've ever seen a full Liverpool team play in front of, in a competitive fixture. 4,500. Hardly the Nou Camp but sometimes these mad little matches are the best for throwing up something a little unexpected. When the final whistle blew, our night changed into one of the strangest post match bevvies for a while.

The ground seemed to empty in seconds and it was then that I thought of my cunning plan. There were hardly any stewards or police so I suggested that we should walk across the pitch, up into the Directors box and into that room with the light on. Halfway across, the floodlights went out and like a shining beacon, our secret room beckoned us.

It felt like we were appearing in our very own episode of Shaggy & Scooby-Doo. Slowly we negotiated our way in the dark, climbing over the seats, telling each other to stop giggling and act sensible. Then we reached the forbidden door. A tentative twist of the handle and BINGO, we're in. Just as I'd thought, it was their boardroom and the table was groaning under the weight of food and wine. Oh happy days. We were like four kids in a sweet shop, licking our lips in anticipation but also knowing that we had to be on our best behaviour or our cover would be blown.

With it being hospitality and free drinks, we were treated to the rare sight of Danny Giles actually going to the bar first. It's one of those once in a lifetime experiences when the boy Giles gets a round in. Up there with the solar eclipse and the type of wildlife spectacular that photographers wait decades to record. You can just imagine people at home watching Corrie or whatever and they cut to go live to Kosice where Danny has just approached the barmaid. Then it goes into slow-mo as he turns around, smiles and then winks into the camera. It would be replayed again and again for years.

Anyway back in the real world we look up to see Danny standing next to our Chairman David Moores. They both stare ahead avoiding eye contact and the conversation goes as follows:

David Moores: "How the fucking hell did you get past security?" (Yep! Our Chairman swore!)

Danny: "Listen boss. When the boys get thirsty there's no stopping us."

David Moores: "Yeah, but how did you get in?"

Danny: "A little body swerve here and a little dummy there and Bob's your uncle."

David Moores: "Look, just promise me you won't let the club down."

Danny: "Fuckin' 'el Mooresy lad, would we do that?"

David Moores: "Well I hope not, anyway enjoy yourselves and as I say, don't do anything daft. PLEASE."

Danny: "Rest assured boss, we're only having a couple of bevvies and a nose-bag and then we're off."

David Moores: "Ok. Take care and look after yourselves."

Now I know Mooresy's not the flavour of the month at the moment, but that night in Slovakia, he was sound. Which is more than could be said of his right hand man Rick, who could easily be the baddie in any Scooby-Doo scenario. He just took one look at us, rolled his eyes skywards and gently shook his head. Then proceeded to turn his back and refuse to speak. Manners Mr Parry, manners.

Anyway we quaffed the finest brandy, filled our bellies and then entered into one of the most bizarre conversations of this or any other season. With us being the only four people left in the room with any LFC connection, the Kosice directors came over. Dressed in undertakers coats and sporting Pete Best blow-waves, they thanked us for coming over and looked forward to seeing us again in Liverpool. Sussing out that they thought we were part of the official LFC delegation, we decided it was time for a little fun. Good old Mooresy would've been proud of us. As soon as his back was turned, we were up and running. In broken English, we'd sorted a five-a-side game out for them against the LFC directors at Melwood, big posh meals out in town all paid by us and a special visit to LFC's very own lap dancing club where mythical babes with liverbirds on their knickers gyrate for all our foreign guests. How we kept a straight face I don't know. We left with handshakes and back slaps and even had the cheek to accept a courtesy car back to the hotel.

The rest of the lads who were still in the hotel bar asked us where we'd been until now. I just said "You're not going to believe this but, have you ever seen the Lion, the Witch and the Wardrobe?. Well once upon a time there was this secret door in a far away land…"

JEGSY DODD

2000/01 UEFA CUP

14 September 2000 First round
FC Rapid Bucureşti   0-1   Liverpool FC

28 September 2000 First round
Liverpool FC   0-0   FC Rapid Bucureşti
Aggregate: 1-0

26 October 2000 Second round
Liverpool FC   1-0   FC Slovan Liberec

9 November 2000 Second round
FC Slovan Liberec   2-3   Liverpool FC
Aggregate: 2-4

23 November 2000 Third round
Olympiacos FC   2-2   Liverpool FC

7 December 2000 Third round
Liverpool FC   2-0   Olympiacos FC
Aggregate: 4-2

15 February 2001 Fourth Round
AS Roma   0-2   Liverpool FC

22 February 2001 Fourth Round
Liverpool FC   0-1   AS Roma
Aggregate: 2-1

8 March 2001 Quarter-finals
FC Porto   0-0   Liverpool FC

15 March 2001 Quarter-finals
Liverpool FC   2-0   FC Porto
Aggregate: 2-0

5 April 2001 Semi-finals
FC Barcelona   0-0   Liverpool FC

19 April 2001 Semi-finals
Liverpool FC   1-0   FC Barcelona
Aggregate: 1-0

16 May 2001 Final
Liverpool FC   5-4   Deportivo Alavés
Liverpool win via 'Golden Goal'

UEFA CUP 2ND ROUND, 2ND LEG.
9TH NOVEMBER 2000
UNISY STADIUM [6808]. LIBEREC. CZECH REPUBLIC.
SLOVAN LIBEREC 2 LIVERPOOL 3

What the hell was I doing in the bleak, remote Czech mining town of Liberec on a (very) dark night in November 2000? With a two year-old son and a six-week old daughter tucked up in bed, I should really have been at home, reading bedtime stories before scuttling downstairs to follow the Reds on the telly. But, at this seminal time of my life, there was a key factor at large which would facilitate a trip to Eastern Europe where previously I had been unable to travel, the two remaining days of my paternity leave!

All I needed was something imaginative and unique, that is, a superior form of bollocks to sneak this Machiavellian long-shot beyond the outstretched arm of my Mrs and inside the post. I had planned to ask my old mate, Dave Allan to be Godfather to our latest arrival, so where best to cement an important friendship and bestow this great honour on a loyal and trusted ally? I settled on Prague, the 'Paris of the East', would be fitting, conveniently located two hours drive from Liberec, the venue for a delicately-poised second-round UEFA Cup tie with the Reds leading 1-0 from the first leg, courtesy of a single Emile Heskey strike. The Czech plan was hatched with Dave over a few pints, fittingly, on the way home from Derby where our very own Czech, Patrik Berger's stunning goal had rounded off a 4-0 win.

Temporary memberships of the Liverpool FC International Supporters Club arranged, and Monarch flights with coach transfers booked with Towns Travel, we flew from Liverpool to Prague early on the morning of the game, dangerously early in fact, given the cheap and ample selection of fine European lagers on offer in the relatively unspoilt Czech capital. Prague is cold in November. A beautiful place, but very, very chilly, especially as a biting wind whips up off the banks of the Vltava River, which dissects the City. With smouldering Czech Koruna's threatening to burn out our pockets it wasn't long before the spectacular spires and delights of Wenceslas Square were forsaken for the marginally less cultural pastime of a day on the swallee.

Dave had recently developed a reputation as something of a gourmet, which in this case went no further than an insistence on eating an awful lot of goulash. I protested at length that he had opted for a Hungarian dish and retaliated with an order for what I vaguely recall to be veal. Suitably fed, the inevitable session with our Czech-mates, Budvar and co. took centre stage. After a few pints of the delicious local brew, conversation flowed and I tried (for the umpteenth time) to get to the bottom of Dave's fascination and support of his all-time Liverpool hero, Steve Staunton. Yeah, I know.

As the hours whizzed by, that familiar, bright idea synonymous with the mid-afternoon of a European away simultaneously entered our scheming heads, sacking the match off altogether.

In the midst of all this, Dave accepted the position of Godfather to my second child, marking the drunken moment with his 39th bifter of the day, no doubt hoping premature death spare him of any of the responsibility accompanying this proud honour. As usual, discretion got the better part of valour and we dutifully boarded a coach at 5pm, encountering fellow Liverpudlians for the first time of the day, for the journey from Central to Northern Bohemia. The sweet, toxic aromas wafting down the length of the coach suggested this select band of Reds were fully engaged with at least one aspect of Bohemian culture. Our immediate plan was moving the drinking goalposts 80 miles north of "Praha".

I don't think I've ever known anywhere as dark as Liberec. An absolutely pitch black sky, without so much as a lone star to cast down a single shaft of light. Floodlight pylons in the distance suggested we weren't far away from the ground, but with a whole hour and a half (this is the European away-equivalent of an entire afternoon) before kick-off there was plenty of time for more bevies. The drawback was that we could see nothing, certainly not anything resembling an alehouse. We set off, intrepidly climbing a steep hill in search of light or just anywhere remotely suggesting human existence and if we were lucky a last port of call before setting off for the match. We traipsed for what seemed like a couple of miles, our eyes adjusting only marginally to the deep gloom, without encountering anything. At one point, we wondered whether we'd actually died, punished for our sins with entry for eternity to this dark vacuum.

Then, I spotted a tiny glow in the distance. Our trudging steps accelerated into a trot, then something passing for a jog as we anticipated connecting back with the human race. As we drew near, a faint yellow burn from inside had us imagining an establishment that could well be a back-street Slovakian torture chamber or a 20 Krona-a-throw house of ill-repute.

However, we'd come too far to bottle it now. As we tentatively pulled open a heavy steel door and peered inside our anxious faces lit up on seeing tables groaning under the weight of ale. Furthermore, this bar was a microcosm of Czech working-class revelry. Ice Hockey on the box, those inimitable, stinking European ciggies puffed by one and all, and poker hands being dealt with alacrity. The men in here didn't appear to give a shit about Slovan Liberec versus Liverpool. Brilliant.

There didn't appear to be anyone serving. Protocol was that you filled your own jug of premium lager and made a small contribution by way of a few Krona lashed into an unmanned till, pre-dating the Stasi, near the bar. Ales in hand we were invited to sit with the locals, and offered them our Liverpool badges, which resulted in the immediate arrival of a second jug of lager. In fluent Czech (obviously) we tried politely to ask which communist stalwart was mounted on an impressive bust (no barmaids remember) at the bar. An attempt that was met with predictably blank faces. It definitely wasn't Stalin, he had too much hair for Lenin, so consensus settled fuzzily on an ageing Leon Trotsky. By this time, the game is about to kick off and we're still quaffing booze in a boss bar. Reluctantly, and fearful of being unable to recount at least a passing description of the actual football on getting home, we staggered off again, downhill this time in search of those old-style floodlights.

116

What we eventually encountered was akin to the approaches of a Third Division ground, think Carlisle, minus a canal down one side but with much better floodies and waiting for us, a line of bored Czech police rather insistent that two giggling, zigzagging latecomers didn't enter.

The great thing about the Czech's and their lager is that they make you feel utterly invincible, capable of bamboozling their constabulary initially with words which would normally resonate only on the streets of Walton. When this approach inevitably fails, you're still pissed enough to try an inelegant dart, risking life and limb, or at the very least a bite on the arse off a rabid Alsatian, to see a bit of the match.

A crowd of 6,808 saw Liverpool win 3-2 (4-2 on aggregate) thanks to goals from Nick Barmby, Emile Heskey and Michael Owen.

MIKE NEVIN

It's about 8.30 pm on a cold Wednesday night in Antwerp, when I take the train from Berchem to Diest, where my mate Stefan will pick me up in his car about an hour later. As I will probably have to do a bit of driving myself later on, I haven't brought any cans of lager with me, so I have to find some comfort in one of the Trotter Guides on Eastern Europe. I discover that there's a chapter on Rumania… now, that would have been handy for the trip to Bucharest a couple of months ago when we went the Rapid game – ahh, the memories come flooding back of three great days in Bucharest, the Tic Tac bar, women with legs as long as the Eiffel Tower, Rapid Bucuresti's so-called 'hooligans' etc. – but let's concentrate on the Czech Republic for now.

The country of Jan Palach, Skoda, Budvar, Staropramen and Pilsner Urquell, and Prague of course, the beautiful city I visited some years ago. All the memories come back to me, as they had done on that Friday afternoon in September when the draw of the second round in the UEFA Cup was made. I was in the office at the time, supposed to be working my socks off, and I was, but not for my boss. I spent the whole time on the Internet, jumping from the RAOTL forum ("the Rattle" as it's now called) to the BBC website, via UEFA and the news site of Belgian telly. And finally it was there: LIBEREC. The Czech Republic, 50p a pint, not really that far away from Belgium – we can drive there, excellent!

A minute later I was on the phone with our pal Minky and Cola as well, who had both made the trip to Bucharest with me, and with a couple of other lads who had earlier expressed an interest in going. By the end of the day we had about a minibus full of lads who would "definitely go".

So how come I'm sitting in the train on my own, knowing that there are only two of us left? The issue of tickets, of course! For some the original enthusiasm had been severely tempered by the knowledge that the Liberec ground had a capacity of less than 7,000 and that Liverpool FC would only get an allocation of 300 tickets, which were then "all taken up by Towns Travel". Nothing there for Reds travelling independently, but that wasn't stopping either Stefan or me. Our mind was made up from day one. This will be too much fun to let go. So there we are then, just the two of us, in Stefan's Rover. The fact that Stefan's passport was out of date wasn't stopping him. "I'll take our kid's passport, we look quite similar, and he's just become a dad so he's grounded", he said. Only to notice that his brother Marnik's passport was just as out of date as his own. Well, I guess we'll cross that bridge when we find it. We hit the motorway to Aachen and turn the radio on, so we can follow the games in the Champions' League. When I hear that both PSV and Leverkusen are out but get picked up in the UEFA Cup, I say "good, that'll do nicely in the next round" and move to the back to get some sleep. We're approaching Frankfurt, and then the German Autobahn will bring us to Wurzburg, Nuremberg and the Czech border.

I wake up when Stefan suddenly pulls up at a petrol station. "Don't know where we are mate, feel like I've been driving around in circles on this main road since we passed Nuremberg." Nuremberg? This means we're already mighty close to the Czech border and Stefan can start thinking about a way to cross it.

There are a few options, but we stay undecided about which one is the best. Simply hand over his invalid (outdated) passport and ask for a two day visa, pretending we don't know that's impossible. Show his Belgian identity card and pretend he didn't know you need a passport. Wave a bunch of Deutschmarks, hide in the back of the car? Suddenly the traffic in front of us comes to a standstill. Are we at the border? We soon notice that the lorries in front of us are not moving one bit, so we switch off the engine and decide to get out of the car to take a proper look. All we see is a long long line of lorries and the headlights of another one shining in our direction, but nothing's moving. Well, one thing's moving and that's a line of ambulances and vehicles of the local fire brigade, all driving in the direction of the border. This could and probably will take ages, we realise. We have a look at the map and have a word with the Czech driver of a Eurolines coach. Stefan thinks about giving the lad some Deutschmarks to smuggle him on the bus, but then we notice there's another passage, some forty miles down South. It'll take us about an hour to get there, but anything's better than just queuing here for hours.

It's about 6.30 am when we reach the other border town and we change drivers. I take over from Stefan who disappears in the back of the car, lying under my sleeping bag, with only his head peeping out. First we get to the German border house. I hand my passport to the Customs man who doesn't seem to notice there's someone lying in the back, then walks into his office, checks my passport and gives it back. The Czech house is only a hundred yards further and I hold my breath when I open the window and show my passport to the Czech Customs man who is casually leaning against his office wall about ten yards from the road. A simple nod of the head means I can drive through and I try not to look too excited and accelerate too fast. "Stefan, lad, we're there mate, in the Czech Republic." My travelling companion is happy as the proverbial pig in his excrements and starts yelling "Every other Saturday is my half day off…" I can feel the buzz myself and start looking for my Wipers tape, it's time I hear some decent music instead of the Bavarian Beerfest crap.

118

We've got the road for ourselves and as the sun comes up we notice how beautiful the Czech countryside is. Maybe I should have watched the road instead because all of a sudden it takes a sharp turn to the left and I realise I'm going too fast. Much too fast for the car's liking and there's a creeping noise of the tyres, and the car starts spinning. Somehow I manage to keep it on the road, and just as I've stopped there's another car coming the other direction. That was close, but we've been lucky again. Stefan must have been reading my mind: "Third time lucky will mean we'll get hold of a ticket, mate. And yeah I know, the tyres need changing."

Without any more hic-ups we reach Prague at about 9am and we head straight to Na Porici, where we see the AXA hotel on our left – we know that quite a few fellow Reds are staying here and at 2pm we'll get on the coach to Liberec with them. We find an underground car park, where Stefan dozes off for an hour or so – since the spin the poor fella didn't dare go to sleep anymore – while I hit the town. It's nearly 10 am, chilly but the sun shines brightly and I'm ready for some fun and games. I'll leave a message for JJP and Johnnie Mac at the hotel lobby, guessing that they will still be in bed, and make my way out again, soon enough finding a little bar in a side street of Na Porici. There I have my first draught lager of the trip. Can't remember whether it was Staropramen, Budvar or Pilsner Urquell but it surely tasted nice. Time to get back to Stefan and wake him up. We spend a couple of hours strolling around the city centre, having the occasional bevy here and there, and end up in that same little bar again, but this time we're not on our own. We're in the company of some of the finest and most loyal Reds you'll ever find, the nicest bunch of chaps you can meet… a band of supporters that would later adopt the name "Irregulars". At that time in Prague, some of them were still called the Herestrau Scousers but that's another story…

It's 2pm now and we're standing outside the AXA hotel, ready to board the coach. We meet up with APB, who's fixing his specially made flag with super glue, and – finally – Johnnie Mac who's carrying a big carrier bag full of bottles. Talk is about two things: you have to buy ale before you board the coach and then of course there's the ticket situation. Rumours are rife: "We met the English consul last night and he told us they don't want 500 ticketless fans hanging round the ground. The part in the ground where the official Liverpool contingent is seated, has a capacity of 1,000, so we'll get a place there." Or: "They are asking up to £100 for a ticket on the black market." "A mate of mine bought two for £25 yesterday." Etc. etc. etc.

It's about 4.30pm when we reach Liberec – on the coach the atmos was good from the start and got increasingly more boisterous as more and more cans and bottles were supped, surprise surprise – and it's already dark. We see the police are out in numbers. There have been plenty of rumours about Liberec skinheads who supposedly want to kick our arses and it looks like the coppers don't want to take any risks. We follow Peter, a Sparta Prague and Liverpool fan who's joined us on the coach, to the main square in the hope of getting our hands on a match ticket. Handy if a Czech lad can do the talking for you. But at that time of the day the price is still about a 100 quid, so we decide to do the decent thing and go for a bevy. We walk into a nice bar, which is completely empty, apart from the lovely barmaid, who serves us 5 pints of the Czech Republic's finest and sells us all the croissants that are left. All three of them. The flags come out, some pics are taken and we sup some more beer. Enter Nige. With a smile on his face he tells us he's got two spares, bought for £25 each the other night. It's more than 8 times the original price, but we weren't really expecting to get in for free, so the money is handed over and a round of whisky is paid by Stefan.

Time to move to another bar, where we have a friendly conversation in broken English with some Polish Liverpool fans (from Lodz – but the fact they once knocked us out of Europe is not mentioned). Apart from them and us it's only Czech people in the bar, mainly middle aged men who've just come back from the day job: painters, carpenters, … a proper workingman's bar so to speak. So it's no real surprise that after about an hour or so I leave this place minus one scarf but wearing the nicest of nice donkey jackets (green with a big yellow patch on the shoulders). I feel posh now. Not as posh as Johnnie Mac with his Chef's jacket in Bucharest but still… Time to go to the match. We have tickets for "Sektor E", which is on the left of the Main Stand. The 300 so-called official Liverpool fans are seated to our left, but on the far side, with a line of policemen separating them from the Liberec fans. There's a huge Liverpool flag on the far side on our right, and we hear Scouse voices in the immediate vicinity as well. We're everywhere. I'm sat between Stefan and an old Liberec fan, who looks surprised when I pat him on the back and wish him a good game.

The Liberec fans make quite a lot of noise, and the volume surely goes up when their team scores the first goal, cancelling out Emile Heskey's late effort in the first leg. Shit! That wasn't exactly planned. Then the Reds seem to find a little bit of form, get some passes together every now and again, and Slovan aren't much of a threat anymore. In fact, when Barmby scores the equaliser with a nice header – Liverpool cheers all around the ground – the game's over. The second half sees goals from Emile Heskey and Michael Owen, who scores about twenty seconds after he has come on. A second Slovan Liberec goal – a well-taken shot from outside the box – is too little too late for the home side, but they deserve their round of applause when they do their lap of honour after the match.

While the 'official' Liverpool supporters are told to stay in the ground for about half an hour after the match, remember the Liberec skinheads we mentioned earlier, we can simply walk out with the home fans and make our way to where the coaches are parked. As I'm standing there, I get a tap on my shoulder and I hear a Scouse voice saying: "Hard luck, mate. Your team did well. More luck next year." When I turn round I see a familiar face from The Albert who simply hadn't noticed it was me. Some disguise this donkey jacket… In the mean time, Stefan is being interviewed by a Czech television crew who ask him about the police presence. The atmos has changed a bit and the coppers look pretty nasty now. Then we hear some noise coming from near the ground. Liverpool fans? No, the infamous Liberec skinheads arrive on the scene. All 15 (fifteen!) of them. Escorted by at least fifty policemen, shouting "Fuck Liverpool" and bringing nazi salutes. The skinheads, that is. While I stand there looking at them, not knowing whether to laugh or cry, a Czech pensioner taps me on the chest and points at my Justice pin. He shows a truly nice Liberec pin. The swap is made. The lad I swapped the donkey jacket with (for my scarf – yes, there was some swapping going on in those days) sees me, shakes hands about a dozen times and keeps rambling on in Czech. It's all very funny and it sums up the spirit of the evening, in fact the whole day, much better than the moronic minority of skins and aggressive looking coppers. I wonder which kind of pictures will be shown on telly…

By now, every Liverpool fan has left the ground, including Johnnie Mac who spent the second half drinking in the director's bar, so he tells us about a dozen times before boarding the coach. We get a couple more lukewarm cans of lager – the service station where we buy them was crowded by Liverpool fans – and find a few more people on the coach than on the way up. No problem, there's some place left on the stairs next to the bogs, where I sip my can of Pilsner before falling asleep. After – as far as I'm concerned – a smooth ride to Prague, we make it to Ché's Bar and next door's pizzeria where we combine red wine, Jameson's and some more lager. It's 3.30 when we head for our beds. Johnnie Mac, APB and Wrighty have been so kind as to invite Stefan and me into their room to get some kip. We are so grateful for our place on the floor that we spend the rest of the night trying to rob their blankets. Or so they say…

NICO VAN DYCK

UEFA CUP FINAL.
16TH MAY 2001
WESTFALEN STADION [48050]. DORTMUND. GERMANY.
DEPORTIVO ALAVES 4 LIVERPOOL 5

Having attended both legs of the home and away UEFA Cup finals of both 1973 and 1976, I was especially keen to be present when the club I supported attempted to win the trophy for a third time in the fourth season since the old format had been replaced by a single match final. Liverpool's presence in the final also marked the club's return to a major European final sixteen years after the horror of Heysel. Almost a new generation of supporters had grown up since 1985. I knew that we would take huge numbers to Germany, especially against a club with a much smaller fan-base, but even I was not prepared for just how many Liverpool supporters turned up in Dortmund.

The day started quietly enough with an early breakfast with a friend at London Heathrow before we boarded a Lufthansa flight to Düsseldorf. The choice of airline chosen by the tour-operator we were travelling with would come back to bite us the next day. Lufthansa pilots had been holding a series of 24-hour strikes over pay demands and although the dispute would be settled in June the next day when they were due to go on strike was the day after the final. But this wasn't a major concern as we boarded the coaches that would take us from Düsseldorf airport to the Ruhr town of Essen, a city located about twenty-five miles west of Dortmund. It was during this short journey that we were handed our precious match-tickets. There might have been growing doubts about how we were going to get home but at least we knew for sure that we would not miss the match.

We decided to make our own way by train to Dortmund in the afternoon instead of waiting for the coaches that the tour-operator had laid on. The weather was absolutely dreadful but it had not diminished the enthusiasm of the thousands of Liverpool supporters who had gathered in one of Dortmund's main squares. We had met my friend's daughter by this time (she had flown in from Liverpool where she was studying) and after we had found somewhere to eat and made our way to the stadium the rain had still not relented and I remember my friend turning to me and saying quite seriously "I think this will be called off". I didn't share his pessimism but I knew it would be a logistical nightmare for the supporters of both clubs if the match was postponed. Outside the stadium … and even though it had been so long since our previous European final … I bumped into people I had known in the days when we used to reach European finals on a regular basis. It looked as if there was some sort of office open for purchasing the few remaining tickets and collecting booked tickets but it was chaos outside that office with hundreds queuing up in a last desperate attempt to secure a ticket.

The rain had eased off and we took our seats in the upper tier of the west stand almost as soon as the gates were opened. Although the capacity was bigger, the stadium didn't look much different from when I had watched Liverpool play a pre-season friendly there in 1975. I looked around as the crowd built up. Our designated end was the enormous south stand but, apart from half of the north stand where the Spanish supporters were, it looked as if we had strong support all over the stadium, a feeling later borne out by noticing the reaction from different parts of the ground as our goals went in.

It was a crazy game, that's for sure. I had been supremely even arrogantly over-confident that we would swipe aside a team that did not have our pedigree. For forty-five minutes I had nothing to worry about. But Javi Moreno's quick double early in the second half made me and everyone around me realise that this was no formality. Even when Robbie Fowler restored our lead, I still had a nagging fear that this was not all over yet … and so it proved. As extra-time began, I was convinced from listening to the comments of people around me that few of them knew that a Golden Goal would apply for this final. That both teams had goals correctly disallowed in extra-time only added to the tension. With the extra thirty minutes nearly over, it looked as if penalties would decide this cup. What happened next will remain etched in my mind for the rest of my life. Away to my left a second Alaves player is dismissed for cynically pulling back Vladimír Šmicer. Gary McAllister floats the free-kick into the danger-area, the ball is diverted by someone and next thing it is in their net and there is an explosion of joy the like of which I have rarely experienced before watching Liverpool as players and supporters realise that the cup treble has been achieved.

Immediate talk centres on the scorer of the winning goal. I suspect an own-goal and although confirmed later it wasn't immediately clear at the time because so many players were in the Alaves penalty-area. The celebrations inside the stadium are long and memorable, especially when all the club's playing and coaching staff line up with the trophy to sing "You'll Never Walk Alone" for one final time before returning to the dressing-room with their prize.

We found our coach in the huge car-park near the stadium and returned slowly by road to Essen. A re-run of the match was showing in our hotel bar but I was drained physically and emotionally and went straight to bed.

We got to the airport as early as we could on the Thursday morning having been told that staff there would re-arrange our Lufthansa flights back to England. However, hundreds had got there before us. My friend's daughter managed to get back to Liverpool on the Thursday but Peter and I decided not to accept the option of seemingly being forced to travel halfway around Europe before we could get back to Heathrow. So we re-booked our flights to leave Düsseldorf on the Friday morning, booked a room at the main airport hotel for a horrendous price of around two hundred quid and went out for a meal in the centre of the city where we could re-assess the final in a rather more composed manner than we had done twenty-four hours earlier.

A week later I went to Anfield to inspect the three trophies in the club's museum. I noticed Phil Thompson, who had been so important in this success, standing talking to a supporter in the area outside the museum-entrance. The museum was almost empty. For all the times I have been there, I have never known it be so quiet. I even had to find someone to take my picture with the UEFA cup. But it was still a special moment seeing that big cup inside. The club had achieved a special place in European club history by winning it for the third time and I had the personal satisfaction of knowing that I had been present at all three finals even though twenty-eight years separated the first from the third.

CHRIS WOOD

2001/02 CHAMPIONS LEAGUE

8 August 2001 Third Qualifying round
FC Haka 0-5   Liverpool FC

21 August 2001 Third Qualifying round
Liverpool FC   4-1   FC Haka
Aggregate 9-1

11 September 2001 Group stage (Group B)
Liverpool FC   1-1   Boavista FC

19 September 2001 Group stage (Group B)
Borussia Dortmund   0-0   Liverpool FC

26 September 2001 Group stage (Group B)
Liverpool FC   1-1   Dynamo Kyiv

16 October 2001 Group stage (Group B)
Dynamo Kyiv   1-2   Liverpool FC

24 October 2001 Group stage (Group B)
Boavista   1-1   Liverpool FC

30 October 2001 Group stage (Group B)
Liverpool FC   2-0   Borussia Dortmund

20 November 2001 Second group stage (Group B)
Liverpool FC   1-3   FC Barcelona

5 December 2001 Second group stage (Group B)
AS Roma   0-0   Liverpool FC

20 February 2002 Second group stage (Group B)
Liverpool FC   0-0   Galatasaray AŞ

26 February 2002 Second group stage (Group B)
Galatasaray AŞ   1-1   Liverpool FC

13 March 2002 Second group stage (Group B)
FC Barcelona   0-0   Liverpool FC

19 March 2002 Second group stage (Group B)
Liverpool FC   2-0   AS Roma

3 April 2002 Quarter-finals
Liverpool FC   1-0   Bayer 04 Leverkusen

9 April 2002 Quarter-finals
Bayer 04 Leverkusen   4-2   Liverpool FC
Aggregate: 4-3

CHAMPIONS LEAGUE QUARTER-FINAL 2ND LEG
9TH APRIL 2002
BAY ARENA [22500]. LEVERKUSEN. GERMANY
BAYER 04 LEVERKUSEN 4 LIVERPOOL 2

The game was a classic and turned out to be Leverkusen's 'St. Etienne' with them scoring the winner with just seven minutes to go, therefore securing a 4-3 aggregate win. Ten minutes before kick-off though and things are looking bleak. Obviously there are a few forgeries knocking about and some lads are being man handled by police as they are sussed trying to get through the outer perimeter ticket entrance.

I haven't got a ticket and the blag ticket I've been passed by an old printer mate from years back has got the reverse printed upside down. Nice one Kev … and you call yourself a printer. He had duplicated a few in a photo-copiers in Cologne a few hours earlier. Desperate times call for desperate measures. So the saying goes.

Five minutes to go before Kick-Off and there's no other option. I need to try the forgery. Around the corner from the main hullaballoo that's going on, as kick-off approaches, I find another entrance for Liverpool supporters. It's quite deserted.

I show the ticket quickly in the hope that no one notices any discrepancy and I'm through. I hastily make my way to the final entrance to the stadium but before I'm just ten yards from it I feel a tap on the shoulder. 'Can I see that ticket again, mein Freunde?' The German guy then susses the upside down printed reverse and tells me to take the ticket back to the tout I said I'd bought it off and get my money back.

'Yeah right!!' My pleas and crying have no effect on the inconsiderate bast@$d. Then the oddest thing happens. It was at this point that someone must have been definitely looking down on me. A Scouser legged it past, obviously having bunked in. 'Wait there, ein minuten' says my escort before racing off in hot pursuit. Is he serious?

With not a moment to waste I proceed to make my way to the main entrance. I can see that there are four or five ticket inspectors. One of the guys looks about 70 years old though, hopefully he's a little short-sighted. 'You'll do' I thought to myself.

I pass my ticket to him, front facing, in the hope that he doesn't look at the reverse and then, to my disbelief, he checks the back, but he's turned the ticket in a way that he's looking at the reverse and it reads the correct way up. A corner is torn and I'm invited to proceed into the ground. Amazing. Come on you Reds…

Now to get in touch with the Mrs who I'd taken as an excuse for an anniversary present. She had left me half an hour earlier to go back to the hotel to get changed so we could go out together to watch the game in a local bar. She had thought my chances of getting in were zero.

This being 2002 mobile phones were still in their infancy but we had seen these walkie-talkies being used by the locals in Florida whilst on holiday and had a set with us just in case we got separated. People go into hysterics when I mention using the two-way radio from the ground to give her the good/bad news depending how she wanted to take it. This may have looked bizarre at the time but just look around now and everyone's got a phone stuck to their ear. It was basically the same thing. Honest. Great anniversary present the Mrs told me later that night. Over and Out.

DAVE HEWITSON

2002/03 CHAMPIONS LEAGUE

17 September 2002 Group stage (Group B)
Valencia CF   2-0   Liverpool FC

25 September 2002 Group stage (Group B)
Liverpool FC   1-1   FC Basel

2 October 2002 Group stage (Group B)
Liverpool FC   5-0   Spartak Moscow

22 October 2002 Group stage (Group B)
Spartak Moscow   1-3   Liverpool FC

30 October 2002 Group stage (Group B)
Liverpool FC   0-1   Valencia CF

12 November 2002 Group stage (Group B)
FC Basel 3-3   Liverpool FC

CHAMPIONS LEAGUE GROUP STAGE
22nd OCTOBER 2002
CENTRAL DYNAMO STADIUM [15000]
MOSCOW. RUSSIA
SPARTAK MOSCOW 1 LIVERPOOL 3

Moscow was cold, very, very cold. This was blindingly obvious five seconds after we stepped out of the concrete monstrosity that was the Hotel Rossiya. It was the kind of scrotum-tightening cold that would make Ranulph Fiennes turn back muttering 'Sod that'. We, however, were made of sterner stuff and had base cravings to satisfy. It had been a long journey and we weren't going to find any semblance of fun in the decrepit time-warp of our hotel that was for sure. The two thousand room Rossiya was the kind of structure that the term 'Brutalist' was invented for. It was also the type of building that the word 'shithole' was invented for. It certainly didn't warrant the title of 'hotel'. It was a crushingly functional, pseudo-modern monolith that was all the rage with totalitarian regimes in the 1950s in Communist states. And Middlesbrough.

Crossing Red Square, our noses and toes began to tingle then quickly started to feel numb. I looked at Wrighty, he'd come to Russia without a coat, hoping the vodka would keep the blood from freezing solid in his veins. He had hair back then, which at least afforded him some insulation. That said, he was soon turning blue. It seemed like a good idea to get him inside a pub as soon as possible lest he be found the following morning, frozen solid, with his mouth open and a can of lager in his hand, like Han Solo at the end of 'The Empire Strikes Back'.

As we hurried past Lenin's tomb the Urchins were posing with their banner, annoying some increasingly irritated soldiers standing guard over the hero of their motherland. A Siberian chill arrived direct from the Urals and it began to snow. We stopped and looked up as what looked like an army of moths invaded from the leaden skies. The Kremlin looked magnificently picturesque as the light faded, in stark contrast to the looming Rossiya behind us, that somehow managed to look even more depressing.

I haggled with a street hawker on the edge of the square and bought a furry Soviet tank driver's hat for $5. I could have haggled but it was too cold to talk. Words would half form on your lips before freezing solid and dropping like a stone to the ground. I jammed the hat onto my head and, not for the first time that night, I wrapped the furry flaps around my ears. It was bliss.

My head was the only warm part of me over the next two days. I even wore it in bed. I say "in bed" but it was more like 'on the bed'. The Rossiya's rooms looked like they'd been home to a convention of chain-smoking bears for the previous 40 years. Everything was sagging and dilapidated; the walls and ceiling stained a sick nicotine yellow. The rest of the room was brown carpets, curtains and bed-spread. And the towels. And the toilet paper. All six sheets of it. And this was a tourist hotel, I thought. This is the 'Russia' they let outsiders actually see. I bet Solzhenitsyn had it better than this in the Gulag. The bed creaked loudly as I sat on it and as I ran my hand over the stiff blankets I thought to myself, "There's no way I'm getting in that". However, after an evening's entertainment drinking Russian beer at 50p a pint in what seemed like a Wild West saloon full of Agent Provocateur models, a surreal meeting of 50 or so loud fellas and a similar number of the best-looking young women in Russia in their underwear, I fell onto the bed smiling at 6am. I slept fully clothed on top, hat on and with my feet a good 18 inches higher than my head, as if lying in an Arctic hammock. I decided in the morning that perhaps I'd been a little hard on Comrade Solzhenitsyn. But then I hadn't used the toilet paper yet.

Matchday. The snow had stopped and as we left reception, Stevie Wright came back in, in his shorts, rubbing his hands together, declaring it was "Freezing me nuts off out there". We spent the afternoon before the game in the incongruous setting of an Alpine-style wooden ski-lodge that had been plonked down in a tarmac car-park right outside the stadium. It was a bar. Mark Briggs and I continued socialising all afternoon, through a power cut, and way past kick-off time. We eventually decided to get in to the ground as half-time approached.

"After all", said Briggsy "there's no point in travelling 3000 miles and not see the inside of the stadium, is there?" It was, it soon transpired, a wildly prophetic proclamation. As we closed the door behind us, zipping up our coats and laughing, I noticed a small group of soldiers turn to look at us. One of them, older than the others, broke away from their conversation and approached us. He stood between us and the stadium, the floodlights shining behind his head, and held out his hand. "Passport" he barked. The word hung in front of his face in a cloud of breath. He looked like he meant business. We handed them over. He never even bothered looking at them, just put them into the pocket of his overcoat and smiled. We stood there for a few minutes in silence, the roar of the crowd and the floodlight glare a reminder of where we should have been. Eventually I asked him, "Can I have my passport? Please."

He held his hand out.

I shrugged, playing daft. It wasn't hard.

"Dollars!" he demanded.

I was buggered if I was giving him anything, especially as we'd been fleeced by a cab driver earlier in the day. I just held my hand out for my passport.

"I haven't got any money" I told him. "We go straight to the airport after the match." He didn't respond. I didn't say anything more. It was a trademark Iron Curtain stalemate, a Cold War stand-off of Bay of Pigs proportions.

"He can't do that" spluttered Mark. Well he is Mark, and we're kind off buggered here so keep quiet, I thought. Mark seemed to calm down but after I'd been refused the passports a second time, he looked directly at the soldier and shouted, "You can't do that! You can't do that!".

"Shurrup Mark", I hissed. Then, smiling again as Mark calmed down, I added "Can we have our passports please."

He stretched his hand out further, grinning.

"I'm flying home tonight. No dollars."

I kept my hand outstretched. Mark meanwhile was rapidly losing all patience and sense, and was muttering, getting very agitated. I tried to calm him down by telling him this wasn't the time nor the place to be arguing with this bastard.

By this time we'd drawn the attention of the younger group of soldiers. They'd been looking on and maybe realised that foreign currency wasn't going to come easily from us. Perhaps the younger generation weren't as hostile to visitors, perhaps this act of wanton extortion was too much even for them. One of them walked over reached into his colleague's coat, retrieving our passports. No words were passed. He shoved them at us and nodded as if to say "Get out of here". We didn't need telling, in fact I was already hurrying away. I turned on my heels, not daring to look back.

"Fuckin' Hell." I whispered. "That was scary".

"That was ... that was ... They can't do that!" said Mark. He's was visibly upset. He looked over his shoulder and shouted back, "You bastards!".

"For God's sake Mark, shut it. You'll get us nicked". I quickened my pace towards the stadium entrance.

"Bastards! You bent bastards!", Mark continued his rant.

"Jesus! Mark, just shut it."

He spun round, and walking backwards on his heels, loudly continued his protest. I put my head down, he's on his own here, I thought, and sure enough and from out of nowhere two uniformed figures appeared and grab Mark. He's marched off briskly and shoved into the back of an army van and driven off.

Shit! It was his round.

I got into the stadium without showing a ticket to anyone and found myself in the home supporters section in the open main stand. With my Red Square, tourist-tat hat they quickly sussed me out as English. To my great relief they turn out to be incredibly friendly and a bottle of vodka is passed round. The scoreboard shows the score as 1-1, but the Muscovites seem uninterested in the match and we talk about anything and everything except football. There's a muffled roar and we all turn and look at the pitch, Michael Owen has scored, it was now 2-1 to the Reds, but they're weren't arsed and carried on joking and generally ignoring the football. Then about five minutes from the end one of them put his hand on my shoulder and said, "The police – they are bastards".

"Oh, I don't know," I said. "Sting maybe. All that tantric nonsense."

"No, you must go now, we are losing and Moscow police are bastards". He gestured off to the far corner of the ground where 700 Liverpool fans stood shivering behind high fencing draped in familiar flags. Ah! Time to leave! He told me to go down the steps at the rear of our stand and get onto the pitch and from there into our section, safe from the local police. As I made my way towards the exit, Liverpool scored again. I hurried down the steps and found myself in the players tunnel. To my left the darkness opened out onto the frosty grass glittering in the floodlights. I walked invisibly to the pitch edge just as the players were leaving. I nodded at a couple of ours, Carragher and Hamann, and say "Alright lads". Then a security guard spotted me and approached. I showed him my passport, keeping a tight grip on it and pointed towards the knot of Liverpool fans on the far side of the ground. He understood, nodded and gestured for me to lead the way across the pitch, flanked by two armed soldiers, and into the safety of the away fans enclosure.

Back at the airport in the early hours we are getting incredibly concerned about Briggsy, but not that concerned that it prevented us from manically trying to spend our remaining Roubles on beer from a tiny window in the departure lounge. The stewards from our travel company know nothing about Mark's whereabouts and we can't find out anything from the airport police. About an hour before we're due to depart, however and just minutes before one of us has to volunteer to phone his mum and report him 'missing', Mark appears in the lounge asking if anyone has his bag. Yes we do. It seems the soldiers kept him in the van for an hour or two then decided to dump him at the airport. The wrong airport. It's taken a panicky half hour dash around Moscow in a taxi to get to the right airport. He sits down laughing and then spots the cans of beer we have.

"Did you get me any?"

JOHN MACKIN

This was a trip that everybody fancied. All our crew were going except Bobby Wilcox who had to go into hospital for his annual checkup and Assy who was probably being a minge bag as usual. For once we were on an official trip and we got to Moscow at about mid-afternoon. After what seemed like ages going through customs, we got our coach to the Hotel Rossiya, the biggest hotel in Europe, which had all the facilities and charm of the Lubyana prison, which was just across the way.

Having finally found our rooms we met up in the hotel bar. The view was incredible, right outside was Red Square, The Kremlin, Lenin's tomb and St Basil's Cathedral. DNA Dave purchased some local ciggies that lit up like fireworks and was instantly renamed 'Chemo Dave'!

We ambled out to experience the Russian nightlife. It was mid-October and the temperature was well below freezing, so we were all soon buying these Russian fur hats. I bet the locals thought that we looked a proper bunch of wools. After a wander around we got the word that everyone was heading to this music bar. It was a good trip away from town so we got taxis up there.

It was a weird place, possibly the world's only Irish/Beatles Bar. The manager was made up and insisted that we sing along to the Beatles for him but the only album that he had was the White album probably the least sing-along-able LP that the Fab Four had made.

After Stevie Crocky had showed him how to pour Guinness properly we left our new friend and headed into town. This is where troubles set in, once our taxi pulled over we had militia men demanding we give them $10 or we'd be arrested, given that we had no choice we weighed them in and went off looking for some safer nightlife.

The club that we ended up in was not much safer to be honest. True the woman were absolutely stunning, most Russian women are, but they were all on the game and supported by Chechnyan gangsters, so we had a couple of shots of vodka (poured out of a bottle kept in a freezer!) and went back to the relative safety of the hotel bar.

The next day was relatively low key, we went for a mooch around by the hotel, had a few pints and then checked out of the hotel and got the coach up to the ground. We won 3-1 but what I principally remember is that it was absolutely freezing, and it wasn't until we got back on the plane home that I had any feeling in my toes.

MARTY PARRY

CHAMPIONS LEAGUE GROUP STAGE
12TH NOVEMBER 2002
ST JAKOB PARK [35000]
BASLE. SWITZERLAND
BASLE 3 LIVERPOOL 3

You often get a European fixture that feels as though all you've done is travel for the whole journey. Whether its plane hopping and being in Airports for hours on end or lengthy coach trips, they seem never ending. Foreign lager always seems to help during these distressing times.

This trip was pretty straight forward but more or less took a day to get there and a day to get back.

We left via car to London's Swiss Cottage where we abandoned the car before jumping the Underground to St Pancras. From there it was the Eurotunnel through to Paris then another train journey from Paris down to Basle for a group game in 2002.

A few crates of Kronenbourg and a few baguettes were secured in Paris for the five hour trip. The effects of the potent brew were to take their toll on our arl mate Ian during the course of that evening. We arrived in Basle a couple of hours before kick off, our hotel was close to the station so we were able to dispose of our bags before grabbing a quick pint before the match. The trip down had been a five hour journey, surprisingly the lager lasted well and by the time we arrived in Basle we were ready for bed never mind an hour and a half of watching football. It was a good job the game was decent.

The match itself was, how the saying goes, a game of two halves. 3-0 down at half time, the Reds pulled it back to 3-3 but couldn't manage the winner that would have kept us in the Champions League. So off to the UEFA Cup it was then.

After the game we met back at the bar that was only ten yards from our hotel. A few more pints were downed before Ian decided enough was enough. Time for bed. 'Where's the hotel?' he enquires. Now Ian's one of those arl fellas who can walk home pissed while blindfolded from his local but step outside of Tuebrook and he needs a guide.

It was on the Paris Metro earlier that day that he had got stranded on his own as the tube train doors closed on him after the rest of us had piled onto the train. We had to get off at the next station and jump the train back for him. Sure enough there he was, not having moved from the position we had last seen him on the platform.

Anyway I digress, so back to the Basle Bar and Ian leaving us for the hotel.

'Next door mate, Out of here and ten yards left'. About an hour later the poor guy appears back in the bar again. 'I can't find the hotel'

He had turned right and walked about two miles around the biggest block of shops, restaurants, bars etc in Europe.

Thats what he tells us anyway. Whether he had encountered a 'Woman of the night' on his little stroll, we have yet to find out. I'm sure there will be one or two tales in this book of mates getting lost and turning up an hour later with a smirk on their face.

I don't think he's touched a drop of Kronenbourg since though. All I can remember is, it was in a white can, it was possibly a 6 or 7% potent brew and not a drop has passed my lips since either. A 1664 hangover and a five-hour return train journey early the next day were not the best of mixes. It was our first encounter with the stuff and possibly the last.

DAVE HEWITSON

2002/03 UEFA CUP

28 November 2002 Third round
Vitesse   0-1   Liverpool FC

12 December 2002 Third round
Liverpool FC   1-0   Vitesse
Aggregate: 0-2

20 February 2003 Fourth Round
AJ Auxerre   0-1   Liverpool FC

27 February 2003 Fourth Round
Liverpool FC   2-0   AJ Auxerre
Aggregate: 3-0

13 March 2003 Quarter-finals
Celtic FC   1-1   Liverpool FC

20 March 2003 Quarter-finals
Liverpool FC   0-2   Celtic FC
Aggregate: 1-3

UEFA CUP 3RD ROUND 1ST LEG
28TH NOVEMBER 2002
GELREDOME STADION [27000]
ARNHEM. NETHERLANDS
VITESSE ARNHEM 0 LIVERPOOL 1

Can anyone seriously remember anything about this game?
A quick search on Google tells me we won 1-0. The abiding memory of the night for me is having a horrible hallucinogenic out of body experience where I was watching myself from the top of the Stand. I was stood below leaning against the segregation partition in an absolute haze. Slumped over whilst eating a weed. Yes, eating it. Incapable of rolling even the smallest of skinners, this is what we'd resorted to.
If I remember rightly the goal, from Milan Baros, woke us up, and the match itself was a bit of a blotch on an otherwise enjoyable evening (as is often the way).
There wasn't a massive Reds contingent who'd made the trip for this game, but having been to the Dam on plenty of occasions this was somewhat of a standout fixture for me. A lesser known town, Arnhem still had a lot to offer the travelling Kopite and is a place stooped in history, most notably for its Second World War involvement with the surrounding towns of Oosterbeek, Wolfehnze and Driel.
Whilst the evening ended in inevitable debauchery, the morning and day did play host to some pleasant historical sight-seeing.
CHRIS MURPHY
*Chris actually said this game was played on the 29th and that Baros had scored. In actual fact it was played on the 28th and Owen was the goalscorer. Strong stuff that Dam weed. Ed.

UEFA CUP QUARTER FINAL 1ST LEG
13TH MARCH 2003
CELTIC PARK [59759]
GLASGOW. SCOTLAND
CELTIC 2 LIVERPOOL 2

After years of doing all the usual league aways we thought it was about time we did a European away, the ultimate trip for a Red. We being Tozza, Philly, Gary, Wayne and me Maca. My first choice was Auxerre in round four which was met with disapproval from the wife. Tiny steps mac, come the quarter final and I was ecstatic to find we had got paired with Celtic. Game on!
After a few phone calls, sorting time off work, tickets and flowers for the mrs, we were booked on a Barnes overnight stay to my first European away!
We met up at Maccy D's on County Road. Quick brekkie of bacon batch's and beer, then we were off.

The driver lobs 'From Dusk till Dawn' on the telly but I only have thoughts about what lies ahead.

A few hours in and countless lagers sunk we finally pull into the services for a well-earned piss and stretch. The usual "Forty five minutes only" shout from the driver. I wish it was! Back on the coach waiting for the stragglers, word gets around that the bizzies have been called. Something's been robbed. Beer, food, what? A kids motorised scooter??

Who the fuck robs a scooter on the way to the game? The local constabulary arrive looking miserable as sin."The coach is going nowhere lads until the scooter is found". "We don't care if you miss the match" says one of the Gestapo. I clock his number on his shoulder... PC 666. I kid you not. PC 666. The devil in disguise!

Time's getting on now. After numerous searches of our coach they finally agree that it wasn't us. It must have been another coach load. A quick phone call to the other Barnes coaches to be aware and we set off again. "Put yer foot down driver will yer" comes the shout as we still have to check in at our digs.

Arrive, check in, bags lashed and straight on it. We send Gary to get some McEwans for later and find the nearest boozer. Nothing special, a few in. An auld fella comes over for a chat. Nice enough saying he was a Celtic fan. Then he drops the bomb. "You wouldn't be talking to me if you knew who i was"."Who are yer?" I ask."David Moyes dad"."Fuck off" Tozza replies with all his usual charm. "Right, photo with him with our scarves around him" shouts Philly. Photo took he wishes us luck and on we continue taking in several Glasgow bars.

On to Parkhead and fantastic scenes before the game. Gerry Marsden blasting out YNWA on the pitch, with both sets of fans in full voice. Absolutely stunning! The match itself came and went to be honest. Took an early lead through Heskey only for Larsson to equalise. The game finished 1-1 with the travelling Kop totally outsinging the Celts throughout the game.

After the game we got talking to some Celts as to where to go for a late bevvy. One of the lads took it upon himself to show us the way. "Follow me lads" was his drunken mantra. After about forty five minutes we arrived at the side of a bar. "I'll handle this" our Scottish crusader says. He knocks on the door and a sliding hatch opens. This is now looking like a scene from a mobster movie."How many?" asks the henchman." There's only 6 of us" the Celt replies. "OK I'll open the door round the corner."

Within thirty seconds of him sliding the hatch shut about twenty Reds appear from no-where! Can they smell the ale? The door opens to The Scotia, Glasgow's oldest boozer and in walks us six and our twenty new best friends. Inside we had nothing to fear. We were in good company. Songs from both sets of fans were in full flow, with Reds flags and banners including 'The Holt Kensington' everywhere.

A few hours later we staggered back to our digs where we were welcomed by a slab of McEwans we had bought earlier. I forget what time we eventually crashed but not a bad European away debut. "if it's like this all the time then count me in" was the shout from the lads! till next time.

IAN McKEVITT

2003/04 UEFA CUP

24 September 2003 First round
NK Olimpija Ljubljana   1-1   Liverpool FC

15 October 2003 First round
Liverpool FC   3-0   NK Olimpija Ljubljana
Aggregate: 4-1

6 November 2003 Second round
FC Steaua București   1-1   Liverpool FC

27 November 2003 Second round
Liverpool FC   1-0   FC Steaua București
Aggregate: 2-1

26 February 2004 Third round
Liverpool FC   2-0   PFC Levski Sofia

3 March 2004 Third round
PFC Levski Sofia   2-4   Liverpool FC
Aggregate: 2-6

11 March 2004 Fourth Round
Liverpool FC   1-1   Olympique de Marseille

25 March 2004 Fourth Round
Olympique de Marseille   2-1   Liverpool FC
Aggregate: 3-2

Liverpool is synonymous with European football. Bill Shankly famously and justifiably heralded the league title as the club's 'bread and butter', yet global reputations and local imaginations have arguably been shaped more by Liverpool's success on the continent. The famous victories secured on European nights at Anfield and on floodlit adventures on foreign soil have underpinned English football's proudest European heritage. Scousers always consider seasons culminating in finals to be the most memorable, signaling a mass exodus of Liverpudlians journeying by whatever means necessary to see coveted cups won (and occasionally lost), on famous May evenings in cities subsequently etched in either folklore or infamy.

In the era of late-modern elite football some of the romance and uncertainty of outcome has been squeezed from the European game. Seedings and group stages framed as proportionate rewards really serve to protect the interests of clubs of wealth and stature, guaranteeing revenues and compensating failures. (Liverpool have been more a beneficiary than a victim, so we shouldn't really complain). Consequently however, the road to today's European finals typically passes through some familiar locations. As unthinkable as it may seem in any barren spell, during Benitez's era of European success at Liverpool some of the continental excursions began to feel almost mundane.

The Champions League is undeniably the pinnacle of club football. As Liverpool fans can testify, football experiences are rarely more memorable than winning a European Cup and rarely more painful than losing one. Yet in eras drenched in success, seasons can now seem saturated with continental contests of variable significance. As the overly elaborate UEFA Champions League draw reveals yet another trip to Eindhoven or Marseille, match-going fans can occasionally find themselves longing for an obscure Europa League tie. When people discover that you follow your club across Europe, they usually ask about the finals, but when you're in the company of those who journeyed with you, nostalgic reminiscences usually centre more on the perilous, incident-packed expeditions to watch less significant matches in unfamiliar territories, experiences that you later realise have helped shape your character.

The Europa League might be the poorer relation of the prestigious Champions League, but no club has won the former trophy more than Liverpool. The club has never tasted defeat in a final, and some of the most memorable trips en route have been in some unremarkable yet unforgettable places. Teams you know you will only ever play once, places you would only get to with a Liverbird upon your chest. If the 1960s had Knattspyrnufélag Reykjavíkur, the 1970s Strømsgodset Iderettsforening, the 1980s Oulun Palloseura and the 1990s Spartak Alania Vladikavkaz, then Liverpool's most obscure European draw during the first decade of the new millennium might well have been Nogometni Klub Olimpija Ljubljana. The season before dramatically winning a fifth European Cup in 2005 under Benitez, Houllier's Liverpool breathed its last breath with four painfully mediocre European ties in the UEFA Cup. Events on the pitch might have been forgettable, but as European trips, they collectively rendered the 2003-2004 season a seminal one for our eclectic group of young and fearless travelling reds. Virtually the entire spectrum of Liverpool postcodes (stretching also to Widnes and Wallasey) was represented by the lads in our group during that character-building season.

With its twenty hour road trip through war-torn Serbia, the Levski Sofia trip in round three was for us probably the most eventful of that campaign, but that's for another chapter. The first European obstacle of the season however, and the focus of this chapter, is the tie against the Slovenian Cup winners from the former Hungarian city of Ljubljana. It was Liverpool's first and only competitive match in independent Slovenia to date and it was to prove Olimpija's last European tie, as the debt-ridden club filed for bankruptcy later that year and was dissolved the following season. (The club continued in spirit from 2005 as NK Bežigrad, achieving four consecutive promotions to gain entry to the Slovenian top flight, seemingly changing its name, crest, legal status, historical narrative and claims to patrimony on an almost annual basis).

After the deregulation of the European aviation industry, airlines such as Ryanair and Easyjet had begun to make life easier for the independent travelling red at the turn of the century. The gradual increase in European routes, ludicrously cheap fares and the availability of online bookings (coinciding with the expansion of European football and Liverpool's modestly successful performances) widened access to the continent. Ryanair were the cheaper and Stansted was their main UK base, and so for us the journey from Liverpool to the Essex border became a fixture of European fixtures. When we arrived at the airport for the Ljubljana game, the small pocket of Scousers gathered were outnumbered by a large group of Perugia supporters who were heading to Dundee for their fixture in the same competition. Fans exchanged knowing glances, respectfully in most cases, certainly a more civilised and cosmopolitan equivalent to the crossing of paths at English rail stations on Saturdays of yesteryear.

We had driven through the night and arrived to find all airport services still closed, so the five of us (Danny Mackinlay, Danny Stainze, David Stead, Andrew West and me) took out a banner each and had an hour's sleep. We woke to the sight of more Italians peering over us, attempting to decipher phrases painted on the red material, covering caps and trackies. 'The People's Republic of Liverpool' seemed the simplest to interpret, sentiment reflecting the romanticised city-state identity of those considered to be from England but not of it. Turning to my left, I noticed a strange man in even stranger attire appear from under one of our flags. Behaving as if it was the most normal thing in the world, he stifled a yawn to utter what I presume was an expression of gratitude in German, then stood up and left. We exchanged nods with the Italians, and headed for Stansted's first flight of the day, a plane bound for Italy. It was time for a Euro away.

We landed in Venice, then picked up the hire car and drove towards Slovenia, confident that the one hundred and fifty mile journey to Ljubljana would be incident free. Hope began to erode at the border however, in the first indication that by heading east from Italy we were leaving Western Europe. As if Slovenia had been reinstated into Yugoslavia, the communist conglomeration it declared independence from a decade earlier, the militaristic Slovenian police looked for any excuse to deport or at least detain us at the border. They searched us for drugs and enquired about our status as 'English hooligans'. They were expecting Liverpool fans, and we were not welcome. With no trace of illegal substance or history of violence however, we were eventually permitted to enter Slovenia, but only after providing proof of match tickets. On this rare occasion, everyone present had a ticket, and we considered ourselves fortunate to have been allowed to proceed beyond the border. We later learned that this privilege was denied to countless other Liverpool fans not in possession of tickets. Within those few minutes at the Sežana crossing, the tone of the trip changed.

Our European away budget rarely allowed for such luxuries as pre-arranged accommodation in those days, and Ljubljana was no exception. We arrived in the capital soon after midday with kick off still eight hours away, so before heading to the city centre we instinctively drove straight to the ground. We were hoping to leave the car there, aware that it might serve as our hotel twelve hours later. To this day I've not seen a worse arena than NK Olimpija's 8,000-capacity Bežigrad Stadium, which as the biggest ground in the country at the time, had also been the home of the Slovenian national team since 1995. The exterior walls of the decrepit arena were covered in graffiti, featuring the work of CSKA Moscow and Hadjuk Split Ultras, as well as Ljubljana Green Dragon Hooligans and the Slovenian Capital Riot Crew – both of whom we were later to encounter. We also saw 'Everton' displayed in foot high letters, evidence that the Slovenians had done their homework and were not out to make friends.

We left the car at the ground, but before walking into town we indulged what had become our group's signature custom of getting our picture taken with a flag on the pitch. Negotiating entry into a professional European ground is often simpler than you might imagine, but accessing the Bežigrad was particularly straightforward. Elsewhere in Ljubljana other established routines were being enacted by touring Liverpool fans, drinking ale, singing songs and swapping stories in bars adorned with Scouse flags. After a few Slovenian pints and a horse burger, we encountered members of the Capital Riot Crew, who had apparently also made their presence felt the previous evening. Groups of fans mixed uneasily at the Dragon Bridge, as tension pervaded the atmosphere. Although the realisation undermined our purported fearlessness, we felt it was time to get to the ground, get a result and get out of Ljubljana.

The match was far from a spectacle, punctuated only by their second half opener, and our equaliser thirteen minutes from time. Michael Owen's strike propelled him above his then forward coach Ian Rush as Liverpool's top scorer in Europe. Our view from the side of the pitch was not aided by the presence of some uncompromising police and the smoke of a dozen green flares, both of which seemed to linger menacingly. Behind the goal to our right a group of fans dressed in green chanted incessantly, noise devoid both of rhythm and melody. They were led by a shaven-headed ultra stood on the fence, forcefully commanding his troops. The group responded to the equalising goal by joining arms and collectively turning their backs on the game. Various intimidating gestures were aimed in our direction, together with the chant: 'England, England, who the fuck is England?' In a context lost on the locals, as I looked at the Scouse collection of separatist banners displayed behind me, it was clear that in this period of shifting identities some of the travelling fans were effectively asking themselves the same question. It was a quiet away end, memorable only for the encounter with some unwelcome nationalistic Dinamo Zagreb fans who had infiltrated our end; and the sight of a lone Scouser who, seemingly out of boredom, climbed the fence separating the supporters wearing nothing but a thong.

After the game we headed back into town, and to the bar where we had spent most of that afternoon. We got talking to a group of Ljubljanian girls keen to practice their conversational English with some 'native speakers', although collectively their grasp of the language was probably greater than ours. In return they offered to let us sleep at their apartment, which seemed a suspiciously ideal arrangement. An unmanned bar provided all the ale we could drink, at an unbeatable rate. We were beginning to get accustomed to Ljubljana, a feeling that spread throughout the vicinity, as Liverpool songs filled the warm September air. Little did we know however, the volume had made us a target. Members of the Green Dragons soon appeared at the outdoor bar, one of whom announced their arrival and took his belt off, proceeding to swing the huge metal buckle around his head. A bottle was thrown from behind us, and then what started as a minor scuffle developed into a mini riot, with glass raining and fists flying. Unfortunately, we were stuck in the middle of the action outside the bar, surrounded by Slovenians intent on attacking Liverpool fans. A further scuffle ensued and it was time to start dodging the bottles again. Scanning the vicinity in a moment of calm between skirmishes, I realised a number of fans had suffered cuts to the head. As some experienced campaigners rallied the troops for a counterattack, we took our opportunity to flee the scene, surrendering our accommodation preference in the process.

We had followed a small number of Liverpool fans out of the bar, and began to walk up a pedestrianized street behind them. As the street narrowed they were met by another group of Slovenians, who proceeded to pounce on the most advanced Liverpool fan, inflicting a number of blows before and after he had fallen to the ground. Having passively witnessed and therefore effectively legitimised the attack that left a man unconscious, the police belatedly intervened. No arrests were made but at least an ambulance appeared soon after. With the threat of attack looming large and local police seemingly intent neither on preventing nor proportionately responding to violence perpetrated by Slovenians, my determination to leave the city gathered momentum, as Thursday gave way to Friday. At that point a few familiar faces appeared, in the form of Southport Reds Jimmy Buck and Greg Pennington, who allowed us to stay on the floor of their hotel room. In light of the day's events, it was the comfiest wooden floor I've ever slept on.

The altercations in Slovenia were the type of incidents English football fans have been

142

repeatedly associated with and considered perpetrators of for decades. There are times when blame is justifiably attributed to travelling supporters, but that night in Ljubljana was not one of them. In contrast to the distorted stereotyping of Liverpudlians in English football contexts, irregular fixtures against unknown European opponents can turn Scousers into minor celebrities on their travels. Alternatively we can be perceived and received as legitimate targets for attack by those who consider The Football Factory a realistic and admirable representation of all English fans. Participation in football violence is something I have always looked to avoid, and in fifty European away matches with Liverpool over fifteen years I've never had to throw a single punch. Yet when a small collection of Liverpudlians are gathered in an unfamiliar city where local fans are not to be trusted and local police are not to be relied upon, in the quest for self-preservation, the safest option is usually to remain with the wider group, even if that means sharing space with fellow Scousers of a more violent persuasion.

The trip took another turn for the worse the next morning, with our hurried attempts to leave the city, aided by the questionable navigation skills of my accomplice, who lay asleep beside me in the passenger seat. The return route inexplicably led us once more into unfamiliar territory, although we eventually stumbled upon an international border. 'Is this Italy mate?' I asked the border guard. 'No, Austria!' came the reply' – an exchange often since recalled when the five of us are together. The indirect return to Venice lengthened the journey, but our route inadvertently took us through Udine, enabling a detour that offered a stark contrast to the chaos of the previous day. After a meal in the picturesque city, we found ourselves at Udinese's Stadio Friuli, an ageing but characterful ground. 'Italy 90' World Cup signage was still visible on the stadium walls, behind which the Alps glistened on the horizon. Fortuitously our visit coincided with the arrival of the club's players, who had just emerged to train on the pitch. No one stopped us from walking onto the turf with them, with everyone assuming someone had given us permission. One of the players even agreed to pose for a photo with us, his teammates probably assuming we were his guests.

We were conscious that our flight home was looming, but made time for a quick stop in Venice en route to the airport. The final photo of the trip was taken at St Mark's Square, the same lads in the same clothes with the same flags. Steven Gerrard captained Liverpool for the first time in the second leg of the tie, a routine 3-0 win for Liverpool. Of the 43,880 in attendance at Anfield, only sixty nine were Olimpia Ljubljana fans, in what proved their final ever European tie. Their club might have died a death (as a legal entity at least), but for me they will live long in the memory.

JOEL ROOKWOOD

One of the greatest compliments you can pay a Slovenian is, apparently, not to confuse his country with Slovakia. It seems a simple enough courtesy, but even those of us with a less than rudimentary geographic sense would have, until very recently, struggled to place Slovenia on a map. The rough consensus was that it was somewhere 'over there'.

'Over there', it transpired, appeared to be any point between Macedonia and Estonia and as far east as Moldova. It's a relatively new country, created only within the last decade, and the Slovenians are intensely proud of the homeland. "Slovenia was," I explained, reading from the home page of www.wherethefuckisslovenia.com, "until the early 1990s part of Yugoslavia and forms the northern most part of that ex-state, bordering Austria, Croatia, Hungary and Italy".

"So where's that then?" asked Paul Stewart, slurping his tea.

"Er … its main exports are hemp, yogurt and ball-bearings, and they are, along with Norway and Andorra, one of the few nations to score nil points in the Eurovision Song Contest".

"Never mind culture, Mackin, how the frig are we getting there?"

How the frig, indeed.

Once again budget airlines came to the rescue. Both Ryanair and EasyJet service cities in neighbouring countries, within striking distance of Ljubljana, Slovenia's capital and largest city. But not from Liverpool. Frig!

Nevertheless, within twenty minutes of the draw being made and the phone-call cum geography lesson for Paul, we'd booked return flights from Stansted to Trieste, on the Italian-Slovenian border, for the return leg in mid October. Feeling pretty smug at securing these for less than £50 return you can understand how we felt later that evening when we learned that both clubs had asked to switch the ties, and play in Slovenia three weeks earlier. To this day we've still had no real inkling as to why these games were switched. The day after the switch, however, after further internet panic, we managed to get flights to Klagenfurt, which though in Austria is actually nearer Ljubljana than Trieste.

There's nothing like a 3:30am mobile phone call to get the pulse racing. It also leaves you sitting on the edge of the bed feeling like your eye-balls have been raped. No matter how early you say you're getting to bed it never quite works out that way, does it. Six hours later, after a breakfast of Maltesers and Diet Coke on the M11, we were checking in at Stansted and my eyeballs were returning to normal. After a few beers we met up with yet another John Mac and his friend Gill, along with Trigger, Archie and Ed. We'd met Ed on the monorail from the main terminal to Gate 32, and Paul was impressed that Ed had on one of Paul's 'Wine for my Men' t-shirts.

"Oh", said Paul, nodding in the direction of Ed's chest, "That's one of mine".

Paul then went all nonchalant and half turned away, but still hung around Ed like someone who once played touring keyboards for T'Pau might do at a music awards ceremony, in the vain hope that he might be recognised. Alas, all Paul succeeded in doing was coming on all desperate and weird like Avid Merrion without the neck brace. Once on board we did a rough head count. There were only about twenty Reds' rough heads on board, which wasn't surprising, even though the flights were relatively cheap. as we would be landing in a different country a mere six hours before kick-off in Slovenia. Still, the view of the Alps as you enter Austrian airspace is spectacular and several large vodkas always help lift the mood.

144

Later, as we stood outside Klagenfurt airport looking for our taxis, we are introduced to Mick Jagger's brother, Chris, who's playing some gigs in Austria. We have a quick chat about cricket as he declares (no pun intended) that he knows nothing about football. The close proximity of a semi-celebrity has sent Paul into paroxysms and he wanders off muttering something about Martin Tyler.

The nine of us are joined by Peter from Prague who'd travelled across Austria by train to meet us. We then split up into three yellow Slovenian cabs we'd booked on the internet (£40 each way) and spend the next hour climbing into the Alps listening to the driver's yodelling cassette. Well, it sounded like yodelling but could have been the soundtrack to a snuff-video about cat strangling. It was hard not to laugh. So we did. The scenery was spectacular, textbook Alpine. At the roadside we'd occasionally pass a steep-roofed chalet with wooden-shuttered windows and the unmistakable, welcoming sign 'Gasthaus'. It was hard to pass but with kick-off time drawing inexorably closer we had to resist the lure of a cold lager and press on.

After a half-hour hold up at border control where our passports were meticulously scrutinised and our names checked against some sort of 'blacklist', as well as being made to produce match tickets, we entered Slovenia and the road began its descent past cascading waterfalls and sheer rock faces amidst fir and pine forest. In the valleys, the meadows were a riot of flowers. It really was ridiculously pretty, but all we could think about was getting to the capital and having a few pre-match beers. As the gorges turned to valleys, and the slopes became less steep, the sun came out and it was hard not to believe you'd just gone on holiday. The driver then turned down the music and pointed out the site of a nazi concentration camp, just a few yards from the roadside. The bare skeletal remains of a couple of dozen buildings looked calm and tame in the lush countryside, like abandoned farm buildings. It was a timely reminder that this region, at the crossroads of the Balkans and 'Western' Europe has, for so long, been the scene of bitter and bloody confrontation. It's almost impossible to believe the existence of such a murderous spot in such beautiful setting. "Nazis?", asked Paul. The driver nodded. After a few moments of silence Paul added, "Bastards!".

Ninety minutes after leaving Klagenfurt we arrived in Ljubljana. Entering the city from the north we passed clean, modern Euro-suburbs and were then suddenly as we entered the city centre traffic thickened and roads grew narrower, buildings taller. Minutes later we drew up outside the three-star Hotel Astral. Our driver pointed opposite the hotel to a hole-in-the-wall fast food outlet. "24 hours!" he proclaimed proudly. How handy was that? A sort of Ljubljanian Lobster Pot within two minutes staggering distance of our room.

After checking in and dumping our bags, we got ready to leave by swiftly changing shirts and grabbing the flags. We meet up downstairs in a smart bar where business types seemed to be enjoying an afternoon tipple. Our first taste of Slovenian beer or 'pivo' was a bottle of the ubiquitous 'Union' pilsner. Depending on where you went in the city it was either in a bottle with a green label or a red label. Like in Gullivers Travels, Brobdignagian-style factions have apparently sprung up in Ljubljana fighting their respective red or green 'Union' corner; marriages have been rent asunder and fights erupted over the discovery that a friend or spouse secretly drinks 'the other one'. All we can say is that the green one is cack: far too astringent. The red was better, but only just. Still we felt the need to reassure the locals that their beer was the best we'd had in ages, then we sat back, sipping our pints and silently joined in prayer that this UEFA cup run took us back to Prague at some point.

Euro travel tip # 1. As soon as you arrive grab a handful of business cards from the hotel reception. They have the name and address of where you are staying in the local language and are invaluable when handed to cab drivers at 4am when you have trouble remembering what country you're actually in. If you're in luck they'll also have a small map of the area. We were in luck and it was by using this crude map that we made our way into the centre of the old town.

KFS – Keep Flags Scouse, Keep Flags Simple(?)

We were heading for a small bridge over the narrow river that cuts through the centre of Ljubljana and divides the old town from the new. "It's a bridge with white pillars on it." Said Mick Smith on the phone, "We're in an alehouse right next to it." There are numerous bridges in this area but we knew we'd hit upon the right one when we saw it and the walls on each adjacent river bank decorated in Liverpool banners and flags. There were about a hundred or so Reds milling about at the riverside cafes and bars. Several chaps from The Holt in Kensington accost me and complain that their wonderful flag never gets a mention. I promised to put that right. Theirs is a simple and yet elegant flag, fully compliant with the KFS and the Boss Wednesday Agreement (See RAOTL passim).

Such simplicity seemed noticeably absent this time amongst some of the newer efforts. The Major was doing his rounds, reviewing the banners, with a sober countenance. "Its all going wrong John," he remarked, "K. F. S. – should stand for Keep Flags Simple as well as Scouse."

The Kingfisher banner so impressed the Slovenian Authorities that Ljubljanan monks were ordered to parade it through the old town on an ancient bannabus (trolley) before it was installed in the Cathedral.

It was hard to disagree. An 'A' level in literature and/or French now seems the required minimum for flagmaking for Euro aways. There are some good and great older flags here but it appears that everyone is now trying to outdo each other in the philosophical stakes. A rethink is required here boys. Our flags are still miles ahead of our rivals but we are falling short of our own benchmarks of originality and wit.

Paul and I retire for a red pivo and resolve, after several 'Unions', that our next flag will say "We love minge."

The display of these bright red flags against the bleached white stonework was eye-catching to say the least, and passers by stopped and stared. Ljubljana is as much a basketball and Ludo town as it is a football town, and some people were completely ignorant as to what what we were doing there making such a mess of their fine architecture. Were we Macedonian refugees, perhaps, possibly selling ornamental tablecloths? Or maybe we were some mad Slavic splinter group protesting at the impending imposition of the Euro? (Slovenia will shortly be joining the EEC). Perhaps 'The Holt, Kensington' looks suspiciously like the Slavic for 'Shove your Euro up your arse, Brussels. All Hail to the Tolar!'.

Some moody looking youths with green scarves wrapped around their faces stood in small groups. I'm not sure they were up to anything, perhaps just trying to look like they were fronting up 'the English'. More likely they were just checking us out. They, no doubt, reported back to the mates later on and told them: "They're all bevvied and hanging flags all over the place. It looks like Wishy-Washys Chinese laundry down there."

An old man in a beret stood looking at the flags as I was taking photos. He said something that seemed obviously to be the Slovenian for "Whats going on?".

"Football." I said. He stared at me; he wanted more.

"Liverpool," I added. No, not enough, he needed details.

"Olympia Ljubljana and Liverpool." I went on. He looked incredulous then with his hand up by his chest pointed to the pavement. It meant, "What? Here?".

I nodded. "Yes. Here".

He nodded, it had sunk in and off he went.

No poetry by Baudelaire or quotations from Conan The Barbarian. (KFS approved)

After a while hunger hit home (we hadn't eaten since 5am and it was now close to 4:30pm) so we struck off into the old town looking for some food. We soon found an old bar-restaurant, reassuringly old-looking, with barrels for tables and a menu written completely in 'foreign'. We settle for several huge platters of chips and several rounds of 'Union'. At around 6pm we decide to head off towards the stadium. As we headed for the nearest main road we stumbled across a bridge flanked by large green bronze dragons, the city's and the football club's emblem. We clustered beneath one dragon with Paul's banner and tried to take photos. A police van drew up and observed us for a few minutes, and then satisfied we were just pissed, sped off.

Taxis were phoned from another small bar we chanced upon, and ten minutes later we found ourselves on the pavement, on the Dunajska cesta, the main road running north from the city centre.

Olympia's tiny open stadium is on this road and gathered all around the perimeter gates, over an hour before kick off, are crowds of Olympia fans. There's no sense of order, just a quiet chaos as they all stake a claim to being first into the stadium. This is the excitable section behind one of the goals, home of the flares and the bulk of the chanting. There's a tiny ticket office window in the wall at this end of the ground where a young girl is also distributing programmes. Paul and I grab a dozen or so each. Programmes intact it was time for more beer so we crossed back over this busy road to a small square, crammed with parked cars and bikes, and looked back at the 'Olympic Stadium'. The stadium perimeter wall is no more than 8 feet or so high with no added security, bar about a hundred fluorescent jacketed stewards manning the wall at one metre intervals. They do this by standing on top of it. They're still there at the end of the game three hours later. It's a feat of physical endurance of almost David Blaine proportions.

Directly behind the 'home' end the perimeter wall becomes slightly grander with a colonnade but it still has all the air of a municipal bowling green. That said it's a damn sight more interesting than the Nou Camp, it doesn't feel like Alcatraz, and has an off the beaten track kind of romance to it that makes you glad you made the trip. It's what Slovan Liberec would have been like if the local police hadn't been on amphetamines. I can remember the other JMac and Gill being with us at this stage but can't recall if Trigger and Archie have managed to keep up. We may also have lost Peter, but to be truthful, I was a bit merry by this time. The other John (MacLeary) has managed to get an Olympia scarf and seeing as they don't sell these outside the stadium, have no club shop and that the locals are loathe to swap is a major feat. We've crossed the square and found a busy bar swamped with locals and a handful of Liverpool fans. It takes twenty minutes of haggling and bargaining by Paul to get one local to swap his scarf for mine. We could relax now and see how many pivos we could sup in the next half hour.

It's gotten dark by now and the floodlights are on across the road, the light also illuminating the square and exterior of the bar. It also lights up a small stall with a barbecue on it where a delightful chap is preparing 'Hot Horse' horse burgers. I have to say that these were absolutely gorgeous gloriously broiled, chewy meat with crunchy salad and a fiery salsa style dressing. We're completely silent for the five minutes it takes to devour them, then just stand there looking smug whilst wiping salsa from our faces. I'd go as far to say that these were the tastiest things I've ever eaten at a football match. I venture as much to Paul. He thinks for a while, then recalls this bird he met in Cologne …

Back over the road we accost a Slovenian TV crew and try to cadge their club press passes from them with the intention of using them inside the ground to go 'for a wander'. The pretty reporter says no, but if we meet her later then she'll let us have them. We agree and march into our 'sektor' of the ground.

We've been given a long narrow section along one touchline that stretches up to the half way line. I'm impressed by the numbers we've brought. There must be close to eight or nine hundred here. The seats all seemed to be full, truth was we couldn't be bothered looking for any empty ones. We stayed at the rear of the section by the perimeter wall where we managed to hang our flags with the help of the fluorescent jacketed 'sentries'. There was a kind of peripatetic party going on along this cinder track at the back. Nico and Stefan appeared, Stef brandishing a huge box of cigars. Pretty soon there's dozens of blokes standing about chatting, smoking cigars and quaffing a weak shandy that a tiny bar was struggling to keep us supplied with.

Cigars, Shandy, Flags and Belgians Nico, Paul & JMac.

It was like a christening. Every now and then we'd glance over at the action on the pitch, but the game was pretty dire. Barely half an hour into the game and there's mutterings from lads desperate to get out and head for the comfort of a local bar where they could watch the game on TV. I'm sorely tempted but Paul persuades me to stay.

At half time I share a portaloo with Danny Giles who's wearing a tweedy overcoat and

148

looks like a gamekeeper. Danny's gibbering and all I can think to say is "Them eels is for his pot." Which, I imagine, confuses the fuck out of him.

The second half livens up only when Olympia score. The locals go nuts and we just shrug; we have played crap even accounting for the state of the pitch. Then out of nowhere young Michael rises to meet a cross and 'nods' home an equalizer, via his shoulder. We almost resent this intrusion into our conversation, but applaud the young man anyway. The game fizzles out and we group up at the back of the stand with the Irregulars and leave for the walk back into town. Outside the TV crew is waiting and I blurt out something about Ljubljana being a wonderful city … lovely people … and what a pretty Stadium etc. They look chuffed and respond by giving us their laminated press passes (a bit late now) and hearty handshakes are exchanged. Our cab driver, the next morning, explains how he'd seen us on Slovenian TV praising the city and especially the Stadium, which he'd found surprising. I hadn't the heart to explain that I was only being nice.

We march back into the city down the main road and under a busy underpass beneath the railway station, classic ambush territory. We were on our guard as several Liverpool fans we'd seen had bruises and cuts caused by flying bottles earlier in the day. However, the journey passed without incident. We reconvened back at the square near the three bridges. It was a very pleasant evening and we sat at some al fresco café tables enjoying a few beers. As midnight drew, people began to drift off across the square to a small alleyway that led onto a courtyard and The Cutty Sark pub. The courtyard was packed, the atmosphere was excellent. Stefan's cigar box made another appearance and the party kicked off in earnest, until suddenly about an hour into the session it kicked off, really in earnest.

A fist fight suddenly erupted and a few bottles were thrown, then riot police stormed into the courtyard, cracked a few heads and restored order. As the bottles flew I stepped back out of the way and fell backwards over someone's holdall. As I lay on the floor someone accidentally trod on my little finger. I clambered back to my feet and saw one or two lads with gashed heads and blood running down their faces. Still, I was indignant that some 'oaf!' had stood on my finger. The bar closed up immediately, shutters down and door locked. The tables outside the pub, though, were still awash with beer and many stayed about finishing off their drinks. Meanwhile the police stood in an immobile line facing the crowd, like stormtroopers from the Death Star. It looked like it might go off again, so we retired to the top end of the square and out onto the busy main road, Slovenska Cesta. Here we found an Irish pub and decided to assault the Guinness.

Outside the bar, a small group of local 'boys' were prowling, eager for a fight. We just ignored them and carried on drinking. One of them came in and approached one of Nico's mates and knocked the cap from his head in a clichéd 'I challenge you to fisticuffs' type of way. He was immediately set upon by a huge bouncer who turfed him out of the bar and into the road. The 'Green Dragons' hung around outside for a while, circling like wolves (excuse the mixed metaphor) and were again soundly ignored by

149

tired Liverpudlians just wanting a quiet drink. Then farmer Danny Giles appeared again, resplendent in tweed, and conversed in fractured Slovenian with the barman. I somehow knew he was talking about eels again. I made my excuses and retired back to the Astral and bed.

JOHN MACKIN

2004/05 CHAMPIONS LEAGUE

15 September 2004 Group stage (Group A)
Liverpool FC   2-0   AS Monaco FC

28 September 2004 Group stage (Group A)
Olympiacos FC   1-0   Liverpool FC

19 October 2004 Group stage (Group A)
Liverpool FC   0-0   RC Deportivo La Coruña

3 November 2004 Group stage (Group A)
RC Deportivo La Coruña   0-1   Liverpool FC

23 November 2004 Group stage (Group A)
AS Monaco FC   1-0   Liverpool FC

8 December 2004 Group stage (Group A)
Liverpool FC   3-1   Olympiacos FC

22 February 2005 Round of 16
Liverpool FC   3-1   Bayer 04 Leverkusen

9 March 2005 Round of 16
Bayer 04 Leverkusen   1-3   Liverpool FC
Aggregate: 2-6

5 April 2005 Quarter-finals
Liverpool FC   2-1   Juventus

13 April 2005 Quarter-finals
Juventus 0-0   Liverpool FC
Aggregate: 1-2

27 April 2005 Semi-finals
Chelsea FC   0-0   Liverpool FC

3 May 2005 Semi-finals
Liverpool FC   1-0   Chelsea FC
Aggregate: 1-0

25 May 2005 Final
AC Milan   3-3   Liverpool FC
Liverpool win 3-2 on penalties

CHAMPIONS LEAGUE
3RD QUALIFYING ROUND 1ST LEG
10TH AUGUST 2004
ARNOLD SCHWARZENEGGER STADION [15000]
GRAZ. AUSTRIA
GRAZER AK 0 LIVERPOOL 2

The excitement was huge for this trip to Graz. It was Rafa Benitez's first competitive game in charge of the mighty Liverpool. Rafa had been at the club for only a few months, so the jury was still out on one of Europe's most up and coming coaches.

It was a day trip with Barnes Travel that I took for my journey to Graz, so it was a nice early start from Liverpool Airport with the lads. Once we had checked in and were sorted it was the usual breakfast for us, "Six pints please mate" was the request at the bar. It was a struggle to drink, with the taste of toothpaste still lingering in my mouth. But that was soon overcome, and it was soon time to board our flight to Graz.

I never knew what to expect from Graz when I arrived, it was a city and country I had never visited before. All I knew was that the weather for that day was going to be approx 28 degrees and sunny, this was courtesy of a brief look on the untrusting BBC website a day before. While we were on the plane we were reading the newspaper and reports were very strong that Michael Owen was about to sign for Real Madrid after the game and Benitez wasn't going to pick him for tonight's game. There had been stories all summer about Owen's future, but I thought that if he was going to go, he would have went in the last month or so, and not now, which would leave us short for cover up front. I didn't want Owen to leave, he was a world-class star in our team, and that's what we lacked, more players of world-class quality. So I read the report but refused to believe it.

Apart from that, the flight was quite quick and we were soon arriving in Graz, which I now know was Capital of Culture the year before in 2003, something which the majestic city of Liverpool would receive in 2008. As we left the plane, we duly got our passports stamped, something that is done on most European adventures if possible. With no luggage to collect our coach was ready and waiting outside the airport terminal to transfer us the centre of Graz. So after, our transfer, which took approx fifteen to twenty minutes, we got dropped off in the centre of Graz. Everyone on the coaches went their separate ways (mainly to the first bars they could find), but we had a little walk around Graz first to have a nose.

The Mur River runs through the centre of this city, and the first thing we noticed was this weird building just built on the banks of the river. It's hard to explain what it looked like, but it looked very futuristic and modern, but also very weird, maybe this is something cities have to do when they get selected for European Capital of Culture. Build weird and modern buildings?

Anyway after looking at this building for a few minutes, which was called Mur Island (bet that name took ages to think off didn't it?), we carried on walking and came up to

Schlossberg. I hear you asking what the hell is that, well this is a very big hill, we got right up to this, and it was someone's bright idea, that we would walk to the top of it. So we did, and it must have took about 30 minutes to walk to the top. When we eventually got there, it was well worth it as the views were fantastic, and you could see the whole of the city of Graz. So after a few photos and a little chat with a few fellow reds, it was time for the walk back down. The sweat was pouring from us, but we had worked up a sweat now for a nice drink in the sunshine. We got to the bottom, eventually, and there was a tiny little café. So we got a table outside and ordered 6 pints and 6 toasties. The café was empty, so after a few more drinks here, we decided to walk towards the centre, where the other fans were gathering, and eventually we came to an Irish bar (time to get ripped off aye?), where we knew quite a few of the lads. So we decided to stay here for a few hours. The songs started to get belted out and the flags and banners started taking over the pub and its surroundings. So it was time for one of the lads with us to put our banner up. He was very tipsy by this time, and we saw someone using a ladder to put their flag up, so we got the ladder from them and put ours up next to it. This was a very nervy moment, I don't know what was more unstable the ladder or my mate on top of it. Anyway both survived. But when he got down I thought, 'how on earth is he going to get that down now'. Especially after a few more drinks. I thought I'll worry about that when we're going. When it was time to go to the stadium, the flag was still 25ft in the air. We waited until the lad who put his flag up first got there, and we just said to him while he was up there, could he just grab ours for us. He duly obliged, much to our relief. This fella was still shaky and taking a chance, but all was well, and it was packed away, and off we went to get the tram up towards the stadium.

We arrived at the stadium, which was called 'The Arnold Schwarzenegger Stadium' and that's not taking the mickey. We all were looking forward to the match now, and seeing Rafa's first proper team selection, and if Michael Owen would play. If he played he would then be cup-tied in Europe. So if the deal went through we could possibly lose a few million or the deal may collapse.

While we were outside the stadium we popped into their Club shop, I got a scarf and a pin badge to take home, which is another European ritual. We stayed outside the ground for a bit talking to other lads we knew, and some Graz fans. We soon ended up with the most ridiculous hats you cold think off. We swapped our Liverpool scarves which we had for these polystyrene hats with Graz and Liverpool badges on. They were that bad, I still have mine in the house. Anyway after wishing their fans luck (not too much though) we went inside the stadium and took a seat. It was a nice little Stadium and quite modern. There were about 15,000 inside and we got the VIP treatment. Drinks, food everything you wanted was brought to your seat. I think we got twelve pints (don't even know if it was non-alcoholic), but they went down a treat in that heat. Everyone was just looking at us and probably saying look at them whoppers with them stupid hats on and all that ale. It's Europe, it's allowed, I would think to myself. Anyway the game soon started and the team Benitez put out was what the papers where saying; Owen was on the bench. So the rumours must be true, because why on earth

154

would Rafa leave his world-class striker out? Another slight surprise was the Hyypia/ Henchoz partnership being broken up at the back. This had been one of Liverpool's team strengths too, but Rafa had seen something in Carragher to put him next to Sami. Apart from that it was a comfortable 2-0 win for the Reds, with Steven Gerrard scoring both the goals. He was robbed of a hat-trick as he had one disallowed for a foul in the area by Cisse. This was also the last time we would see Michael Owen for Liverpool, he never came off the bench, but he warmed up, so we sang his name, hoping we would somehow persuade him to stay. But basically the deal was done and he was off to Real Madrid. It was sad for Benitez, because Owen never gave him a chance to prove what he could do for this football club. But it was a blessing is disguise, because with some of the money we purchased Luis Garcia and Xabi Alonso. Rafa was left in the lurch really because we didn't have time to replace Owen, Cisse and Baros had potential but would or could they fill Michael Owen's boots? The answer was 'No', but both played a big part that season for Liverpool. The game came to an end, and we walked back to the coaches which were ready to transfer us back to the airport for our flights back home to Merseyside. It was a long day, but a good one. Rafa won his first game in charge, and Liverpool were one step closer to the group stages of the Champions League.

STE TRAYNOR

A trip from Farce to almost tragedy!

What should have started out as an easy lift from Northampton to Stansted on Monday morning for the flight to Graz, could have led to Gareth and I not actually making it at all. All this after the date of the game was changed and various alterations to flights, at much extra cost, made us fly direct to Graz rather than taking the cheap route. It saved us going via Salzburg and an eight hour round trip on the train mind!

It all started on Sunday when Gareth had a problem with his starter motor. Come Monday morning at 08.00am and no car, no lift and two old gits panicking about the flight leaving in less than four hours. A quick ring round from both of us for a lift or taxi fares ends up with me heading off in a taxi down the M1 to pick him up and a desperate hope that we could get to Stansted in time for the flight.

Three hours later after (luckily) a pretty good cross country trip and we arrive with over an hour to spare only to get held up at check-in due to various numpties in front of us. For a change none of them were known to us.

I still hadn't collected my match ticket yet as it was currently sitting with a lad that I hardly knew who had collected it for me and was presiding in Wetherspoons having a pint (well what resembles one). Various misfits were spotted in the bar otherwise known as Olly, Aidan (The Dave version), Alan and John. There was time for a quick pint before the flight and a near crippling of myself when a kid ran in front of me as I approached our gate at speed. I already had a strained side muscle, so falling over, coughing, sneezing or sleeping well were completely out of the question (and that's before my world renowned snoring before pot-kettle-black members of this forum comment).

I don't think I've ever been on a flight which was so quiet so I decided to have a sleep before an anticipated two days on the piss. Arrival at Graz and out was pretty quick although the so called bus service into town was a minibus and was full which was solved ten minutes later by taxis for the same price as the bus. Twenty minutes later and in search of our hotel we tried to get somewhere cheaper. The hostel was full and the cheap-looking hotel we tried wanted the same money as the one we'd booked. We decided to slum it at the Hotel Weitzer at a cheap 150 euros a night, as Gareth obviously thought we were both about to win the lottery. After various discussions between Gareth and the receptionist we couldn't haggle down the price, but did find out we were in the same hotel as the press, various members of the club and some players' family. We luckily made it to the hotel in time before the heavens opened and after an hour decided to brave the lashing rain to walk about two hundred yards to a bar. We spent a couple of hours "staying dry", before venturing out into bright sunshine and having a walk around to look for decent bars in what turned out to be a beautiful city. After a quick bite of food we met up with the aforementioned Olly, Dave et al and decided to continue drinking as you do in various establishments (no Irish bars for a bleeding change) although we did seem to end up in a right dodgy old man's gay bar. As the other four decided they'd get a taxi to a bar called Venus (not sure why but I think the comment of naked ladies won it for them). Gareth and I wandered off looking for somewhere else to drink and found a nice small local bar. Unfortunately on this night it was inhabited by a pissed Austrian bloke whose grasp of the English language was slightly better than mine, as all he could mutter was 'FUCK YOU' and laughed. Charming lad, so before I got arrested for hitting him I left.

We decided to call it a night, but not before Gareth decided to buy a fucking kebab on the way back and a beer that he put in the minibar to chill. I'm assuming this was the night he sent the usual text messages complaining about my snoring. At least this time he used his own phone instead of using mine the sly get.

Match day was a late start, not out till noon, and the collection of tickets for others who hadn't received them was being organised in our hotel by the lovely Ged Poynton (or not if your names Gareth). A five minute walk into town led to whatever kind of sausage sarnie was available. Not for me, I'm on a diet and didn't eat till much later that night, plus I didn't want to fill the beer carrier up. The arrival of Dan Lloyd added another drinker to the gang, only for us to lose one as Gareth fancied getting changed and joined us again later. More bars and then over to an Irish bar to meet up with others. The singing and drinking got started proper. Banners were hung outside in the back street with the police looking on and thankfully not concerned about the red hoards massed in the street.

Song after song were sung and some of which I only know parts (in fact only about three people on the face of the Earth know the full words for), but the ever willing Luke the Songmeister sang everything. Does he have a job? He can't have as he must spend all day checking his singing talents.

Match time and why pay for the tram to the ground when you can just get on and off? Helped by a GAK fan within fifteen minutes we were at the ground. As usual with half an hour to go, chaos in the queue caused mainly by the muppets we seem to drag along who seem to think it's fun to push people around to try and get in quicker, not realising if they waited we'd all get in more quicker. They never learn. As already advised by text if Owen wasn't in the squad then he was off to sunnier climes, but wait he was on the bench albeit to not come on and nigh on confirm the rumour from the night before. Wouldn't say it was the greatest match I've seen and to be honest wasn't much better than last season, but it'll take a short while before this Rafa's team starts to come to fruition. The tie should have been over and done with for the second leg. We could and maybe should have scored more, but two cracking strikes from Gerrard ensured that the leg was won (with a third strangely disallowed).

Back into the centre on the 'free' tram and to the Irish bar for more singing and drinking until they closed at about 2am, when the fat duo decided to bugger off for some nice and healthy hot dogs, but only after the silly cow selling the food said nicht hot dogs, but then that's all she had. Learn to speak your own language, oh sorry it's German not Austrian.

Back to hotel by 3am or thereabouts to see Hoonin getting his lager, from the night before, out of the fridge the jammy fecker.

Highlights of the tour? Well copious amounts of drink, lovely sunshine which gave us some great views of some stunning women dressed in as little as possible and of course the win on the night. Graz was a lovely city which I hope to go to again, and the people were very very friendly apart from the knob in one bar.

JONATHAN HALL

CHAMPIONS LEAGUE GROUP STAGE
3RD NOVEMBER 2004
ESTADIO RIAZOR [32000]. LA CORUNA. SPAIN.
DEPORTIVO LA CORUNA 0 LIVERPOOL 1

Another day trip with Barnes Travel to Deportivo was arranged for this match in La Coruna. A victory would be a huge boost for Liverpool, but without the influential Steven Gerrard for the trip and Xabi Alonso not fit enough to start, this was going to be a huge task. Deportivo had some well-known players in their ranks and were one of Spain's top clubs at the time along with Barcelona, Real Madrid and Valencia. It was the usual arrangements for me and the lads going on this trip, they would pick us up in a taxi on the way to the airport, and the last minute checks were made to make sure we all had our passports and tickets, and a bit of money would help. So we checked in at the Airport and after getting a Burger King for breakfast, it was the usual round at the bar. I also checked the BBC website again the day before to see the weather, and to this day it said sunny and twenty degrees. I told all of the lads about the Spanish heatwave, so not one of us took a coat.

Once we arrived at the Airport, we were greeted with rain, and lots of it. So everybody turned to me, and said I thought you said it was going to be sunny? Well I'm no Michael Fish but that's what the BBC website said. Never again did I take their word for it about the weather on a European trip.

We got the usual transfer from the airport to the ground, and we said we were going to buy a jacket just to keep dry, but from the airport to the ground, the rain stopped and the weather turned and yes it was sunny. See I was right. After buying the usual stuff in their club shop, we had the full day to explore, drink and just let Deportivo know that Liverpool were in town.

We went for a walk along the waterfront, and the beach, yes there's a beach in La Coruna, even though it's in the north of Spain! Then we went for a few drinks, and set off again. Most fans stayed around the ground I think, because we didn't see too many were we were. Whilst having a few drinks, one of the lads said he'll be back in a minute, he was just going to get some fridge magnets (this is usual for a European away for him), so we stayed in this café/bar and had a few more drinks.

While we were in the café/bar one of the lads spotted a sign saying car for sale, ring this number. Well that was it, my mobile phone was out and the number was dialled. Little did we know it was the woman's phone who was working in the bar/café. She answered, and we couldn't stop laughing, we done this a few times, and she just kept on answering her phone. I honestly don't know how she never knew it was us. We were all drinking our beer while laughing and spitting it back out.

Anyway the lad who had gone for the magnets still wasn't back, so a quick phone call to him was made, but no answer. We all wanted something to eat and so we walked up to the next block, and thought he will find us in here. Food was ordered, apart from me as I wasn't hungry. I think they all got chicken in a basket. I rang the lad again, he

158

answered and said he would be back soon. After about forty minutes in this food place, I went outside, and found our mate. He was sitting in the back of a Police van, and said he got a lift back from them. Madness. He ended up in the back of a police van after asking them (police) how to get back to the harbour (where we all were), so they gave him a lift back, and that is when I/we found him (some two or three hours later I think it was). So I got him and we walked to the food place. As soon as we got in there, all the other lads were leaving, so we walked out with them, little did I know, they hadn't paid (I think they must have though, because no one came out after us, and it wasn't really busy in there!).

Anyway we were all back together, at last, when I received a phone call from one of my mates who travelled to Porto and then drove up to La Coruna. He said they were in this tapas bar by the ground, so we took a walk back up to the ground.

Once we arrived, we saw the mascot who seriously looked like Dennis the Menace in a Deportivo kit, so we all got our picture took with it/him, you have to don't ya? The bar my mate was in was right opposite the ground on the corner. It wasn't as busy as the Albert on a match day, but was a traditional Spanish tapas bar. A few more beverages were ordered, and the food was placed on the bar for us to eat. I'm not quite sure what some of the food was, but I ate some as I hadn't eaten since breakfast.

The Kick off was about an hour away now, so we decided to go into the ground and get our seats (not that you have any at a European away game). The Riazor Stadium was fairly big and has got a decent reputation in Spain, but it wasn't full. Once we got in the ground, we walked around to the Deportivo end (which was next to the Liverpool section, just too see if we could sit or stand in there) basically just to try and get a better view than what our end was offering. The stewards seemed relaxed and let us stand there. We were in the front three or four rows, and had a great view.

With standing here, I thought this could be very hostile and stupid, but it was great, it was empty by us as well. Anyway to the game and what a game Igor Biscan had in central midfield. It seems he took responsibility for Gerrard and Alonso not being there and for our goal Igor broke up the play, spread the ball wide to Riise who played in a low cross for Baros to score. Well that's at least what I thought, but in fact it was an own goal from Jorge Andrade in the 13th minute. Once Liverpool took the lead our end went wild, and us few in the Depor end went mad too, only for one of the lads to sit down and break the seat, I didn't think he was that heavy. The stewards moved in and picked up the broken seat and left us to it. About 20 minutes later I sat down, and guess what? I snapped the seat. Either these seats were made of some dodgy Spanish material or I was putting some weight on? It was definitely the first option I said!!

So with a comfortable 1-0 away win to take back to Liverpool, in Rafa Benitez's first return to Spain since joining Liverpool, qualification from this group seemed possible. There was still a long way to go though and it wouldn't be easy - is anything ever easy with Liverpool?

STE TRAYNOR

CHAMPIONS LEAGUE Last 16 2ND LEG
9TH MARCH 2005
BAY ARENA [23000]. LEVERKUSEN. GERMANY
BAYER 04 LEVERKUSEN 1 LIVERPOOL 3

"Is this anyone's ticket?" enquires the guy outside the Leverkusen Club Shop as he picks it up from the floor in front of us. We allow two seconds for the rightful owner to claim it, but as no one comes forward we claim the precious ticket as our own. Seven of us had travelled with only six of us having tickets. Now Alan, the unlucky 'odd one out' found himself the owner of one Hospitality ticket.

He decides to go into the ground there and then, before the ticket is reported as lost. We decide to leave him to it and head off to the outdoor drinking area for a few more pints and some bratwurst. There was still an hour or more before Kick Off and in European time that's three or four pints.

Anyway you're never sure if the beer inside these Stadiums is non-alcoholic so best bevy outside. Once we had had our fill we headed into the ground close to Kick Off. As we take up our seats, there, four private boxes in from the right, behind the goal is Alan, smirking and waving with beer in hand. The spawny bastard.

By half-time the Reds are two up and the night is going well for us all. We give Alan a bell to meet up after the game, but there's no answer. He's probably tucking into some half time scran with free ale.

How wrong could we be? At the final whistle we head outside the ground to be met by our mate looking somewhat flustered. It appears everything had not gone to plan. Don't get me wrong, it had all started so well. A free Hospitality ticket, which included a three-course meal with wine or beer with the permed mullet of Rudi Voller for company on the same table. In fact the view from the private box was, like the meal, excellent … for fifteen minutes that is. It was at that point that the police entered and asked Alan to step outside the box, then outside the Stadium, then into the police van. He was taken to a police station until being released 10 minutes before the end of the game and thrown onto the street not knowing where on Gods earth he was.

This was only after being fingerprinted and asked various questions on how the ticket had come to be in his possession.

A few weeks later a summons turned up at Alan's door from the German courts. No one's got a clue what it says, but we imagine it could be a fine. Obviously as yet unpaid. Alan still refuses to travel via Germany in case he gets locked up for none payment of fine.

The remainder of the evening included grabbing Ian Rush for a photo in our hotel. We had got that Steve Morgan to take the photo, which was funny as he wanted to get on the photo. This was when he was rumoured to be interested in putting money into the Club and he obviously thought he was well-known enough to spoil our Rushie photo. We were having none of it.

Bizarrely Didi Hamann's parents and sister, who were staying in the hotel and all had his name on the back of their shirts, became minor celebrities during the course of the evening as Eric asked for photos with them.

DAVE HEWITSON

In 2005, me and the Mrs ventured out to Leverkusen. It was planned months before but by February she was twelve weeks pregnant!!
We had tickets guaranteed but got let down at the last minute, gutted to say the least.
We stayed around the ground to try and get tickets but to no avail.
My old man had got in touch with his friends who were there as well, to try and help.
Tom Foley (legend) gave me a ring "Get down to gate A1, I'll sort you out" he said.
So we did, however he was already in! He passed a ticket through the fence.."I know you need two" he said, "Just do what I say. Walk to the turnstile and listen".
Although confused we complied. As we approached the turnstile with one ticket in hand, a gang of about sixteen Scousers including Tom made a commotion. At this point my pregnant wife and I made our entrance. We were In! Unbelievable. It topped our week with the result making it even better. Unforgettable.
I decided to buy my sixteen new best friends a beer in the ground, but after spending about 50 Euros it became apparent that it was alcohol free!!.... Typical!
Worth it nonetheless

JAY SHERIDAN

CHAMPIONS LEAGUE FINAL
25TH MAY 2005
ATATURK OLYMPIC STADIUM [70024]
ISTANBUL. TURKEY
A.C. MILAN 3 LIVERPOOL 3 (2-3 Pens)

It started in the Crystal Bar the night that we had lost to Monaco, Liz turned round, full of confidence and vodka, and stated that not only would we beat Olympiakos but we would win the European Cup. At the time I thought that the poor girl was in need of another trip to the Betty Ford Clinic. And then the roller coaster started up. Olympiakos went down to a beauty and Andy Gray became a Kop Icon for a milli-second. Leverkusen came and went in a daze of projectile vomiting, non-free champagne and the wonderful Ritzy bar. And then there was Juve. To no one's great surprise the press trawled through the dark side of the eighties. There was a very emotional pre-match presentation before Juve were blown away in a wall of noise to give us a narrow lead that we managed to hang onto in Italy. The Special One did not trouble us at Stamford Bridge although a snide dive by Gudjohnsen saw Alonso suspended for the second leg. With every game approaching St Etienne status some people thought that, against Abramovitch's noveau-riches, we would not surpass the legends of Olympiakos and

Juventus. Not a bit of it. We had left the Globe over an hour before kick off to get into the ground. We sang, Garcia scored and Chelski huffed and puffed. We sang louder, confidence grew, thoughts of the Bosphorous were taking hold of the imagination when Dudek flapped at a cross, Gudjohnsen controlled the ball, looked up and, as 41,000 reds collectively said,' Fuuuuuuuuuuuuucking hell', he blasted wide. We sang, partied, made plans, lied to our partners about the cost and crossed our fingers.

Fast forward three weeks and we are flying to Cologne on the Monday afternoon before Istanbul. We have a relatively quiet night in the Alt Mart, clearly saving our powder for Turkey. We arrive in Istanbul in the early evening and taken to our hotel, which is just behind the Blue Mosque, by a taxi driver who is, judging by his driving, under the influence of a powerful narcotic.

A tad shaken we arrive at our hotel. To be fair about the accommodation, both the roof and the shower were in working order, but that is all that can be said for it. We leave our bags to the tender attentions of the local insects and head off to sample the night-life of Sukhtamet.

Within minutes we have met up with both the Globe and Holt crews, all of whom are going out of their way to quadruple the profits of the Efes Brewery. Sitting resplendent at the head of the table is the legendary Bobby Wilcox who is giving out stick and tickets with equal abandon, surrounding the table are various bar-owners who are hustling for our custom. Dennis takes over, haggling with them for the most favourable price for our shipping order sized round. A deal is struck and we repair to what is to become known as Jimmy's Bar, where the barman splendidly attired in a Milan Baros shirt, is climbing out of a second storey window to string the 'Globe Ratpack' banner across the street. The night becomes a blur, ale is supped, songs sung, people who should know better whirl like dervishes, and a damn good time is had by all.

Match day morning, and while the Muezzin is calling the faithful to prayer we awaken bleary eyed and parched of throat. We breakfast on Metzes with Turkish coffee, and return to Jimmy's Bar. Everyone is in high spirits but as the afternoon progresses we are becoming more and more conscious of the fact that soon we will be watching the biggest game in the club's history for the last 20 years. We are getting reports that the facilities around the stadium are non-existent so the nearest off-licence is visited and armed with a couple of dozen Party Seven sized cans of Efes we charter several taxis and it's off to the match we go.

We are out of the city in relatively short time but soon we are going at a crawl, Going over the crest of a hill we look down on the road ahead, it is yellow with taxis as far as the eye can see, for a surreal moment I think that we are off to see the wizard, but then from over the next hill we see the ground in the distance. My first impression is of how grey everything is, the stadium, the sky, the gravel, everything is grey. We abandon the taxi and yomp over the surrounding fields. We make base camp at the back of the stage and begin to work our way through the Efes. Let's face it there is nothing else to do except drink the beer and listen to the music which is excellent. The facilities here are non-existent, a couple of portaloos and that is it, no food, drink, souvenirs or pro-

162

grammes. Just a grey stadium, in the middle of grey volcanic nothingness, thank you Sepp Blatter. Yet, like an enormous Jackson Pollard painting, all this grey monotone is broken by vast splashes of red, red shirts gyrating madly in front of the stage, hundreds of red banners coming over the hill behind us, like something out of Mao's Long March, and a red sun slowly sinking in the west. All around are people you haven't seen for ages, Peter Crilly, Wayne Morris, Kevin O'Rourke, Fred Sephton and Kevin Crowley. These are Reds that you may not have seen for a long, long, time but you knew that tonight, of all nights, they would be there.

We finally get into the ground. There is nowhere to hang the flag so we give it to the stewards to place on the red running track. Out on the pitch there is all manner of pre-match 'entertainment' going on but everyone around me seems to be solely focused on making as much noise as possible, because we know that tonight is going to be our night. That implacable belief receives an enormous dent after only fifty-two seconds, when Maldini's cross shot bounces over Dudek's outstretched hand. There is a milli-second of silence from the 50,000 odd Reds in the ground, followed by a blast of support. There are eighty nine minutes left, plenty of time to pull two goals back. We push forward, Riise has a shot blocked and Hyppia could have done better with a header. We are pushing forward again, Garcia breaks into the box, the ball hits a Milanese defender's arm and, with the appeals for a blatant penalty ringing from three quarters of the ground, Crespo breaks to score a second. Hell may have no fury like a woman scorned, but the seventh circle of the pit knows no anger like a Scouser denied a penalty. Around me tumult abounds. The police and the stewards look more than a tad uneasy, and, as we are coming to terms with this latest injustice, Crespo is played in behind Carra to score a sublime third.

Winny is sitting next to me. His eyes are beginning to water. I feel physically sick. We hardly notice the half time whistle has blown. I wander off in a daze. Around me there are all kinds of kick offs breaking out. Some people are walking out into the black, velvet night. I sit on the steps, head in hands, cigarette in mouth, and look around me. Those that are not fighting, arguing or walking out are looking around with the same dumbstruck expressions. Then from the terracing to my right I hear the strains of 'You'll Never Walk Alone' .

I joined in, Stevie Quinn next to me joined in. Everyone in the ground joined in. They seemed to be of the same collective thought,

"Sod this, we've come thousands of miles, spent hundreds of pounds, ok we're getting hammered three nil, let's get behind the team, let's show the watching world what supporting a football team is all about."

The song echoed around the ground. Judging by the number of camera flashes coming from the Milan end they were impressed, perhaps it was the knowledge that they were in the presence of their betters.

The teams came out. Everyone was relieved that Hamann was on as sub. Could he make a difference? At first it appeared not. Schevchenko nearly made it four from a free-kick that Dudek saw late. It looked like things were going to get worse, a lot worse,

And then .....

There are a lot of things in this world that I do not understand. Why, for instance, do people think Gareth Gates is talented, or why do ITV consider that Andy Townsend knows something about football ? What I do not understand, even now, is what happened during what the Italian media termed 'Six minutes of madness.'

From 3-0 down to level terms in six minutes. No wonder the Rossoneri sat shell-shocked behind the goal, they had seen the most odds-on favourites to win brought down to earth with a resounding bump. At our end of the ground Stevie Quinn and I dance improbable jigs of joy. We were back in it, there was no way we could lose, was there ?

The rest of the game went past me in a blur. All that I can recall is that extra time was a flurry of red shirted bodies blocking every shot and cross from a Milan player. Then came that awful slow motion moment when Shevchenko rose and headed for goal, Dudek parried, and 50,000 reds watched in horror as the ball fell to the best striker in the world, unmarked and six yards from goal. The entire world knows what happened next, Dudek threw up a despairing, flailing arm, and in a moment that is indelibly etched on our memory, the ball flew over the bar. It was at that moment that we knew that the European Cup was won.

To me the penalty shoot-out was never in doubt. The Milan players looked drained, their fans were silent, we were obnoxiously loud, we knew the cup would be ours. When Dudek saved the penalty, Stevie Quinn threw himself down the terracing, I was screaming incoherently as I strangled the lad next to me. The cup was presented, the players danced and capered, we sang ourselves silly and then it was back into town.

It was the bus journey from hell. An hour and a half of monotony. God knows what would have happened if we had lost. Finally we landed in Taksim Square, I jumped a taxi, (No not literally, I leave that kind of thing to Duncan McKenzie) and was soon at Jimmy's Bar, and that was where the party started. All our crew were there, Bobby, Mary and Sheila Wilcox, Lenny Woods, Azzie, Alan Taylor and Colin, Marty Parry, Dennis and Cabaret, Ged, Winny and Jimmy, Peter and Neil Hughes, Tony Tavs, Frank and Mono, Kieran, Peter and Steve, and last but not least Philly Hawksworth in his jarg shirt. There were big, mad smiles, a few tears of joy,and renditions of every song in the book. My abidng memory is of Woodsy, drawing deeply on his Embassy No.1, and repeating the word 'glorious' at fifteen second intervals The bar's night staff went home suitably shattered, and were replaced by the day staff. Me and Dennis still had time to write down another verse to the 'Sloop John B' song.

It was at this point, with the sun coming up and the ale going down, that I realised that my flight was in three and a bit hours time. I got back to the hotel, showered, woke Liz and found yet another narcotically influenced taxi driver to take us to the International Airport. We were lucky there was none of the chaos here that was going on at the other airport down the road.

We flew to Cologne, I slept the entire way. We flew to Speke, I slept the whole way. The newsagent at Speke did a roaring trade, as we snaffled every paper going, then we

164

headed into town.

The Globe was rocking, Liz and I were the first two back and we were greeted as if we had brought the cup home ourselves. Cains Bitter had never tasted so good. Liz and a few others tried to get to St Georges Hall but it was too chocker so they came back and we watched the homecoming on the telly. Beer flowed, they ran out of glasses. Lindy-Lou behind the bar managed, between serving several thousand customers, to play 'You'll Never Walk Alone', 'Sloop John B' and 'We Are The Champions' times too numerous to mention. People just stood there smiling, big, red, mad smiles. It doesn't get any better.

DAVE HARDMAN

We've been to loads of European aways and we were a bit pissed off to have missed Rafa in the pub at Leverkusen by just a few minutes in 2005. However we made up for it when about twenty minutes after buying a new camera in Istanbul we met the team! On the morning of the game we had been arguing with the hotel staff about the advertised pool not being available and we wanted to know why! The girl wouldn't tell us so we headed off to the bar and set about setting up the camera we'd just bought. As we were sorting the camera I looked out of the window straight into the face of John Arne Riise. It was about half one in the afternoon and I suddenly realised that the whole team and staff were in our hotel! That was the reason why we couldn't use the pool. We had a good chat with them all and shook hands with Jerzy and Smicer. I had a cuddle from Rafa and my photo taken with him while my husband had his photo taken with Jerzy. I remember telling Rafa to win it for us and he smiled and said they'd try!! There was a lad and his old fella there as well but apart from that no one but us. I have the photo of me and Rafa in a big frame at home! I have met the team at other times before and since but that one is obviously the most special.

SARA LAST

Well was Istanbul the best ever?

Of the five, I mean. The only other contender shares the same magical date.

May 25th. Rome 1977 was special. Well they say you never forget your first time.

After Monday night in Cologne, a lot of Reds were gathered on Tuesday morning for the Turkish Airlines flight to Istanbul Ataturk Airport. The first real tingle set in when we saw 'Istanbul' on the Departures board.

A taxi to Taksim Square gave us some idea of how visually stunning Istanbul is. Our first sight of Taksim Square was equally stunning, a mass of Reds, flags waving, lit flares, Reds up trees, Reds on rooftops and every building draped with red flags. The sound of 'Rafa Rafa Benitez, Xabi Alonso, Garcia and Nunez' filled the balmy air, driven by the insistent beat of a rooftop drum.

Wednesday afternoon in a bar, one Red made the 'Comment of the trip' when he tripped on a wrinkled-up rug trying to reach a window seat. "F...in' carpets here are shite!" Outside, Batman and Robin were entertaining the crowd, Robin sporting his 'Gotham City Reds' suit. Later I saw Batman being sick all over the toilet floor, something you don't see everyday.

At about 6pm we got a taxi to the ground. As it hurtled west out of town, another taxi full of Reds swerved wildly past then right in front of us, yelling 'Ring of Fire' as we entered a tunnel. We returned the call.

After about half an hour, we hit the traffic. Miles of it. Bus after coach after taxi full of Reds. Down in the valley below, we could see the brilliantly illuminated Ataturk Stadium. It looked like they were holding the European Cup Final on the moon.

We finally got into the stadium at 9pm. If there'd been a bar (or anything) outside, or any way of getting back into town, it might have been half-empty for the second half. Kind of glad we stayed. We had our precious Number 5. Magically, it also stirred the other four back into life, they'd become a bit cut off in history. Now they were all current again.

Back in town, each returning Red was greeted with hugs, like returning warriors. The narrow cobbled side streets were full of song, flags and thick with the smoke of coloured flares burning brightly in the night sky. Unforgettable, even for us veterans.

The sons and daughters of those I started going to the match with all those years ago now had their own dreams and songs to sing.

CHRIS ROWLAND

My Istanbul Story or Why Do Musicians Have To Act Like Knobheads When You Take Them Abroad

Everybody has an Istanbul story, but please indulge me for a few minutes. Hopefully mine is sufficiently different to merit a few minutes of your time. And I'm not going to talk about the match itself because: A) you already know all about that and B) because, for reasons that will become clear later my memory of the game is something of a blur (and this has nothing to do with alcohol for a change).

So, like everyone else, immediately after the Chelsea semi-final my thoughts turned to Istanbul. As usual there were the smart arses who had just assumed we were going to win and booked stupidly cheap flights before the semi's. Then there were the boring bastards who didn't celebrate the Chelsea win but legged it straight home to jump on the internet and book the last of the cheap flights and then smugly told us all about it the next day while we were struggling with Champions League sized hangovers.

As usual I was in the dilly dallying, shilly shallying camp being swayed by people who came up with the stupidest possible routes to Turkey. ('Yeah, it'll take us three days to get there but it's dead cheap and it'll be a boss laugh, la'). Even my normally sensible mate Phil suggested going on holiday to Greece for a week with a sojourn to Istanbul in the middle. I knew I had no chance of getting that past my Missus so I had to gently break the bad news to Phil that although this sounded great in theory sadly it was a

166

non – starter for me.

So there I was wrestling with increasingly complex or expensive ways to actually get to the final when I was saved by an old friend. Someone I knew worked for the Premier League, was a Liverpool fan, and had good links to the club. Liverpool were looking for someone to manage a stage for them in the Fans Arena by the stadium. The club obviously had far more important things to do and just wanted to hand it over to someone who wasn't going to give them any trouble while sorting it all out. Apparently I fitted the bill perfectly because I appeared to be a sensible human being, while also having something of a history in the music industry. You may find this hard to believe but that's actually a pretty rare combination.

So calls were made in which I did my best to confirm that I was sensible and convince the nice man at LFC (hi Jonathan) that I had some idea of what I was talking about. He fell for it and I was in.

Happy days you may well think. Well I certainly did – but how wrong was I? On the plus side I was guaranteed a flight and a ticket. So obviously that was brilliant. But the downside was that I had to actually decide which musicians to take and then ensure that they all returned from the trip safely without causing any major international incidents.

So who to take? The club had given me ten flights and match tickets which sounds like a lot. But the reality was that we were meant to provide entertainment for a few hours in the Fans Arena so what was needed was a line- up that was as flexible as Rafa's team selections.

With that in mind and with every space absolutely vital I obviously chose my mate Phil first. I went the match with him and he was my mate so it seemed like an obvious choice. He wasn't a musician who could actually contribute to the festivities but to my mind this minor weakness was balanced by the fact that he ran a venue, understood musicians, and well, he was my mate so he had to come didn't he?

Next up we needed a proper grown up. I know I had managed to deceive that nice man Jonathan at LFC but honestly I had no clue as to what I was doing. In theory Phil could be the nominated 'adult' but I knew that in practice he was likely to be even more unreliable than me. So we called up our mate Kenna. Now Kenna is something of a legend in Liverpool. He has been working with bands since as a young lad he helped out The La's. He then went on to provide tech support or tour manage a number of bands including local lads like Cast and The Coral.

So three places down and still no musicians. But at least we now had someone who knew what he was doing. I felt like I was making progress.

The first real musician I asked was Pete Wylie. Why him? First off he was an old friend. Secondly he'd based himself in my office for the previous six months so I saw him nearly every day and couldn't avoid him. And finally he was one of my all-time favourite musicians with a real passion for the football club and the city.

I love Pete but he is typical of many musicians in that he can be incredibly difficult to deal with. So even though we'd been mates for years and I knew he wanted to do it, actually getting him there involved several days of extensive negotiations. While this was going on I talked to other bands. A couple of the Zutons were going to do it but then suddenly they weren't. Tommy Scott (singer from Space) would have loved to have come but at that time didn't want to do any of the old Space songs. There was one musician I was really keen to bring but everybody around me warned me off saying it would only bring trouble and pain.

All the while I was in regular touch with the nice man at LFC reassuring him that everything was under control and throwing random names into the hat with a confident " yeah, I'm just waiting for them to commit inside the next few days".

Being Liverpool word quickly got out that I had access to tickets and I was being pestered by every musician/LFC fan around who all assured me they would be perfect for the stage in Istanbul.

The lovely Danny Hunt from Ladytron was one of those who offered his services. I'd known Danny for years, he was something of a 'name', and an all-round good lad to boot. So that was it. Danny was in. At last I had a genuine musician signed up.

Four places gone and now finally we had a musician. Things were looking up. Obviously Danny wasn't going to bring all of Ladytron with him. But he was an actual musician – well he stands there on stage looking cool and pressing a few buttons when Ladytron are playing. I'm actually not sure any of them actually really 'play' anything. But in Istanbul he was going to be our DJ so whether or not he actually had any musical skills was irrelevant. He was our mate and he was coming with us to Istanbul.

Gary Bandit of the recently defunct Bandits and just general man about town had been in touch. He'd already sorted out his tickets and travel but wanted me to take John Bandit so they could play a short set there. The fact that The Bandits were no more didn't seem to bother either of them. John was another good lad and to this day I still regret that I didn't make space for him. Rafa apparently caved into pressure and had the useless Josemi on the bench that night rather than the far more deserving Warnock and I think John Bandit was my Warnock/Josemi moment.

John Power once of The La's and then leader of the hugely successful Cast was another one who was going under his own steam. At this time Cast were no more and John was pursuing a solo career and playing live with Jay Ireland. Jay was someone I knew to be sound and it was agreed that he would come as one of the lucky ten and that John would meet us at the Fans Arena where upon he and Jay would do their stuff.

I really should have known that this was complete bollocks.. It was well intentioned but bollocks all the same. In the resulting chaos I'm about to describe I may fail to mention this particular episode so for the sake of completeness let me tell you how this panned out now.

Jay was a brilliant traveller and the least troublesome of our group. For a kick-off he wasn't a vegetarian. You'd be surprised how whiny vegetarians can get even when you have sorted them a flight and ticket for Liverpool's biggest game in years. But I digress. Jay made it with us to the Fans Arena and was ready and willing to play. John Power also turned up at one point. He was very 'happy' having spent some time with his Dad in the bars around Taskam Square. He was so overcome with happiness that he could barely stand let alone sing. Singing and playing bass at the same time as standing was definitely something that he was far too happy to do at the point we met him. But God love him for at least making the effort to turn up.

Now back to the real story. Somehow I also ended up taking Ian Prowse on the plane. To this day I'm still not sure how this happened. I like Ian and he has written some nice tunes but I'm not a massive fan. And he supports Tranmere. But there seems to be some sort of rule that says Ian has to play at everything. I'm not sure how this rule came about but on this occasion I just went along with it. So by my reckoning that was six of us. Although if you have been paying attention at this point only Ian Prowse could actually get up on stage and play some songs like.

At this point I caved in and gave Wylie everything he wanted. He was coming along with a keyboard player, a drummer, and a bass player Marin Campbell who I'd known for years and was best known for stints with the Lightning Seeds and Richard Ashcroft. Wylie and his ego only counted as one person. So that was that. We were the ten.

Did I get any thanks for taking people? Not really. Although to be fair the likes of Jay and Danny can be excluded from this moan. Did I get hassle from the people I had been kind enough to pick to escort me on this trip of a lifetime? To fucking right I did. To be honest by the day of the final I'd had enough and I'd have been happy to leave them to it and not go at all. Although I had a sneaking suspicion that even if I'd tried to duck out of it the musicians would have come to my house and forced me on to the plane so just so they could inflict more misery on me.

After sorting out the final ten I'd spent much of the few weeks left before the final dealing with the knobhead musicians I'd stupidly chosen as well as LFC, and the Turkish people who were running the Fans Arena. The musicians kept wanting more things. The Turks went out of their way to be helpful while LFC stood their ground and refused to cough up a penny more for any additional gear that might be needed. I couldn't escape from it. I was either on the phone dealing with LFC or talking to the Turks or increasingly dealing with members of our ten strong party who just kept turning up in my office slowly doing my head in.

Finally the fateful day arrived and it was like a well-oiled machine clicking into gear. Of course that is complete and utter bollocks. It started to fall apart before we reached the airport. The plan was that I was to get a taxi from Walton, pick up Ian Prowse by the Tunnel on Dale Street, then pick up Danny from Duke Street and then get Phil in Wavertree on the way to Speke. Of course it was me who was paying for the taxi, obviously. The first couple of steps were fine. I got the taxi from my house, picked up Prowse and then went on to pick up Phil at his. Luckily Phil was more on his game than I was and his first words as he got in the cab were "Where's soft lad?"

I'd only forgotten to pick up our DJ hadn't I! What an idiot. Disaster averted, we had to turn round, go back into town, pick up Danny who was oblivious to my error and then hotfoot it back to Speke along with every other Liverpool fan in the city.

The airport was chaos and the next challenge was getting my unruly group and their assorted musical equipment on to the plane. The crew wanted us to stick the guitars and keyboards in the luggage hold whereas my boys wanted to keep their precious guitars etc close to them in the overhead lockers. A quick call to that nice Jonathan from LFC led to him jumping off the plane so he could negotiate on our behalf with the airline. I think by this point Jonathan was beginning to get wind of the fact that he may have been wrong to trust me to pull this thing off! Anyway due his intervention we got to bring our stuff onto the plane with us. Musicians one – Airline nil.

At this time you could bring liquids including alcohol through customs and on to the plane. Prowse's mum and dad had just come back from Greece and the Metaxa brandy they had brought him was open and finished off with in about ten minutes of the plane leaving the ground.

The nice stewardess on hearing that she had a bunch of musicians on board asked if we'd like to lead a cheery singalong. Never one to be backward in coming forward Phil rose to the challenge and some had everyone joining in with 'You'll Never Walk Alone' and 'Team of Carraghers'. Interestingly Phil had printed out some songsheets for such an eventuality before we'd left but for some reason thought he needed to write down every work of the Carragher song, which I thought was a little over the top given its lyrical simplicity.

I've just realised that this story is getting to be as long as the flight so I'll speed up now if that's OK?

We finally arrived in Turkey. By this point I already felt like I'd done a days work but next was the first real hitch I'd had to face. The club had assured us that there would be buses going from the airport to the stadium all day so that when we arrived we could just jump on one of these free buses so we could get there in plenty of time to do soundchecks and all that boring stuff.

Obviously they lied to us. At this early stage of the day no other bugger wanted to go out into the wilds to the stadium. They wanted to do what any right thinking football fan would and go to Taksim Square and drink far too much too quickly. Unsurprisingly Phil and Danny wanted to go on a research trip into the city centre along with every-one else. But in a rare spate of common sense I forbade this splitting up of the group. Prior experience told me that if I let Phil and Danny enter an area with bars full of beer then I would probably never see either of them again until maybe in the airport for the return journey. And more importantly I didn't want to be left to deal with a bunch of knobhead musicians on my own in a strange country for the best part of a day. Also I couldn't afford to let Danny, our DJ, out of my sight, because we were really going to need him if everything else went west.

Taxi Drivers

This bit deserves a separate heading because it was a saga in itself. Having worked out that no buses were going to the stadium I now had to convince the doubting musicians that I could handle this mini crisis.

My brainwave was to get taxis. See, problem solved. But nah, it was never going to be that easy. The problem was that there were ten of us plus assorted musical instruments.

We were in a strange country and none of us had a fucking clue about anything really. And to top it off me and Phil seemed to be the only ones with any money. Let me just be clear about this. There were ten adults here. It had been explained very clearly to them that LFC were not providing any sort of expenses. However, despite this very clear message most of them had thought it would be ok to go on a journey across the continent with no more than three quid in their pocket in case they needed to get a bus home.

Negotiating with this bunch of taxi drivers was almost as bad as working with the bloody musicians. I seem to recall that they started off by asking for around the equivalent of about one thousand pounds per head but after several hours of heated discussions settled on an eye wateringly extortionate but just about affordable fee to transport us to the stadium. After the three drivers had finished laughing between themselves at how much they had extracted from us they set out on the journey to the stadium. To be honest I'm still staggered that I survived this trip. I have no idea if everyone drives like this in Turkey or if we got three mad men who posed as taxi drivers for the day just to take our money and scare us to death. We bobbed and weaved across lanes of traffic at incredible speeds and I just gave in and assumed death was just moments away. It was one of those moments when you remember your catholic upbringing and I'm not ashamed to admit it but I prayed. 'Oh dear God, I've generally been a good person and I don't deserve to die with a bunch of knobhead musicians. And if you let me live I will be a much better person' was the gist of it.

Anyway I survived so thank you God. And I really am trying to keep up my end of the deal, honest.

The last bit of the journey was surreal as we went down the dirt track (or 'road' as UEFA called it) towards the Stadium. Suddenly we were in the middle of a bunch of hills. Look there's some sheep. (I still think the plural of 'sheep' should be 'sheeps' but that's for another time). Look there's some military looking men with machine guns next to those sheep. Look there's a bloody great big stadium in the middle of nowhere. Oh aren't those nice men at UEFA so clever choosing this lovely place for a final.

Me and Phil paid off the taxi drivers who no doubt immediately went and bought sizeable mansions or at very least treated themselves to exotic holidays with their ill-gotten gains. I was just thankful to be alive and out of their cars.

If it had all ended there I'd have been happy to tell you the truth. We'd had a bit of an adventure and we'd all survived. That wouldn't have been so bad would it? But we had to go and do the bloody gig didn't we. I know that was the reason we were there but it didn't half cause a lot of trouble.

You all know the scenes there. There were thousand of us in this scruffy bit of countryside with no ale (unless you'd brought it in a bus or taxi yourself) and nothing else really apart from this stage made from bits of wood and sticky backed plaster. The musicians obviously started moaning as soon as we got there. They wanted food and they wanted beer. My good Turkish friend who I'd been talking to for the previous month about the arrangements provided both but not in sufficiently large amounts for the musicians and obviously not to the satisfaction of the bloody vegetarian. I'd thought ahead (as befitting my status as the Leader of this motley crew) and brought a bottle of whisky with me, which I generously shared with 'The Knobheads.'

We all saw mates in the crowd and people came over to us and suddenly with the amazing atmosphere building and the musicians not moaning for a few minutes it all seemed worthwhile.

Phil liked getting on the mic so he made the first announcements and then young Danny was on stage in his role as our official DJ. He played a few well received tunes and I particularly remember a rapturously well received 'Teenage Kicks', favourite of the late, great Liverpool fan John Peel.In a stroke of genius he then played the Kop favourite 'Ring of Fire'. The whole place went bonkers and Danny realising he was on to a good thing and sacrificing his art for the greater good, basically just kept on playing the same tune for most of the time he was on. And believe me it worked.

Chaos was all around. The Coral who were doing a corporate gig nearby sent someone over to borrow a guitar. Some fella with a CD said he sang at all the clubs in Liverpool and wanted to get up and do a turn. People turned up asking us to announce they needed a ticket or had spares. Someone came up who had burnt their trouser leg off when accidentally setting off a flare. Luckily he was fine but he was so drunk I don't think he would have known if he wasn't. And somehow in the midst of this madness we managed to put a show on as well.

Prowse had the unenviable task of coming on first and I think he did ok. It's hard being one man with an acoustic guitar in front of 30,000 mad Liverpool fans who just want to sing and dance. I think he did a Clash song and a few of his own and then he was gone. The crowd was getting bigger and more excitable as more arrived from the bars of Taksim Square. And up stepped Wylie who was simply magnificent. He loves the big occasion and like a striker at the top of his game he responded to the challenge of entertaining an increasingly rowdy but good humoured mob. Wylie, with his great band, pulled out all the stops, including a version of the Ramones 'Blitzkreig Bop' changed to 'Blitkrieg Kop'. The place went absolutely mental and lots of our friends and thousands of people we didn't know suddenly they decided they wanted to join us on stage.

The Turkish stage manager understandably got a little upset and began yelling down the mic "THERE WILL BE A CATASTROPHE. PLEASE GET OFF THE STAGE. THERE WILL BE A CATASTROPHE".

At this point a very emotional John Power staggered to the stage to do his turn but by that point there was no way we were going to be allowed to go back on. So that was it. It was all over. We managed to get everyone off stage but there was to be no more. Still it had been a brilliant experience and one that everyone who witnessed it will remember forever.

At this point things got worse for me. I was on a real high and relieved that somehow we'd got through it. And, with my work done I stupidly went wandering with Gary Bandit who introduced me to that Colin Murray chap from the tele and radio. Then we wandered some more. Then I fell over and blacked out. And for me that was it. Game

172

over.

I still don't really know what happened. I suspect that Gary is partly to blame (he normally is) along with the rocky terrain around the stadium. I'd barely had anything to drink as I'd shared what I had brought and let the musicians have the beer provided by the Turkish organisers.

Anyway I woke up at some point. It was dark, I was cold and groggy and had no idea what was going on. I had big cuts and bruises on my face and to this day my Istanbul scar on my nose still appears every year on the 25th May. The lovely first aid people patched me up and when they thought I was ok they let me into the stadium. But that epic match was wasted on me I'm sad to say. I can truthfully say I was there but none of it made much sense. It really was a blur.

I somehow got myself back to the airport where the medical team patched me up some more and my beautifully battered face was there to greet my travelling companions and many other friends as they arrived for their flights back to Liverpool.

So that's my story and I'm sticking to it. I was there but that epic match passed me by. I swore I'd never do anything like that ever again. Even without the blackout all the hassle of dealing with the musicians took the pleasure out of it. It was like work but without the pay.

But move forward two years and we'd just beaten Chelsea on penalties in the semi final. Within half an hour of the match finishing I'd had a text from Danny Hunt. 'We on for Athens Kev?'

Of course I should have said no but like a proper knobhead I ended up doing it all again. Well I couldn't let the musicians go there on their own could I? They'd never have survived without me.

KEVIN McMANUS

2005/06 CHAMPIONS LEAGUE

13 July 2005 First qualifying round
Liverpool FC   3-0   The New Saints FC

19 July 2005 First qualifying round
The New Saints FC   0-3   Liverpool FC
Aggregate: 0-6

26 July 2005 Second qualifying round
FBK Kaunas   1-3   Liverpool FC

2 August 2005 Second qualifying round
Liverpool FC   2-0   FBK Kaunas
Aggregate 5-1

13 September 2005 Group stage (Group G)
Real Betis Balompié   1-2   Liverpool FC

28 September 2005 Group stage (Group G)
Liverpool FC   0-0   Chelsea FC

19 October 2005 Group stage (Group G)
RSC Anderlecht   0-1   Liverpool FC

1 November 2005 Group stage (Group G)
Liverpool FC   3-0   RSC Anderlecht

23 November 2005 Group stage (Group G)
Liverpool FC   0-0   Real Betis Balompié

6 December 2005 Group stage (Group G)
Chelsea FC   0-0   Liverpool FC

21 February 2006 Round of 16
SL Benfica   1-0   Liverpool FC

8 March 2006 Round of 16
Liverpool FC   0-2   SL Benfica
Aggregate: 0-3

CHAMPIONS LEAGUE 2ND QUALIFYING ROUND 1ST LEG
26TH JULY 2005
S. DARIUS AND S. GIRENAS STADIUM [8300]
KAUNUS. LITHUANIA
F.C. KAUNAS 1 LIVERPOOL 3

After the glory that was Istanbul, TNS didn't have the same ring to it so when we drew Kaunas I reckoned that the plastic might just stretch to get me there, wherever the hell Kaunas was.

At first everybody in the Globe was quite enthusiastic about the idea, but one-by-one, including one of the editors of this book, Mr Hardman, they dropped out. In the end there were four of us, but Bobby Wilcox dropped out at the last minute saying that he would just do the day trip.

So there we were, me, Tony Tabs and Fraudulent Frank. The first two thirds of the journey were easy, well Easyjet anyway. Liverpool to Berlin, then Berlin to Riga. The final third of the journey proved problematic as what the Latvians termed motorways, we termed dirt-tracks. There was something disconcerting about driving through the mountains along a rubble strewn road with a stomach churning drop on one side.

We finally got to Kaunas to discover that we had been booked into the Hotel Romantic, which it definitely wasn't. If it had been called the Hotel Cheap and Cheerful it would be more appropriate. We had arrived very, very late and there was nowhere open so we emptied the mini-bar, and were presented with an extortionate bill between the three of us of just under £5!

I don't remember that much about the game except Bobby getting on the TV singing the Peter Crouch song, and Jamie Carragher scoring.

Coming back was a wee bit disconcerting, as Latvian road signs leave something to be desired, and it took a lot of hand signs and talking rubbish to find our way back to the airport.

All in all a normal week of watching Liverpool.

LIZ WATTS

CHAMPIONS LEAGUE GROUP STAGE
13TH SEPTEMBER 2005
MANUEL RUIZ DE LOPERA [45000]. SEVILLE. SPAIN
REAL BETIS 1 LIVERPOOL 2

Bear with me. This little yarn will take us to Seville, all in good time, but first I must drag you back to Istanbul, a few months previously. I know. Rubbish, eh?

Everyone has their own epic tale of magical times in Constantinople. Ours involved a journey so convoluted that we didn't get back until the wee small hours of the following Saturday. We flew Manchester to Gatwick; Gatwick to Varna; drove overnight from

Varna to Sofia, then flew from Sofia to Istanbul. The return journey would have been hell if we'd lost. Anyone who's braved the pot-holes and hairpins of Bulgaria's mountain passes will understand how unforgiving those roads are. Even after the miracle of 'Number Five', we were feeling it in every bone by the time we got home.

We'd missed the homecoming, of course, so on the Sunday there was a low-key 'Second Coming' down at The Pump House. A few dozen hardy souls laid their flags out, enjoyed a pint or two in the sunshine and that was that. I came home and near-electrocuted myself with a hedge-trimmer. A bit of the plastic casing on the cable had eroded, exposing a live wire. I gripped it, and became part of the electric circuit. Those everyday hedge-trimmers are not sharp, as such, but their 'teeth' move at a frightening speed. It was like the machine had turned into a little velociraptor, snapping away at me. My right hand was melted to the live wire. I couldn't control my own movements. Until I passed out, my main aim was to keep my head back and keep my jugular away from the chopping teeth. My last conscious thought was,

"Ah well. Istanbul."

When I came round they'd pinned my shredded shoulder and strapped me up. I was on ultra-powerful, codeine-based painkillers. For months, I couldn't do a thing. Physically, I had to wait for the various bone grafts to knit. Mentally, my sleep pattern was all over the place. The month-long argument as to whether Liverpool or Everton would be England's fourth representative in the 2005-06 Champions League passed me by. History has it that both, eventually, qualified though I don't recall Everton taking part. I can barely remember the TNS games. I was disappointed to miss out on Kaunas, as it's the kind of 'proper' Euro destination you long for and if I'm honest about it, I was half-relieved that, physically, I wasn't up to going to CSKA Sofia. Having been there only weeks before, it might have felt like a 'wasted' trip. This is how blasé we get, as Liverpool fans. A few consecutive years back at the top table and we're going: "PSV? Kinell! Not again. Can't we go somewhere new?" Sitting here writing this, with the Champions League glittering like some elusive mirage that might possibly have been real, once, but probably didn't exist at all, I would absolutely fucking love to be pushed about by the Eindhoven police once more, and spend 90 minutes penned into that shitty little end after a functional 0-0 draw. But back then it was:

"Sofia. Thank fuck I've got an excuse…"

By the time the group stages had been drawn, I was well into the physio stage, gradually getting my fingers to wiggle again. I was also gagging for Euro action. We'd got Anderlecht, Chelsea and Real Betis in our group, with Betis first up. Again, it seems crazy to think back to how we considered Betis (who had spent heavily in qualifying for the CL) more of a threat than Chelsea. Anyway, with partial use of my right arm restored, nothing was going to stop me travelling to Seville for the game.

The motley crew that met at Speke Airport (or was it JLA by then?) consisted of Giles, Danny 'King of the Swallee', Parsons, Brian Parso aka "The Truth." Buckley, David Bucko and Jegsy Dodd, who, being christened Jegsy, needs no playful handle. As the firm's token invalid, I'd been saddled with all the booking arrangements and Danny gave it a full five minutes before telling us that our compadre Sconch had booked the same Malaga hotel as us for 11 Euro less. I wouldn't say it drives me potty that, but when you've done all the work, loaded the cost onto your own credit card and had to do the chasing-up to get each intrepid voyager to cough up, it can be mildly irritating that instead of thanks and free drinks, what you mainly get is the insinuation that you've diddled the lads out 11 Euros.

It was a nice, low-key flight to Malaga, followed by a brief but very serious discussion about driving 40 km down the coast to join up with a rum bunch of scallywags in Fuengirola. Smigger from Kirkby was on the phone and, unless he had his "Now That's What I Call Boss Pub Atmospheres" CD turned up to 21 in the background, it sounded like they were having high times in Outer Marbella. But it was midnight, the game was the next day and there was the small matter of a lengthy drive to Sevilla to factor in. For once, common sense won the day. Us crazy amigos bought every last mini-tub of Pringles from the hotel reception and toddled off to bed.

It took a while finding the right road out of Malaga. I'd taken a glance on Goggle Maps and it looked straightforward enough. Head for Antequerra, turn left for Osuna and follow your nose to Seville. That's where the problem lay, Bucko's insistence that Osuna was where Sammy Lee had once plied his trade. We knew he'd played for Osasuna, and myself and Parso were sure, but not that sure, that Osasuna were based in Pamplona. Pamplona is, in Spanish terms, 'Up North'. We wanted to head due South-West. We didn't have a roadmap. Debating whether Osuna and Osasuna were one and the same, we drove around in circles for over an hour, but it was all very pretty.

Got to Seville. Found hotel with miraculous ease and we're all made up to find it had a pool (and bar service) on the roof. It being match day though, we thought we'd save that treat for tomorrow. There was a vague agreement that we'd head for a bar called The Bodega Santa Cruz, right in the heart of the old town. The sun was at skull-splitting intensity, making regular stop-offs for shade and cold-cold Cerveza an absolute necessity. If Estrella Dam ever decided to make a TV advert, they could do worse than film our thirsty pilgrimage under a scintillating sun. The perspiration was running freely down necks, arms, legs, finding its way into little crevices behind the knees, creating mini-lagoons of sweat in our elbow creases. Our tongues were literally stuck to the roofs of our mouths. We would have handed over small fortunes for one cold bottle of beer.

And then, the mirage. A little bar called Sa Placa, sheltered under a massive old palm tree, cradled in the corner of a…well it wasn't a square, to be honest. More of a triangle. Let's call it a plaza. It was very old and oozing with charm anyway, and in we went. By God, a drink has never tasted so good. I tilted my head back and walloped the first bottle in one ravenous swig. We ordered another, then another. The phones were going, different carloads and gangs of mates starting to arrive and assemble in the Old Town, but we were fine. We were on 'manana time' and everything but everything could bide its time.

The splendidly fat owner/waiter/barman (who, to our extreme surprise, was called Juan) brought over another tray of icy Estrellas and tiny little portions of black pudding, olives in chili oil, crispy little whitebait, piquant chorizo, cubes of garlicky lamb, shave-thin Serrano ham… then more Estrella again. Eventually we toddled off, but, bludgeoned by the afternoon sun once again, only as far as the next bar. This is the best way to discover any new town, especially in unfamiliar nooks of Europe. Stumble from bar to bar at a leisurely pace, with no particular plan in mind other than just enjoy the moment. It's what Europe with the Redmen is all about. Memories in the making.

By now it was around 3pm, with the match kicking off at 8.45. Through squiffy eyes and propelled by many a burp and trump, we set our controls to a distant but familiar cacophony and followed the singing past a grand old Cathedral, all the way to the Bodega Santa Cruz. A fine selection of seasoned Reds had clearly had a good afternoon. Among the throng were Dave Hewitson and Co, John Mackin, Jon Guard and amigos, and a healthy smattering of lads I have known for decades as "mate", "lad" and "sunshine". After all these years of bumping into one another on trains, in bars and outside grounds with a nod and an "alright lad", it'd be weird to toddle over and go,

"By the way. Been meaning to ask. What's your name?"

Flags are laid out on the pavement outside. Johnny Mac notices that Bucko's pride and joy reads as follows:

BOOTLE RED'S

Like a patient supply teacher, he tells young Buckley why the apostrophe has to go. Shoulders back, he looks him in the eye, clears his throat and says:

"Bucko. You leave me with little choice. I'm seizing that apostrophe…"

And that's it. The apostrophe goes.

Betis fans come over to take photos, buy us drinks and try to get us to sing YNWA. It's after five now, but the sun is still high in the sky and the drinks keep coming. The waiters start bringing out these bucket-sized glasses of beer (which, later, will mysteriously morph into bucket-sized buckets of beer; the glasses become plastics.) With every round of drinks they bring us little plates of cheeses or shrimps or miniature casseroles in tiny dishes. They've been great with us all day, but they're starting to worry about us making kick-off. Tapping their wrists they're explaining that taxis are hard to come by in this pedestrianised part of the Cathedral area. If we head for the river, turn left and follow our noses, the stadium is a 30 minute walk away. I head for the latrines for a tactical slash.

Some of you reading this will be familiar with what happened next. Inexplicably, I lost twenty minutes, maybe even five or ten, I can't be sure. but it felt longer. It's a phenomenon that seems to go hand-in-hand with long days on the plonk in sultry countries. I've had similar in Barcelona, Porto, Marseille, where you find yourself startled, not quite sure where you are or how you got there, but very aware on some deep-seated level that you've been there for a while, time has shuffled on and the air feels different, colder. In short, you have fallen asleep on the bog.

When I come back into the bar, I get a round of applause from the barmen and waiters. Refreshingly, none of them speaks English so, with much gesticulation, they indicate to me that my friends have, how-you-say, "done one." They lead me down to a big plaza where horse-drawn carriages await. They seem to be telling me that my comrades have used this method of transport to get them to the ground. It's 8.20 pm. I have 25 minutes to get there, but I'm severely allergic to animal fur. Horses are worst of all. There's no way in the world I'm going anywhere near, so I hug my hombres farewell, promising we'll be back after the game, and set off on foot for the Estadio Benito, that, at least, has a happy ring to it.

If I were to have the pleasure of observing my progress on CCTV, I would note that I am walking in an S trajectory. If the Oxford Dictionary of English Phrases ever wanted a 3D performance of that old nugget "one step forward, two steps back", here was my game rendition. I was bladdered. I can't see without the help of milk-bottle lenses when I'm stone cold sober, so if you'd care to stand up, put your arms out like an aeroplane and whiz yourself round and round and round until you're nearly sick, that's how Seville looked and felt. There was no way I was making that match, there was no way I'd find my way back to the Bodega Santa Cruz.

And yet, and yet…what was this, before me? Yes! YES-YES-YES!! A taxi, no less. There was a white-with-green-stripes taxi cab, pulled over, letting a little old lady out and I was mere paces away. With a fixed "I'm friendly, me" grin, I eliminated any misunderstanding by thrusting a 20 Euro note into the driver's hand and uttering three words. "Stadio, por favor."

He did what taxi drivers often do in these circumstances and, aware that neither of us was familiar with the other's mother tongue, gabbled away like the fella from Rapido, throwing his arms around and, every now and then, craning his head right round to make eye contact. He reserved these moments for the busiest roundabouts, when cars were flying at him from every direction. I carried on grinning.

He got me as close to the ground as he was able. The roads were closed off with barriers and manned by what looked like militia. They had guns and batons, for sure. At this stage you must indulge me while I take on the persona of one such riot cop. You've been waiting and training for this day for a while. Liverpool are coming. You've been told to expect the worst. For the last two weeks, in pulverising sunshine, in full kit, you've been going through full battle manouevres; drill after drill with riot shields, water cannon, snarling dogs, tasers…whatever it's going to take keep the invading Liverpool thugs in line, and keep your beautiful, historic city safe. You've been told what they're like. They'll be out of control, and you're primed and ready to quell them at the first sign of menace. Imagine the disappointment when all that materialises is a smattering of portly pissheads wassailing the locals with songs that have slightly too many verses. All that preparation - for what?

But then a taxi rolls up. The match kicked off twenty minutes ago, Liverpool are already two goals up, so whoever is in that cab can't be a true fan. It'll be an Ultra. one of the top boys, trying to avoid detection. On your mettle, lads. Here he comes. He appears to be kissing the taxi driver…don't be fooled by that. They'll use any decoy in the book to get behind enemy lines. Oh dear. Oh no. He's wearing shorts. It's after 9 at night and the imbecile is wearing shorts…

I got out of the cab to see six very young, very surly men in grey military uniforms, fingers on triggers. Behind them there are another dozen or so Policia. Local, green uniforms, no guns; and one hundred yards behind them is the stadium, rocking to the sound of joyful Redmen.

"A-RA-RA-RAFA BENITEZ, XABI ALONSO, GARCIA AND REINA!!"

I smile to myself. I've sobered up, all is well, still an hour of top-notch Euro footy to partake in. I study the stadium plan that came with my ticket. All is well. That's the Liverpool section, right ahead of me, I think. Eager to impress upon the militia that I pose no threat and, on the contrary, am quite the internationalist, I stride towards them with a beatific smile stretched across my grid. I'm trying to emit an air of cheery bonhomie. What the police see is a gurning halfwit heading their way, an idiotic grin sloping across his stupid, punchable face. I sense they don't like me very much, and I have perhaps three paces to turn the game around.

I smile even harder. I need to convince them that, far from being a threat to security, I'm a tipsy tourist, slightly lost, who just needs pointing in the right direction. To emphasise my friendliness, I add the internationally recognised convention of "wide open arms" to the simpleton's smirk.

I hold my ticket out, to let them see I'm not trying to bunk in. And then I make the biggest mistake I've made since grasping that live wire, back in May. I put my arm around the militia-chief's shoulders and get as far as pointing at my map. I don't get as far as asking him my question, "which entrance please for fan of the Liverpool?"

He shrugs me off aggressively, pushes me away. I hold up the flat palms of both hands in the internationally recognised convention of "I mean no harm." He thrashes me across the back of my thighs with a riot stick. For a second I feel nothing, then the hottest, most shocking pain shoots right through me. He draws his baton back again and skips towards me, taking a run-up this time. In spite of the pain, in spite of the drink, in spite of not having done anything akin to exercise in three months, I leg it. I sprint like a hare, and feel like one as riot police run after me, whipping my back and thighs with batons.

I tripped and skidded across the track, tiny nodes of gravel embedding themselves under a raw flap of skin on my knee. I was getting up even before I hit the deck, and carried on running, pell-mell. Ahead of me, the green uniforms drew their batons, too, and formed a line across the road. I've never been much of a fan of rugby or any of those American sports where they have massive shoulder pads and plough into one another for hours on end, but I had no choice. I just ran at them and hurdled them and carried on sprinting and, for whatever reason, heat, exhaustion, heavy uniforms, they stopped chasing.

I got inside the ground just before half-time to be greeted by John Mackin, eyes all slitty with drink, saying:

"What happened to you? You missed all the fun."

He took a breath then, as though it was a matter of deepest human sadness, said, "Bucko's lost his apostrophe. He's gutted. He loved that little comma…"

Betis pulled a goal back but we won 2-1 and went on to win the group, easily. Three wins, three draws, 12 points. Later that night we went back to the Bodega Santa Cruz where, standing outside and taking a moment to watch the moon high up in the Andalucian sky, I spotted a scrap of off-white material billowing gently on the kerb. It was Bucko's apostrophe. I paraded 'The Lost Apostrophe' of Seville around the bar, where it was feted and toasted with copious apple brandies. That punctuation mark, as much a part of

Liverpool FC's glorious history as any badge or pennant or last-gasp winner, now resides in the (comparatively newish) Museum of Liverpool on the waterfront. Pop along and say hello one day.

KEV SAMPSON

All the Betis are off!

And once again my first proper European trip of the new season, as I don't really think I can class going to Wrexham as being a Euro away and no, neither is Chelsea. This time due to lack of holidays caused by an unexpected four days extra off work in May (woohoo) I could manage only a fly into Seville on match day and back home the following day.

Pre-match eve and I get home from work looking for an early night, so a bath to relax the muscles (or possibly fat) and off to bed early to get up for the 4.15am train via London to Gatwick. What a shock, I can't sleep and I stay up until the taxi arrives at 3.45am on match day. The train to London was very busy for the time of day. On arriving at Euston it's straight over on the Victoria line to Victoria for the Gatwick Express.

Now I've never used online check in before and Terri kindly booked both of us in the previous day. I got off the train at 6.44am and had to get the connecting train thingy from South to North terminal, print off a boarding card, go through security and get to the bar. This took a massive eleven minutes. Not sure how long it would take when a lot busier but I was impressed. Not so impressed by Jon G being fucking slow in getting the beer in, as I had just got off the train. Ample time in my book.

A few faces I recognised as usual along with the likes of Jon G, Mivi, John Mac and Terri who looked well wrecked (it was still early for her).

On the flight over I had to stop myself berating some Swedish knob in business NOT to pick on any Liverpool players, but apart from that and me irritating someone trying to sleep, it was a decent flight for an early start.

Now I've been to Sevilla before but only for one night and used the train from Madrid on that occasion, so we were hoping for a decent taxi journey in. No probs for Jon G and I getting to our hotel but knobhead taxi driver wasn't taking Mivi and Terri any further. After trying to ask for more money, he was advised to go away by the lovely female of the group (no not you Mr Guard).

A quick change and back out. After trying to avoid the Irish bar near the Cathedral we find a few of our lot are still in there, so pop along briefly. (strange how over twelve hours later we end up back there).

Luckily we have a local for a guide, well local as in he's Irish and lives in Sevilla. He's known as Patrick on RAWK and Figaro on YNWA. So off we go for a bar/tapas crawl and first stop is Bar Giralda, which I've been to before and think is a great bar. Then off to Bodega Santa Cruz where we stay for a while drinking what can only be described as halves of Cruzcampo but since we drank them so quickly we always seemed to have someone at the bar buying the next round. This is what I really love about some Euro aways and especially ones in Spain, as I find them so much more relaxing than other games, and the fact that you can as a rule drink for basically fuck all helps even more.

Time for a bit of food at Casa Robles which was just off the beaten track back towards the Cathedral. I had stewed bulls tail amongst other things and to be honest it neither tasted bad nor anything brilliant.

We then head back down the street to the Irish bar for more beer and a few songs with the flags coming out. The RAWK flag whore got her Luis Garcia one out to show to everyone. A while later, outside another bar, that same flag owner was so pissed she didn't even notice the flag being taken down whilst being half covered by a parked van. Luckily I had noticed and got there just in time as some old Spanish bloke was attempting to grab himself a souvenir of our time in Sevilla.

Leaving it late, as if we were still on the veranda at the Sandon, we wander off for a taxi. We don't have much luck, so we kept on walking only to be called over by a local who got us to go on the bus, and many thanks to the bloke for that whoever you were, and thanks for directing us to the ground.

Yet again another hike up fucking Everest to our end, mind it still felt like a molehill compared to St James fucking Park where on a bad day you can see Norway and a good day Moscow.

The game starts and within two minutes we have gone one up with a sublime piece of skill from Florent Sinama Pongolle. To then go two up was more than I could have asked for. In the Second-half we were well under the cosh and they duly got a goal back and we had to struggle to keep it down to the one. Highlight of the night was Patrick shouting Cero – Dos to the Betis fans as deep down he is a Sevilla FC fan after Liverpool. Maybe too much Cruzcampo for his own good, or was it Olly, Aidan and Jimbo for yet again dressing up and going to the match by fucking Horse and Cart. I would say more money than sense. Yet again I found out Olly was caught sleeping in bars. Wouldn't be a Euro away if he didn't.

Off for a wander when they finally let us out and a bar was found for a beer, surprisingly half full of reds celebrating. Now others got taxis back to town, but no, Patrick, Will, Jon G and I walked back to the centre. Patrick says "See those traffic lights down there?" "Yep" we say, "Well after those it is a five minute walk." What the numpty didn't tell us it was five minutes to another set of lights and three weeks later we finally got back to the aforementioned Irish bar for some more beer for the night.

One thing I do hate about turning up on match day is there's no chance to have a good beer and wander around a place the day/night before. On this trip I only had one hour or so the next day to get a taxi in from the hotel and do some sightseeing. Ok, I dragged Jon G back to Bodega Santa Cruz for an hour or so for a beer, before heading back to the airport for the trip home.

It was nice to make it onto the plane as probably the last passengers because when in Spain you have to get the red wine from the duty free to at least take some kind of souvenir home with you.

Next one is more comfy, Eurostar to Brussels and some 8% Belgian ales please. If any of you come with our lot we're heading to a nice bar ten minutes from Grand Place for some easy drinking before the sing songs later that day.

Adios.

JONATHAN HALL

CHAMPIONS LEAGUE GROUP STAGE
19TH OCTOBER 2005
CONSTANT VANDEN STOCK STADION [21824]
BRUSSELS. BELGIUM
RSC ANDERLECHT 0 LIVERPOOL 1

From French to Flemish – have a Leffe Blonde and drink to it.

I'd never done a Euro away by Eurostar before, so I had no idea what it was going to be like. The ale ban that people talked about wasn't in force but after a few the night before I didn't really fancy starting at breakfast time.

A good start to the day, the normal London Transport travel chaos! On arriving at Waterloo I had this feeling that Terri was sitting on a tube train going nowhere, which she had been. Not as many Reds as I thought there would be but that was mainly due to the fact that most were travelling mid-morning, so it was just Terri, John & Shazz and myself from the normal bunch travelling by Eurostar.

Due to the fact that we were in different parts of the train, Terri had to put up with me as usual, mind you at least I had a decent guidebook unlike the ones she had got from the library, not sure if Belgium existed when her books were printed.

It was a nice relaxing train ride as normal with Eurostar and due to being early no one was acting up, though the group of lads in front of us changed their watches as an excuse to go to the bar earlier than normal, but when you have a whole day of drinking stronger stuff than usual my plan was to keep off it as long as possible. Well, OK, it lasted until about just outside of Brussels Midi but that was better than usual. Off the train and past quite a few police who were stopping quite a few with colours on and checking for tickets and there were rumours of some getting their phones checked in case they were arranging a fight.

We met Pheeny just after this and he had overheard one officer telling a probationer the difference between Liverpool and Chelsea fans, which was that Chelsea fans are more interested in hooliganism but the Liverpool fans are more adept of going into shops and removing items free of charge. If only Pheeny had asked them where the nearest Lacoste shop was.

What was going to be a quick beer turned into two glasses of Leffe, as it would be rude not to, and then John and Shazz went to find their hotel, while Terri, Pheeny and I got the PreMetro into town to go to our respective hotels. 'Confusing those hotel lifts aren't they Tony?' As both of us pressed the button which showed as occupied so we waited and waited until we realised the fucking thing was there all along and this was before we'd had too many.

Hotel staff aren't half sharp these days, as we'd booked a triple room and due to Jon.G deciding not to go, the guy checking us in said there's only two of you? Hadn't realised mate, really you don't say…

So the usual quick piss and freshen up and off to the second bar of the day, a nice little bar called BierCircus, a short walk uphill from the Grand Place (or Grotemarkt) part of town. I had sent this bar suggestion to a few that I personally know as I didn't want it to turn into a place I'd get barred from, so we get there and Lee, Ali, Brenda and Christine are already in there, with bottles of water (I nearly cried) and their excuse was getting in at 5am after the previous nights drinks. They were also eating and from the text Lee had sent me he must have been wasting away. Also in attendance was Andy Mac who a few on YNWA will know. I thought I recognised him and then he said 'I saw you in Istanbul at 4am, after the game, amazingly outside a bar drinking.' 'Andy mate, you were well on the way to being slaughtered and it hadn't even got to 2pm.' More of Andy later no doubt.

Mmmm, did someone mention beer, a couple of weak ones to start with at 5.5% as we're waiting for a few others to turn up and the food looked nice, so we waited for Terri to arrive only she'd got lost and this was not long after taking the piss out of me and transport and directions. Cheers girl. Food didn't happen after the bar owner said 'If you are only drinking please use the bar side', so Pheeny orders food five minutes later to be told the kitchens closed as the bar shuts at 2.30pm till early evening. BUGGER. The Jim Price duo had already arrived and I'm sure it was their fault for us not getting food. Decision time was easy and once Terri had finally turned up we headed back towards the Grand Place and to Café Delirium which was just off Rue Des Bouchers which is full of seafood restaurants. Why Café Delirium I hear you ask and not an Irish bar or one on the Square. Well this bar has a beer menu which is as thick as the yellow pages and has over 2000 beers listed. How the hell you are supposed to pick one is beyond me. I left the rest in there and headed for food with Terri, and later joined by Raj who wasn't eating, so we got a steak. Whilst sitting outside eating, certain members of RAWK went past and it was lovely to see Cowtownred being the outstanding member of the surgical community as normal. Shaun (or is it Nigel?), what have the people of Northern Ireland done to deserve you? I have never seen him so out of it.

Food did the trick for a change and even slowed my drinking down which on Belgian ale can be a good thing with the match not too far off, but back to Café Delirium for some more beers where we were joined by Dan.L, Paul Davies and Paul.

184

Finally off to Grand Place for a beer or two, lovely Square with brilliant architecture, which wasn't very busy when we got there due to most already heading off to the ground, but as we had seen a few times Andy had somehow cottoned onto a woman and stood there for ages talking to her. If only she'd have known the police were close by to save her. By this time the flag that Will had taken had been removed by the Irish branch (JimmyLibel will claim it's a lie) and how thick do you have to be to get loads of hints of where the flag is and even feel up the stomach of the person who was hiding it there. Mr Neville yer plonker.

By now we'd been told to avoid the Metro as the message had got back that it was chaos and the police were out in force, so a taxi was the option but nope we went for the Metro option, and getting there was not much of a problem and getting to the ground was easy. If only it had been as well organised at the ground and after. Getting in past the police was easy and no checking of tickets, which led to problems with fans trying to go back out to pass tickets to people they were meeting, but the police in their ultimate wisdom were having none of it. Why the hell they didn't have the first ticket check there and that problem would have been eliminated. It turned out that anyone inside this section without a ticket was held there while the game was played so didn't even get the option to go back and watch it in a bar. A fair few arrests had been made, I can only assume it was people trying to get in without tickets and kicking off about it. A point made to me after the game is that there appeared to be fans who didn't look like the normal Euro away traveller, so maybe some had gone from wherever on the off chance of kicking off.

The novelty at this game was not having four thousand steps to walk up to the away end. Not a bad little Stadium but a typical European seating arrangement of shite seats with no backs, not that we were going to use them unless of course you are known as Lee.B and fancy a kip.

At the end of the match quite a few of the Anderlecht fans stay behind to listen to our songs and clap all of us which I suppose you could say was nice. I'd have personally been off and down the bar but there's some strange ones out there.

Twenty minutes or so and we are let out and have an escort down towards the Metro station. I can understand why they would hold us outside the station to filter people in but yet again they decide after a long wait to let a large group all at the same time try and get down an escalator two at a time. Once the mini crush was over in the station it was down onto a special Metro train heading back to town and a chance for more beer. We get back to Café Delirium for a few more beers for the rest of the night, and the barman asks if we are going to sing. Only if you pay us mate and no he didn't offer.

We finally left at about 2.30am and got back for a few hours sleep. Up at 8am and I was now wishing I'd booked a later train but it was too late now and Terri and I meet to get the PreMetro tram to catch the Eurostar back to London.

Terri has now acquired the whole of the Belgian chocolate production for the next few years. I still think when she packs she assumes she is going for two weeks and not a one night stay. Women…

It was a quiet trip home as Terri decided to sleep for almost all of the journey and with a slight delay of twenty minutes on the journey I'd missed two trains by the time I got to Euston and the next one got cancelled, so I decided to sod going to work for the afternoon and went for a couple of pints and some lunch.

Another decent trip with funny moments.

JONATHAN HALL

CHAMPIONS LEAGUE LAST 16 1ST LEG
21ST FEBRUARY 2006
ESTADIO DA LUZ [63702]
LISBON. PORTUGAL
BENFICA 1 LIVERPOOL 0

Fifteen of us flew to Faro in Portugal on the day of the game. We hired a mini bus to drive to Lisbon with the Sat Nav saying three and a half hours. So we set off and the Super Bock started to flow.

The designated driver, who was one of the lads, was getting really pissed off because his son had changed the voice on the Sat Nav to Cartman from South Park. He was getting so wound up that we were pissing ourselves laughing. We didn't want to tell him that you could turn Cartmans voice off or even change it.

Anyway, an hour into the journey and he has had enough. He suddenly throws it out of the window on the motorway.

Now it was just a case of following the signs that would get us close to Lisbon. As we got closer we see what we thought was the team bus. This will be easy enough, we'll just follow it to the ground. So we follow it for ages.

By this time the match was nearly kicking off. The bus pulls over, so we do the same, only to realise it wasn't the team coach but it was a load of disabled school children.

A policeman then came along in his car, so we ask him for directions to the ground and he said for Fifty Euros he would take us with his lights flashing . We got to the ground and dumped the minibus.

By now it was half-time. When we got up to the ground the local police/stewards wouldn't let us in until a LFC steward appeared.

Eventually we got into the ground for the final twenty minutes. Only to see us get beat 1-0.

We went to Albufeira for two days following the game which actually made up for what would have been a wasted trip to the game.

JOHN CORLAN

2006/07 CHAMPIONS LEAGUE

12 September 2006 Group stage (Group C)
PSV Eindhoven   0-0   Liverpool FC

27 September 2006 Group stage (Group C)
Liverpool FC   3-2   Galatasaray AŞ

18 October 2006 Group stage (Group C)
FC Girondins de Bordeaux0-1   Liverpool FC

31 October 2006 Group stage (Group C)
Liverpool FC   3-0   FC Girondins de Bordeaux

22 November 2006 Group stage (Group C)
Liverpool FC   2-0   PSV Eindhoven

5 December 2006 Group stage (Group C)
Galatasaray AŞ   3-2   Liverpool FC

21 February 2007 Round of 16
FC Barcelona   1-2   Liverpool FC

6 March 2007 Round of 16
Liverpool FC   0-1   FC Barcelona
Aggregate: 2-2
Liverpool win on away goals

3 April 2007 Quarter-finals
PSV Eindhoven   0-3   Liverpool FC

11 April 2007 Quarter-finals
Liverpool FC   1-0   PSV Eindhoven
Aggregate: 4-0

25 April 2007 Semi-finals
Chelsea FC   1-0   Liverpool FC

1 May 2007 Semi-finals
Liverpool FC   1-0   Chelsea FC
Aggregate: 1-1
Liverpool win 4-1 on penalties

188

23 May 2007 Final
AC Milan   2-1   Liverpool FC

CHAMPIONS LEAGUE GROUP STAGE
18TH OCTOBER 2006
STADE CHABAN-DELMAS [31471]
BORDEAUX. FRANCE
GIRONDINS DE BORDEAUX 0 LIVERPOOL 1

The cheapest way to get to Bordeaux was to fly from Gatwick with BA. I didn't realise how far away Gatwick bloody was though! Anyway whilst in the departure lounge we bump into Ray Wilkins who was commentating on our game for Sky. We had a good chat with him before Tozza says "Give us a mention on the commentary", "Will do" replied Ray. "He won't do that, I bet he gets asked that all the time" I said. After a quick photo with Ray we were on our way.

We then found out off the lads watching the game at home, that to our surprise in the second half commentary Ray uttered these words "I'd like to say a quick hello to some Liverpool fans I met in the airport. At first I thought they were gonna beat me up but they turned out to be thoroughly nice chaps!". Get in Butch lad.

Unfortunately any photo evidence was lost when I left my bag with my camera in it, in one of the many Bordeaux bars we visited. My guess would be the one where we were sampling Wheat Beer, White Beer, Cherry Brandy Beer and Strawberry Beer!

IAN McKEVITT

CHAMPIONS LEAGUE GROUP STAGE
5TH DECEMBER 2006
ATATURK STADIUM [23000]
ISTANBUL. TURKEY
GALATASARY SK 3 LIVERPOOL 2

Dead Body Floating

We knew before we went to Istanbul that this was a dead rubber. However, more of the dead body later on.

There are people out there who wouldn't go to Istanbul and the Ataturk again because it diminishes their memories of our fifth European Cup win. Absolute bollocks that is, does that mean that if you went to the first final in Rome, you wouldn't have gone to the second? Aye I bet you wouldn't.

However, less of the whining from me, I had a trip to go on. As usual these days, once Liverpool have played somewhere a no-frills airlines then starts flying there after the event.

Monday started off well, I was down in Northampton on the Sunday doing some jobs for my mother then I was on an early train back to Liverpool. The train got as far as Crewe before being cancelled due to the line being shut. More importantly would the line be reopen for the afternoon journey down to Milton Keynes and the coach to

Luton Airport? Thankfully come mid-afternoon and things were back to normal. So I settled down with the paper and some red wine and headed south to eventually meet up with GlentoranMark and Will for our evening at the Holiday Inn Express by the airport.

Not much to say about the night as we'd been bored to death watching the Man City v Watford game on the telly. Mind you things looked up once the takeaway curry arrived. So not long after midnight the three of us buggered off for a few hours sleep before the early flight on match day.

For a change after check-in at Luton we didn't bother with the bar but as usual loads of Reds were around, so the airport can't complain about the takings being down. With it only being a quick two-day trip with just over 24 hours actually in Istanbul I fancied being 'half with it' by the time we got to Istanbul proper. Easyjet must have been happy with the extremely quiet flight due to most on board probably thinking getting extra sleep a better option for what would be a long day for most of us.

After landing at Sabiha whatshernames airport, it was off to get the visa in the passport time. There was just one man with a book of stickers and a long queue of about a hundred people to sort. Considering you had loads of officials hanging around doing fuck all, could you at least open the second window yer fuckwits, some of us have a bar to go to.

The plan was to taxi it to Kadikoy on the Asian side, and hopefully to see the Fenerbache ground on the way. Well we got the taxi but didn't see the ground, and the taxi driver pointed us to where the ferries that plied the Bhosphorus went from.

Now here's where the dead body comes in. The Ferry leaves and stops at the jetty covering the train station before heading off towards Eminonu which is the terminus into Sultanahmet. All was going well until the ferry decides to stop and turn back towards the Asian side. All the locals look at each other as if to say 'what the fuck?', and full steam ahead to whatever had been spotted in the water. A small dingy appears alongside the article and what we suspected as someone floating in the water, but they have a grab and miss and don't seem bothered, only to turn round and have another go. This time they manage to pull out a lifeless body and drag him onto the boat and by the look of him and his colour he must be dead, only for Will to ask would it be bad form to take a picture as, after all, we are on holiday.

Anyway, He didn't take one.

What's that floating in the water.
What's that bobbing in the sea.
Just turn the ferry around and pick the body out.
Oh what a way to start a Euro away.

Not quite Ferry Across The Mersey but there you go.

Now that we'd finally arrived to the other part of Istanbul, we're off on the tram to Sultanahmet proper to meet up with the normal gang. Take a bow Brenda, Lee and Ali, Jon.G and his mate (memories gone so can't remember his name) Scongil and Shazz, Dave (Anny Road) and Andy. Think that covers that lot. Mind Scongil had fucked off to get his obligatory Turkish shave, mainly to get rid of his ear and nasal hair I reckon, the old get. So finally after a long trip some beer and then the need to go to the hotel to check in.

Well the checking in part was easy, it was just the getting there. We thought 'ah great Brenda is going back and she can show us the way'. First mistake was following Brenda, second mistake was when she admitted she was lost we should have gone back and gone the way the map seemed to show. Now geography isn't obviously her strong point, confirmed by the fact she left Liverpool to move to Corsica and ended up in Jersey… Less said about the bloke who showed us the way, does anyone in Istanbul actually know where streets are, as I don't believe they do.

At the hotel we meet Colin who seems a nice lad so how the hell is he unlucky to know Tiger Tony is beyond me. It's a lovely hotel but we're perturbed with the heart shaped cushions that seem to be in every room, but it was cheap enough and also the rooms had mini bars which might have come in handy unless your names Jon Guard.

Five minutes later and it's back to a bar in Sultanahmet called Sah Bar. We went in and then realised I'd been in there before on the Monday before the European Cup Final and we spent the next few hours in there apart from popping to the local kebab takeaway round the corner.

It's off to the match we go, well it would be if the buses laid on were in the right place. Sultanahmet Square was the place, but they weren't there but further along past the Blue Mosque. The local bizzies seem to think that beer wasn't allowed, not that any notice was taken, so an hour later after a sing song and beer, we were back to the Ataturk and the end Milan occupied. Yes the losers end, which might explain why we lost this game.

As usual in these reports the game barely gets reported as such apart from any strange goings on from within the ground. Notable mentions to the polystyrene sheets to sit on which ended up being turned into snow and thrown around. Whatever the reason for Jon.G and Ali to start doing 'Walk Like An Egyptian' is beyond me, and no really I don't want to know. The last thing of note was Lee and Ali fetching their banner and not actually realising Robbie had scored his second. Obviously deafness rules in the family as they missed us cheering and chanting Fowler just after this.

After the game it was back to Sultanahmet once they'd let us out and then tried to kill us off with diesel fumes. Back to Sah Bar to while the hours away singing, dancing (well if Dave actually thinks that's called dancing) and finally having to be eased out at 3am. As we were leaving it appears one of our entourage had helped himself to a bottle of wine from the rack next to the door, but promptly dropped it outside and left the others to pick up the pieces. No names mentioned to save the embarrassment for Jon.G.

JONATHAN HALL

CHAMPIONS LEAGUE QUARTER-FINAL 1ST LEG
21ST FEBRUARY 2007
CAMP NOU [88000]
BARCELONA. SPAIN
BARCELONA 1 LIVERPOOL 2

Whenever the draw is made, phone calls and texts are quickly sent. Numbers need to be confirmed on who's going. Their trust is then with the organiser who will obviously try to get everyone there as cheap as possible. Then it's the dilemma of a single or a two night stay. This fixture pairs us with Barcelona, not only a brilliant team but also a great place to visit.

The texts keep coming thick and fast. Everyone fancies this one including John, who is spending as much of his redundancy as possible on seeing as many European away games as it will afford. It appears that if ever there was a football ground bucket list, then this is up there near the top. It's also one of those places on quite a few flight paths and expectations are of a cheap journey. So after many hours trawling different routes, that may save us a tenner here and a tenner there, it's sorted.

Click … that's it done. The most up to now. Nineteen of us, all booked for Barca. Liverpool to Glasgow Prestwick by train, Ryanair from Prestwick to Reus, Reus to Barcelona by coach. I just hope I've booked the correct dates and nothing goes wrong. Worst nightmare would be such a major cock up of my doing. I can't relax until we're on the plane. We arrive at Prestwick and all's fine as I herd everyone together to pass in their passports. Then young Joes friend Anthony passes over the mintiest passport you've ever seen. Scuffed cover, pic hanging out, water stained. 'Oh shit' I think as Passport control tell him 'Sorry, You can't fly with that". His mother had put it through the wash. Apparently not just the once but twice. My leadership tendencies had to take over, so I pointed him back towards the train station 'Liverpool's that way' and went for a beer. Five minutes later there's a plan being hatched by the young lads, Joe, Rob, Jack, Dan and Anthony. 'We'll bunk him onto the plane'. This is post 9/11 not 1977 I think. So as we head towards the departure lounge and start boarding Anthony gets in between us all. We show our boarding cards and make our way onto the plane. I get on and as I'm fastening my seatbelt, I can see Anthony's made it onto the plane before a young stewardess asks for his boarding card. A quick thinker in the party passes him his own and Anthony turns to show the stewardess the card. 'No problem' she says. He's onboard but obviously there will be a head count and now there's an extra person on board who should be on the train back to Liverpool. No worries, we'll hide him under the seat. Have you seen the gap under the seats on Ryanair? Well remember them contortionists getting into boxes on Opportunity Knocks. This lad would have won the show. He gets curled up in a ball and Joe puts his coat over him.

The plane takes off and once we're airborne it's 'All clear.' He gets up a bit dazed and looking the colour of boiled shite, but unbelievably, in this day and age, it's job done. On arrival in Reus,there's no showing of any passports, we walk straight through and its away we go. Airport security. A doddle.

We arrive at our hotel, the classy Hotel Silken next to the famous gherkin shaped building. In fact, the gherkin is that famous I can't remember its name, but it looks great from the terrace as we take in the surrounding cityscape and decide whether to take a dip in the rooftop pool. The hotel is perfect for us old fogeys, stylish and comfortable. Not one of them cheap and cheerful, 'it'll do, it's only a bed for the night!' type places for us. The younger element thinks it's cool too, apparently the Arctic Monkeys recorded a video up here.

Anyway back to the day in hand. The luggage is abandoned in the rooms and we head off in numerous taxis to join the inebriated at the world's best Champagne bar, La Xampanyeria, located down a small side street close to the port. It's a cool Bodega, a typical working class Spanish place, where the local Cava and Tapas are cheap. The tables are barrels and everyone stands.

Our taxi arrives ten minutes after the first one and already arl Ken is sitting outside in the mid afternoon sun getting some fresh air. The first couple of glasses had gone straight to his head. We did hope he wasn't too hot as his string vest could soon be on show. Typical Englishman abroad was Ken, God rest his soul. String vest, hanky on head, white socks with sandals etc. The afternoon is spent quaffing a glass or three whilst enjoying the odd tapas, plus we also get involved in a photoshoot and chat with some journos from the Champions League Magazine, which made for a pleasant afternoon. It's gonna be a good day.

The younger lads disappear early on. They want to go to the local square to kick a ball 100 foot into the air. A bizarre ritual that seems to amuse everyone after a few pints. Later we journey along the Ramblas to meet up with them before heading off to the game.

Oh yeah, the game, that ninety minutes that always seems to get in the way of a great day. A magnificent 2-1 victory against the reigning champions, topped off a magnificent day. Bellamy and Riise hitting the net. Ironic given the fact that rumour had it, both had a falling out after Bellamy struck Riise with a golf club. Craig's goal celebration couldn't have been more apt.

The following day on the journey home Tony was asked the same question about his passport by Spanish Airport security. The answer was simple, it had fallen into the hotel swimming pool.

DAVE HEWITSON

After missing out on Rome in '77 due to gross dereliction of duty, I developed a sixth sense for legendary European nights abroad. Nights when absence was not an option. Wednesday 21 February 2007 in the Nou Camp, against the best team in the world, in the Champions League knock-out rounds, was one such night. Many fellow Reds felt the same. We'd only been given 3,000 tickets for that boy's pen spec, so far up in the Gods your head rubbed against celestial beards, but 10,000 of us paid homage to Catalonia. I'd made my mind up I was going as a fan, not a journalist, on the day the draw was made in December, when a famous national sportswriter said, in that patronizing way a section of scribes have perfected, that Liverpool had done well to reach the last 16 but now they were out.

"Seeing the world's best team in its pomp, on home turf might be something for Liverpool fans to tell their grandkids about. Just don't expect them to win," I was told. But I did expect them to win, and decided to let our Phil tell any grandkids about it. He was seventeen at the time, and needed a few more big European nights on his CV.

Strolling down Las Ramblas on the day of the game was magnificent. Virtually every cafe table had been hijacked by Liverpudlians, and every square off it decked out in red flags, echoing to red songs, with 25-a-side games going on. It felt like the day of a European final, which it was in a way, as the two previous Champions League winners were meeting. They had Ronaldinho, Messi, Deco, Iniesta and Xavi. We had

Rafa Benitez's tactical genius, and a squad motivated to shove tales of disharmony back down critics' throats after Craig Bellamy had enjoyed a friendly game of post-karaoke golf with John Arne Riise's legs. Deco gave Barca an early lead and it looked like we were in for a hiding. Instead (thanks in no small part to debutant Alvaro Arbeloa taking Messi home in his pocket) Rafa's men staged a remarkable comeback, with scripted goals from Bellamy and Riise. As the huge colosseum emptied at the final whistle you could make out clusters of Liverpool fans dotted around the lower tiers doing congas in the aisles and joining in the sing-song emanating from the Gods.

We were locked up there for twenty minutes. But as I stared out at the majestic city below, bathed in a neon-glow, rattling though our entire repertoire for the tenth time that day, it was the most enjoyable lock-in I'd ever had. And back in the pre all-day drinking days of the 70s I'd been locked in strange places more times than Harry Houdini.

The rest of the night was a blur. But the next day I remember with a fond smile. We walked down to the harbour to clear our heads, only to find a quayside cafe taken over by jubilant Reds, who were battering their credit cards paying for celebratory lobster and champagne breakfasts. Now that's style. As we descended into Liverpool Airport I recalled that classic couplet from John Toshack's infamous poetry anthology "Gosh It's Tosh!" (currently riding high at 4,285,919 in Amazon's best-seller charts) describing how he felt landing at Speke after scoring the winner in the Nou Camp in 1976: "Just got back from Barcelona, now I'm going for a sauna." I just went for a pint. Which tasted good.

BRIAN READE

CHAMPIONS LEAGUE FINAL
23RD MAY 2007
STADIUM ATHENS [63000]
ATHENS. GREECE
A.C. MILAN 2 LIVERPOOL 1

After what seemed like an extortionate amount of 'Money well spent' for the Istanbul final, it was decided that we could book this trip on our own without paying a 'rip-off' Travel Agent. What could go wrong? We now had six years experience of booking flights via Ryanair and Easyjet to all of Liverpool's European games.

The plan was hatched. The cheapest route seemed to be via Koln, then an overnight stay in Thessalonika, before an early morning flight to Athens on match day. Eric would book the Koln-Thessalonika flight whilst I would book Liverpool to Koln and Thessalonika to Athens.

I also had to scour the internet for a hotel or somewhere for 11 of us to stay. The easy part was the flights. Between the two of us we sorted the flights for a lot less than the package deals on offer. Little did I realize though, that every Travel Agent would have all of the hotel rooms in Athens sewn up. After many hours searching every hotel website, a penthouse apartment was found close to the centre of Athens. I had to pay for the three nights even though we were only staying for two but who could complain? We had a twelve berth penthouse apartment for just £100 each. Amazing, as things had been looking bleak with every hotel and B&B seemingly booked up.

Our flight out of Liverpool was early Tuesday morning and the first cardinal sin was realizing I had forgotten my passport as myself and Daniel headed down Queens Drive bleary eyed. Surely not the first or last to do such a thing. There's a quick U-turn to pick up the forgotten item and we're on our way back to the airport only 20 minutes late. Little did we realize that the check-in desk would have a queue almost out of the door. It seems like another five thousand Scousers had decided to leave Liverpool at the same time. No time for the English etiquette of queuing, it's straight to the front to plead with staff that my flight is leaving in forty five minutes. Luck sees us through and we meet the rest of the lads in the bar.

Fast forward four hours to Koln Airport.

"Pending? What does he mean 'Credit Card Pending'?" I wasn't the only one looking a bit pissed off. Here we were in Koln, 1,600 miles from Athens. Eleven of us, questioning the airport check-in assistants meaning of the word 'Pending'. Apparently 'Pending' comes before 'Credit Card Declined', which was the next email our intrepid Travel Agent Eric had received weeks before the journey when booking, but with it being in German he had failed to translate it's meaning. Well that was Eric's story. At that moment though German Wings are not in our best of books.

The check-in assistant then directed us away from the departure lounge. We weren't getting this flight. He obviously doesn't realise some of us have been to every European Cup final Liverpool have appeared in. We can't just walk away.

196

Panic sets in. We have got to get to Athens by hook or by crook.

The conversation then goes a bit bonkers as it sometimes does in these situations. It went something like this,

Me "You lot go and look for a Travel Agent and find a flight and I'll see how much a car will be. We'll drive through the night"

Eric "But you've had ten pints and no-one's got a driving licence with them."

Me "Bollox!!"

That was the end of that great idea.

Eventually we find a kindhearted Travel Agent in the Airport who takes pity on us and also takes a fair amount of money from us. She books us on a 5.30a.m. flight from Dusseldorf, which is thirty miles away. Off we then go to catch a train to Dusseldorf, but not before two of our company, Billy and Carl, are told their credit card booking has been accepted. They skip off into the sunset like Morecambe and Wise. When will we see them again I don't know. They along with us have Hotel rooms booked in the Northern Greek resort of Thessalonika for the night. Now the pair of them will have a choice of 6 rooms in a hotel overlooking the beach.

We, on the other hand, get to Dusseldorf pretty late. In fact we book into a hotel where we can only get about three hours kip before jumping up to get to the airport on time. By 5.15am. we are in Dusseldorf airport. Our flight to Athens is about to board. Bleary eyed [again] we approach the departure gate. Suddenly we all hear our names called out over the tannoy and have to report to the desk, where a lot of German is being spoken and phone calls being made. I fear the worst. The Travel Agent who gladly took our money the previous evening has over-booked us on a full flight and now someone has to stay in Dusseldorf whilst the flight departs. That someone being us. As there were absolutely no other flights available to Athens our only option is to try and get this flight.

Panic sets in [yet again] but there's no time to hang around, it's time to move. I wouldn't say it was 'with military precision'. It was more a case of 'Let's just try and get on the plane'. We had been allocated boarding cards at the check-in, so I tell the others I'm boarding. I hand in my card and the attendant scans it but the machine lights up red. There's a problem. She turns to the other attendants but they're busy making calls. I take my card back and tell the others to follow and they all hand their boarding cards in and again the light turns red, but there's no stopping us now. If we don't get on this flight then we're going to be watching the Mighty Reds in some German Bierkeller. Everyone makes it on board. We then find some empty seats and begin to pray for the doors to close. This takes what seems like half an hour, but was probably 5 minutes. During this time it's noticeable that some bags are being removed from the hold. None look like ours. Suddenly the doors are closed and the cabin staff prepare for take-off. The sigh of relief can be heard back in Liverpool. We are on our way to another European final. Athens greets us with morning sunshine and would you believe, Billy and Carl arrive through customs, as fresh as daisies, from Thessalonika ten minutes after ourselves. **DAVE HEWITSON**

197

So what do 40,000 odd fans of an English football club do when their team has just lost Europe's most important match? Lay waste to the city? Attack rival fans? Start fires? In the backstreets of Monastiraki, Athens, Liverpool fans showed what you do. You have a bloody great all-night party.

'The best midfield in the world', sung on the move by an endless procession of reds running through the narrow streets (check it out on youtube).

The Greek guys who wanted the full lyrics of YNWA written down so they could learn it.

The Milan fans arriving, initially fearful, have their hands shaken and are told 'Well done'. Them teaching us anti-Inter songs and Olympiakos fans teaching us their songs. 'Oh campeone, the one and only, we're Liverpool' echoed round, and then the distant sound of a burst of 'Ring of Fire' being played in cartoon bad style on a bouzouki, accompanied by raucous cheers.

The three of us had arrived the day before the game, via a Monday all-nighter in Berlin. Cheap flight from East Midlands to Berlin Schonefeld, then a flight from Berlin Tegel to Athens. The two Berlin airports are close to each other like Gatwick and Stansted are. The rest of our mates had gone by ferry from Bari in Italy to Piraeus and were staying at Glifadha – a long way out. We had a room right in town. On the Tuesday evening, after the nth change of plan - we're still paying off the mobile bills - we got a train half way to Glifadha to meet them, only to be told they were now on a train from there into town where we'd just come from. After a bit of a nark we gave up trying to meet up (it was one of the lads' birthday too!), arranged to meet on match day morning in Syntagma Square and just got a train back into town and stayed around ours. We overheard one lad saying he'd been to the Parthenon that afternoon but not to bother, 'it's shite, just ruins basically'. Reminds of the WBA captain on a pre-season tour of China who said after being shown The Great Wall' 'well once you've seen one wall you've seen them all really haven't you?'

In all those famous victories in Rome, Paris and Istanbul, I don't think I've ever had a better night than after we lost in Athens. A Milan fan summed it up best during the post-match all-nighter.

He said 'Your wake is better than our party'.

That's how to lose.

CHRIS ROWLAND

2007/08 CHAMPIONS LEAGUE

15 August 2007 Third qualifying round
Toulouse FC   0-1   Liverpool FC

28 August 2007 Third qualifying round
Liverpool FC   4-0   Toulouse FC
Aggregate: 5-0

18 September 2007 Group stage (Group A)
FC Porto   1-1   Liverpool FC

3 October 2007 Group stage (Group A)
Liverpool FC   0-1   Olympique de Marseille

24 October 2007 Group stage (Group A)
Beşiktaş JK   2-1   Liverpool FC

6 November 2007 Group stage (Group A)
Liverpool FC   8-0   Beşiktaş JK

28 November 2007 Group stage (Group A)
Liverpool FC   4-1   FC Porto

11 December 2007 Group stage (Group A)
Olympique de Marseille   0-4   Liverpool FC

19 February 2008 Round of 16
Liverpool FC   2-0   FC Internazionale Milano

11 March 2008 Round of 16
FC Internazionale Milano 0-1   Liverpool FC
Aggregate: 0-3

2 April 2008 Quarter-finals
Arsenal FC   1-1   Liverpool FC

8 April 2008 Quarter-finals
Liverpool FC   4-2   Arsenal FC
Aggregate: 5-3

22 April 2008 Semi-finals
Liverpool FC   1-1   Chelsea FC

30 April 2008 Semi-finals
Chelsea FC   3-2   Liverpool FC
Aggregate: 4-3 Chelsea win after extra time

CHAMPIONS LEAGUE Last 16 2ND LEG
11TH MARCH 2008
SAN SIRO [80000]
MILAN. ITALY
INTERNAZIONALE 0 LIVERPOOL 1

Going away is always a test of endurance. For this trip, a group of us used the Dam
as our travel hub (to give us more for our money as the official trips there and back
worked out at the same price as what we had planned). Flying out the day before the
game, having blagged our way into the airport executive lounge for some early morning
French coffees, we spend the day and night doing what you do in the Dutch
city. The Dam normally has lads from Liverpool knocking about whenever you go. And
they are normally in Stones café in the RLD. This trip was no different. Having crashed
in the Delta hotel on the Damrak in rooms that resembled a Dutch cell (with porn), we
set off early doors for the airport for the hop over the Alps and into Milan.
I'm not going to dwell on the trip to the centre, drinking in Piazza del Duomo and the
trip up to ground on the metro. There were a few Ultras mooching about but they were
all pretty pleased with us after our antics against AC Milan back in 2005 so we did not
have to worry about throwing rolled up newspapers into our back pockets. The road up
to the ground was a long curve and it seemed to go on for age and when you got to the
end it was one of them football moments that you live for … The San Siro.
Sometimes things are built up that disappoint. Not this place. It is a football Mecca and
one of the Holy Trinity of Euro aways (the others being the Camp Nou and the Berna-
beu). Inside the stands fall steeply to the pitch, and it's noisy.
Thousands had made the trip over, all wanting a piece of this part of the trinity. On the
night Liverpool excelled and a goal from Torres gave us a well-deserved win. We came
out of the ground with the objective of getting back to Milan airport to catch the early
morning flight back to the Dam. This was when the endurance element kicks in.
We got back to the Central Station at about 1am and touched for a joey [taxi] to the
airport. It was amazing how comfortable the marble floor was as we managed to get
a couple of hours kip. Unbeknown to us at the time, storm force winds were shutting
airports and causing delays all over Europe.
Our flight back to the Dam was delayed a good few hours before Easyjet realised they
would have to fork out for a load of Scousers that had missed their connecting flight
back into Liverpool. The decision was made. Now I am not the best of fliers, so when
the captain came on to say that the last hour into the Dam was going to be bumpy,
I grabbed my bottle of Diazepam and self-medicated a few extra pills for good luck.
Anyone that has seen Castaway will know the type of descent we had into Amsterdam.
I was just rolling with the punches on my nice warm rollercoaster, eyes closed and
feeling warm. Others where in a blind panic, spewing up and praying. Even in my high
as a kite status I knew it was bad. As we were coming into land, the Torres song was
being rasped out as a final show of defiance to the elements. It worked. The landing was

met with thunderous applause and there where many imitations of the Pope kissing the tarmac when we got off.

We spent the rest of the day around the bars of the Dam before the final leg back into John Lennon, which was nowhere near as hairy. Three days, four planes, six trains, two buses, one taxi and three hours kip. You can probably tie that ratio to any of the Euro aways.

MIKE HOUGHTON

2008/09 CHAMPIONS LEAGUE

13 August 2008 Third qualifying round
R. Standard de Liège   0-0   Liverpool FC

27 August 2008 Third qualifying round
Liverpool FC   1-0   R. Standard de Liège
Aggregate: 1-0
Liverpool win after extra time

16 September 2008 Group stage (Group D)
Olympique de Marseille   1-2   Liverpool FC

1 October 2008 Group stage (Group D)
Liverpool FC   3-1   PSV Eindhoven

22 October 2008 Group stage (Group D)
Club Atlético de Madrid   1-1   Liverpool FC

4 November 2008 Group stage (Group D)
Liverpool FC   1-1   Club Atlético de Madrid

26 November 2008 Group stage (Group D)
Liverpool FC   1-0   Olympique de Marseille

9 December 2008 Group stage (Group D)
PSV Eindhoven   1-3   Liverpool FC

25 February 2009 Round of 16
Real Madrid CF   0-1   Liverpool FC

10 March 2009 Round of 16
Liverpool FC   4-0   Real Madrid CF
Aggregate: 5-0

8 April 2009 Quarter-finals
Liverpool FC   1-3   Chelsea FC

14 April 2009 Quarter-finals
Chelsea FC   4-4   Liverpool FC
Aggregate: 7-5

CHAMPIONS LEAGUE GROUP STAGE
9TH DECEMBER 2008
PHILIPS STADION [33500]
EINDHOVEN. NETHERLANDS
PSV EINDHOVEN 1 LIVERPOOL 3

As with most Euro jaunts, this was a trip most memorable for the journey as apposed to the match itself. A trip to Holland is always a good one and this was no exception. It started early Monday afternoon for a few pre-gig swigs in Pogues. The gig in question was Kings of Leon down at the Echo, and whilst not everyone's musical cup of cha, it was a decent start to a Euro trip for this group of intrepid Kopites. We were finished for midnight then it was a quick hop foot over to the Pier Head to meet our accommodation for the next few days – the SOS bus.

Having already secured a qualifying spec from the group, this was much of a nothing game for the Redmen but the prospect of a pre-match night in the Amsterdam (red) light was too much to resist for our small group of lads. The journey down was as good as you'd suspect, everyone in high spirits and the ferry a boss laugh as usual. There's always something nostalgic about boarding the ferry en route abroad to follow the Reds. Due to the nothingness of the match Amsterdam wasn't its usual hive of Scouse activity which accompanies a Liverpool game in Holland. This suited us and we pretty much had free reign of the city. The lure of the lights, however, was too much for most and those of us actually heading on to Eindhoven were seriously in the minority. It was a non-entity for most of our group to up sticks and dive on the train and they were happy to swerve the match completely.

The match itself, as usual, was a bit of a non-event. Like with most of our matches in this neck of the woods the away end was awash with a thick, black, narcotic smog. The bizarre looking Albert Riera scored a screamer; I do remember that much. The match couldn't finish quick enough and it was full-steam (on a tightly packed train) back to the Dam. The lads who'd remained there had done us proud and were rightfully, royally smashed upon our arrival! It all boded well for a long arl coach jaunt back to Blighty the following morning. And as promised the ride back home was more of a hoot than the match was ever going to be. Fresh off the back of a two day Dutch bender the party was in full swing, and for such a low key, somewhat unnecessary Champions League fixture, this one will go down as one of the more memorable European jaunts.

CHRIS MURPHY

2009/10 CHAMPIONS LEAGUE

16 September 2009 Group stage (Group E)
Liverpool FC   1-0   Debreceni VSC

29 September 2009 Group stage (Group E)
ACF Fiorentina   2-0   Liverpool FC

20 October 2009 Group stage (Group E)
Liverpool FC   1-2   Olympique Lyonnais

4 November 2009 Group stage (Group E)
Olympique Lyonnais   1-1   Liverpool FC

24 November 2009 Group stage (Group E)
Debreceni VSC   0-1   Liverpool FC

9 December 2009 Group stage (Group E)
Liverpool FC   1-2   ACF Fiorentina

I got a text saying we had Debreceni of Hungary. Perfect, was the first thought, we'd never been to Hungary, probably because the Reds hadn't played there since Ferencvaros in '74. It was the sort of place we had hoped would come out of the hat in the group stages. A new place to visit and a victory over inferior opposition. Anyway we had frequented the likes of Madrid and Eindhoven far too many times for my liking. The second thought was 'Where about in Hungary is Debreceni?' This became less of a problem once we heard the tie was to be switched to the capital, Budapest. A 'Godsend' as Easyjet flew straight there from Luton. So after a few days of organizing, it was a car to Luton, a few or maybe more than a few pints, a curry, then cheap digs next to the airport in preparation for the early morning flight.

Now I'm sure you will have heard tales of 50p pints and meals for a quid in far flung former Eastern Bloc Countries during Liverpool's European excursions over the years, but not having come across such delights, this was to be our turn. The fact that Hungary did not use the Euro must account for something. We did hear the price may have increased with inflation to 60p but I'm sure this £20 I got changed into Hungarian Forint will see me well.

We arrived in the capital early morning on match day and jumped a taxi to our hotel on the banks of the Danube. The view across the river from the hotel was amazing. Budapest is described as one of the most beautiful cities in Europe and has an extensive World Heritage site, which is what we could see before our eyes over yonder. We'll save the visit across the Danube until the following morning though. A leisurely stroll to walk off our hangovers will be had then. At the moment there was the more pressing matter of getting pissed on this £20s worth of Florint burning a hole in my pocket.

We arranged to meet in the hotel bar after throwing our bags into the room. Carl was down first and as we approach he tells us we should move on. There are no 60p pints in this four star gaff. £3 they were asking, robbing bastards.

We wander off, heading through the Christmas Market, picking up a mulled wine en route, as you do. Liverpool attempts these International Christmas Markets now but it will never match drinking mulled wine in a foreign city as you pub-crawl your way to a Liverpool Euro away.

After a visit to numerous bars and £2 being the norm for a bevy, we suddenly realize that we haven't eaten for a few hours. We turn up a side street and see what could be our mecca. £10 for a two-course meal, surely the ale would be damn cheap. Now this was no cheap looking joint. For a start they had cool chairs, not the plastic or cheap aluminium style made famous by England yobs abroad with their throwing antics. We enter to be greeted by Art on the walls plus waiters and waitresses looking very smart in their black suits.

We sit and peruse the menu. Salivating at the pleasures in store. The thoughts turn to local Hungarian Lager at abnormally low prices but wine connoisseur Eric has other ideas. 'Shall we get a bottle of Red?' Obviously we will. We order beers first whilst Eric discusses the virtues of the local grapes with our host [waiter]. He then picks out a local 'Red' and shows me the price. It's one of the most expensive but I think it works out at about £8. The waiter assures us its one of the best Hungarian wines they have.

The meal is a work of art, the type hipsters take photos of to put on Instagram.

The wine is poured into a carafe by the waiter plus a small touch is placed into Eric's glass, who tastes it and nods his approval to the guy.

We simply distribute the carafe amongst fellow Reds and before we get started on the starter, another bottle is needed.

The waiter is called and is quite bemused that the carafe has been emptied. We were supposed to give it ten minutes to breath. Ahh well, 'Another bottle of your finest, Sir' we jovially retort, the mulled wine, lager and red wine now beginning to take effect.

An hour later, stomachs replenished, we split the bill, which is something like £40 each. This seems a bit steep for a £10 meal, two bottles of wine plus a couple of pints but we're well on the way to that merry stage of the afternoon where no one questions such trivial matters as the cost of having a good time. I put the receipt in my pocket and we toddle off to the next fine hostelry.

But hold on a minute. Maybe we've been 'had off' for a tenner or £20 each. That's not on, no matter how pissed you get. 'They definitely saw us coming'

I've got the bill in my pocket I tell Carl, so we begin to analyse it.

Two-course meal £10 – Check.

£2 a pint – Check.

£80 per bottle of wine x 2 – Check.

WHAT??? £80 a bottle??

'Fuck me Eric, that wine was £80 a bottle not £8'

Eric takes the flak for the next few minutes or was it the next few years?

It still gets brought up now whenever he orders wine in Europe.

'Make sure you've checked the price there Eric, remember Debreceni? Has anyone got a calculator for him?'

It may not have been so bad had it been some French or Spanish vintage, but who would pay £8 for a bottle of Hungarian wine, never mind £80?

Anyway let bygones be bygones. An hour or two later and we are approaching the Ferenc Puskas Stadium. It looks great from a distance, the tall floodlights making the light drizzle glisten in the night. It looks better close up, with proper old style pylon floodlights in each corner. The type of traditional ground that is diminishing in England and being replaced by dull, nondescript stadia.

The game is watched as usual through a drunken haze. It's at times like these that you promise yourself you'll watch the recording in the next few days to see what was missed. But you never do. Especially as we only win 1-0.

It was another boss trip, although not the cheap one we were expecting.
DAVE HEWITSON

I decided to treat myself (being 50) and book a swanky pad to watch the once mighty Reds, as it happens, crash dismally out of Europe. Still never let the match get in the way of a good jaunt out of Blighty eh! This plan was quickly scuppered.

On arrival in Budapest the advanced party, namely a founder member of the N.M.C (the fearsome North Mersey Casuals, Hightown branch), who on second thoughts I won't name, informed me that there was a spare bunk in his room. Too much, for this chancing door hinge I have worryingly become, to resist. Yes, my great no expense spared trip hadn't involved booking a room. In fact I had only jumped, at the last minute, on some other poor souls flight who was having problems with a court order which carried a bit of weight shall we say.

I'll start somewhere near the beginning. A couple of sparks from Litherland (a little known borough on the posher side of Bootle) kindly took, Billy no-mates me, under their wing. As mentioned previously, their buddy was bare knuckling bailiffs. Another addition to the posse as well as me was a chain smoking Kopite (more about him later). Nottingham International Airport is an awfully gruesome place. Proceedings were briefly livened up by a bulky Birkonian on the arm of a buxom traveling companion with a fondness for cider. To this day he is nostalgically remembered as Davey Apples although not to his face.

The hotel foyer can be a tricky place especially if you are trying to outwit the can lad who's onto you.

Keep up!... we have now touched down in a foggy BUDAPEST. The postage stamp hotel reception area meant you had to negotiate the serial killer behind the counter dishing out the keys (the concierge, Norman Bates, whatever JEEPERS. What if he thought I was the new bitch on the block. Anyway I was in! 90 squid is 90 squid isn't it ?

Literally outside of our, yes it's now our hotel, taking in the gloomy Danube air, I bumped into a lad who uttered the immortal line "What are you doing here??" I thought everyone knew about the by-annual gypsy violinist competition of the year. Anyway we retreated to a nearby Magyar bar to sup hot wine which even met with the approval of the Litherland sparks or should that be sharks? My asthmatic lungs gave a thumbs up too.

As normally happens on such a trip to far flung mysterious cities full of local tradition and intrigue, you quickly embrace a Sports Bar with frothy lager served up by busty totty. This trip didn't break with tradition.

The Sports Bar was its charming name, packed to the rafters it seemed with punters from the North Liverpool region… NOT citizens of BUDAPEST. When I say North Liverpool I can pin it down geographically tighter, to the greater BOOTLE area. Maybe there was a holiday declared by the stout yeomen at Bootle Town Hall? (yes there is such a place)

The night ended more or less as it had begun, back at Dracula's Castle negotiating the cold eyed killer on reception. I waved a cheery good-night as I left the niceties to Hightown's top boy who was an official guest. I woke in a cold sweat!.. the nightmare still vivid. The hotel concierge swinging the ice pic towards my skull. Maybe I had too much hot wine?

Day 2.The St Andrews bar. Another non Hungarian haunt. More members of the Bootle Independence Movement. This time a younger more dynamic element. A good little crew of cheery souls displaying a banner topped or should that be bottomed off with a liver bird sporting a pair of samba. An un-doubted homage to the 80s when some of their own dads (actually on this trip) made the Dassler bruvvers a few more Marks. Later in the day we stumbled into a bohemian Jazz Bar thick with ciggie smoke. "Just like the old days", the chain smoking Kopite said emotionally. Soon, the aromatic aroma of home-grown Mersey backie infused the premises. No one seemed to bother or care. The Budapest Metro beckoned, the rain came down, and the Reds went out.

After the game the Litherland three struck up a friendship with an ex bizzie, now full time piss artist, who told nasty stories about Ferencvaros Ultras. He insisted on driving them back to the city centre. A precarious journey were loved ones flashed before collective eyes. We all met up surprise surprise, in the Sports Bar. There was only one more thing to endure.. Norman Bates in gloomy towers.

Definitely not the swanky hotel I had dreamed of.

I did and lived to tell the tale.

MICK POTTER

Micks tale first appeared on the website the-end-fanzine.blogspot.co.uk

Can you remember what you did on your 18th birthday? For many young and old, it was spent in a drunken haze either in some snide function room amongst family and friends with a host of 80's classics providing the soundtrack for a night that often ended in tears… and your bathroom covered in vomit. But mine was somewhat quite different (although it did involve a lot of drink and vomit) as I headed East to watch the Reds play the mighty Debrecen in Budapest. Along with my Dad and uncle, we headed east to a place which was home to the Magnificent Magyars of the 1950's, and one that would ultimately see our Champions League dreams die. Arriving the day before the game, we set about exploring the various watering holes of this weird yet interesting city. With tall, dark buildings wherever you looked and trams straight out of 1950's Blackpool wherever you looked, it was a place that appeared to be stuck in the dark ages. However that only served to make Budapest even more appealing with every bar we visited. For all the glitz and glamour of your Milans, Madrids and Barcelonas, a lot of Champions League aways are now the same monotonous types Redmen have grown accustomed to over the years. Ultimately it is of course the price we pay for having such a rich and gloried history on the continent, but every now and then we're given the opportunity to travel to places which we wouldn't think twice about going to.

As the night wore on, it was safe to say the cheap but strong Hungarian ale was going down rather too quickly and before too long it caught up in a big way. Happy in the haze of a drunken hour, the old man passed me a shot of jagermeister as the clock ticked midnight and announced to the bar that his lad had turned 18. Queue more shots and pints being bought by strangers and sometime after I was dragged back to the hotel where I preceded to spew it for what seemed like an age. Just your average 18th then…

The next morning, I awoke with quite easily one of the worst hangovers I ever had and after finally coming round I stumbled out of bed to try and figure out how I'd came to be an intoxicated mess. After stumbling downstairs for a quick breakfast (which I spewed up) and meeting some of the Liverpool side who just so happened to be staying in our hotel (get on us being posh!) we were soon back on the ale. From back-street bars, to old-style coffee houses that were crammed with familiar faces young and old who'd made the trek over, there was a healthy following Reds despite the fact that the odds on our Champions League survival being against us. Requiring a win and hoping that Lyon did us a favour away to Fiorentina; thoughts were already turning to the Europa League and the potential trips that lay in wait.   But such thoughts only dampened the mood on what was an otherwise feel-good day of personal celebration filled with lager and goulash, as well as a surprise signed shirt from Jamie Carragher which was sorted by Vinnie Garrigos – a top bloke and one of the old school reds from Kensington.

With kick-off approaching, it was time to bid a sad farewell to our adopted locals and head to the Ferenc Puskas Stadium. Compared to your Wembleys which are soulless and look like a Lego-built monstrosity, the ground looked a bit moody and had some character about it, even if it was a shit-hole. The most vivid memory I had was walking through a field full of mud and cow-shit in order to find the away end which was only accessible via a steep staircase.

As always the match got in the way of an otherwise great trip with David N'Gog's early strike proving the difference between a poor Liverpool side, and an even worse Debrecen side. With the news coming through that Fiorentina had beaten Lyon, our stay at the top of European football was over, and little did we know at the time it would take us five years to climb our way back to the promised land. The only other highlight from a grim 90 minutes was a 50-odd year old Red began ranting about Rafa Benitez and how he couldn't wait for the club to "sack the cunt." After being challenged on his views by a mate of mine (who was also 18) he proceeded to profess about he'd seen it all and just because we were younger knew "fuck all" compared to him. You know the type, one of those who just because he's seen more success than we'll probably ever see he's always right and our views mean nothing. In fact the row escalated to the point where the divvy was close to raising his fists! Eventually common sense prevailed even if he persisted with his views. However that argument was a sign of the times in terms of how Liverpool fans had been divided and became a shadow of their former selves in the face of what was happening to the club under the ownership of George Gillett and Tom Hicks. Nevertheless, that was all soon forgotten about as we beat a hasty retreat back to the city centre and more ale to wipe out the pain of what we'd witnessed earlier. Making the most of an extra day, we spent the rest of our trip drinking and getting excited by the prospect of visiting more European outposts in a competition which many turn their noses up at.

With an extra day allowing us to spend more time drinking down by the Danube, I was left to lament what had been a pretty enjoyable trip despite the one reason for us being there letting us down. After all, how many Reds can say they went on a Euro away for their 18th?

JOEL RICHARDS

2009/10 EUROPA LEAGUE

18 February 2010 Round of 32
Liverpool FC   1-0   FC Unirea Urziceni

25 February 2010 Round of 32
FC Unirea Urziceni   1-3   Liverpool FC
Aggregate: 1-4

11 March 2010 Round of 16
LOSC Lille   1-0   Liverpool FC

18 March 2010 Round of 16
Liverpool FC   3-0   LOSC Lille
Aggregate: 3-1

1 April 2010 Quarter-finals
SL Benfica   2-1   Liverpool FC

8 April 2010 Quarter-finals
Liverpool FC   4-1   SL Benfica
Aggregate: 5-3

22 April 2010 Semi-finals
Club Atlético de Madrid   1-0   Liverpool FC

29 April 2010 Semi-finals
Liverpool FC   2-1   Club Atlético de Madrid
Aggregate: 2-2
Atlético win on away goals

EUROPA LEAGUE LAST 32 2ND LEG
25TH FEBRUARY 2010
GHENCEA STADION [21065]
BUCHAREST. ROMANIA
UNIREA URZICENI 1 LIVERPOOL 3

One trip, three cities! After finding flights totalling £87 and match tickets for just £7.50 this trip was now a goer. Quick call to Tozza, Degsy and Eddie, two finals and it was booked. Liverpool - Rome on the Wednesday, Rome - Bucharest on Thursday and Bucharest - Liverpool via Venice on the Friday.

In Rome we did the usual sights for the lads who hadn't been before. Trevi Fountain, Colosseum etc. Pasta, pizza and peroni then hotel ready for early flights the next day. Upon landing in Bucharest we had to fight our way through a shed load of taxi drivers trying their best to rip us off. After finally cutting a decent deal with one of them, he dropped us off on the opposite side of the road to our hotel because it was too busy. A proper ball-ache that road. Four lanes either way and chocker. It took about twenty minutes to cross the bastard. Ended up like frogger!

Bucharest must be the greyest city I've ever visited, the constant rain didn't help and dog shit everywhere as well. After a quick visit to Dinamo Bucharest's ground we started at a Romanian Liverpool supporter's bar. Great atmosphere, friendly and very hospitable. Then it was a taxi into the city centre to try and find some other Reds. On hearing The Troubadours "Gimme love" blaring out of one boozer made it easy. Some lads already in there had the barmen playing some Scouse tunes via Youtube. So we got Shack, The La's, Cast, Pete Wylie and The Real People to listen to whilst downing our cheap beer. Quality!.

With time getting on we needed to get to the ground. Enter Nello our taxi driver/chauffeur for the next few rides. He was a big Liverpool fan who wanted to go the game but his wife told him he had to work cos they needed the money. Degsy felt sorry for him so asked Nello if he would pick us up after the game and also take us to the airport the next day. Deal done.

There was no roof on our end and the torrential rain meant it was a hard match to watch. With the game comfortably won at 3-1, we decided at about seventy five minutes to jib it and find a cheap boozer to dry off and wait for our henpecked chauffeur. The first bar found us a 50p pint. Sound. "Degsy tell Nello to take his time, we're goin' nowhere fast!". Eventually Nello turns up and takes us back to town. Swerving the Goblin Club we instead end up back at the hotel for some late bevvies.

The next morning Nello turned up bang on time and dropped us off at the Airport. He got a good tip off the lads to keep his missus happy. "We'll give you a moment Degs,-dont be long!" we said as Degsy and Nello said there last goodbyes. Another holiday romance gone.

Walking into the airport and we all just started pissing ourselves. Playing over the tannoy was that Michael Bolton song "How am i supposed to live without you?" You

213

couldn't make it up. I'm sure I saw a tear in Degsys eye!

Next stop Venice. we had time to kill before our connection to Liverpool so we got a return coach to Venice centre. A mix of small alleyways, bridges and obviously water-ways. Not many pubs as such but we sniffed one out. Again the barman was another big Liverpool fan and took a shine to us. He gave us a large shot made to look like the Italian flag, which was downed in one obviously. "Lovely that what was it?", "The green bit was absinthe" he laughed. "Same again" we said, several times, earning us a place on his wall of fame for drinking the most shots. I think at one point we ended up behind the bar serving the locals! the absinthe was kicking in.

"What time is it?" Eddie 'Two Finals' slurred. "I think we've missed our coach back". Shit we had. Panic. "Don't worry" said the barman calmly "I'll get my brother to take you to the airport"

The rest was a blur to be honest. Apparently his brother dropped us off in the nick of time. A close shave cos the next available flight back wasn't for three days.

A quality trip with quality lads, which is what these European aways are all about.

IAN McKEVITT

2010/11 EUROPA LEAGUE

29 July 2010 Third qualifying round
FK Rabotnicki   0-2   Liverpool FC

5 August 2010 Third qualifying round
Liverpool FC   2-0   FK Rabotnicki
Aggregate: 4-0

19 August 2010 Play-offs
Liverpool FC   1-0   Trabzonspor AŞ

26 August 2010 Play-offs
Trabzonspor AŞ   1-2   Liverpool FC
Aggregate: 1-3

16 September 2010 Group stage (Group K)
Liverpool FC   4-1   FC Steaua Bucureşti

30 September 2010 Group stage (Group K)
FC Utrecht   0-0   Liverpool FC

21 October 2010 Group stage (Group K)
SSC Napoli   0-0   Liverpool FC

4 November 2010 Group stage (Group K)
Liverpool FC   3-1   SSC Napoli

2 December 2010 Group stage (Group K)
Steaua Bucureşti   1-1   Liverpool FC

15 December 2010 Group stage (Group K)
Liverpool FC   0-0   FC Utrecht

17 February 2011 Round of 32
AC Sparta Praha   0-0   Liverpool FC

24 February 2011 Round of 32
Liverpool FC   1-0   AC Sparta Praha
Aggregate: 1-0

10 March 2011 Round of 16
SC Braga   1-0   Liverpool FC

17 March 2011 Round of 16
Liverpool FC   0-0   SC Braga
Aggregate: 0-1

EUROPA LEAGUE QUALIFYING PLAY OFF
26TH AUGUST 2010
HUSEYIN AVNI AKER STADIUM [21065]
TRABZON. TURKEY
TRABZONSPUR 1 LIVERPOOL 2

It started with a phone call as it usually does, "Its Wayne here, have you heard who we've got? Trabzonspor," I knew what was coming next. Could I book the flights and hotels for the rest of the lads? Macco, Andrew, Wayne & me (Phil)..So as I have been doing this since 1977 it was my job to get everything sorted. Lucky now that we have the internet, so it was straight onto there and I booked some brilliant flights.

Stanstead to Istanbul and then a connecting three hour flight to Trabzon. So the day before the game three of us left North Wales by train to Euston, where we met up with Andrew and got the EasyBus to Stanstead..

After landing in Istanbul we had a three hour wait for our connecting flight to Trabzon. As we waited to board we noticed that we were the only Liverpool fans on the flight. No problems though as all that the locals wanted was photos with our scarves and flags etc We stayed at the hotel next door to where our team were staying and after meeting up with a few of our lot, including Dan whom we had met at Galatasaray and who had flown in from Ankara, we went to see the team. We thought it would be rude not to, as we had hundreds of Hicks and Gillette 'Not Welcome Here' flyers to give out. We had some great photos with the flyers on display in front of the players and Trabzon locals which were shown all over the world..

When we got to the ground the heavens opened and we were all given ponchos, only trouble was, they were all BLUE! Then I asked one of their officials did they have any programmes, he disappeared and next thing was he comes back with a cardboard box and gave it to me. I opened it up and inside were about two hundred programmes. After stuffing about twenty down my jeans I gave the rest away to our lot.

After the game as we were waiting to be let out, a couple of lads came over and asked me would I take their flag to Anfield. They had driven six hours from Tiblisi in Georgia and it was their dream for their flag to go on the Kop.

I told them 'Yes, no problem', so after the game the flag was hanging up in a bar with us and all of the legendary LFC banners. It was a little bar that the fifty of us who had travelled all ended up in..

After a few ales it was time to head back to the hotel to pick up the bags, as our flight was at 5.00am from Trabzon to Istanbul. We didn't have time for a sleep. I think we arrived back home late on the Friday night.

Two years later we played Galatasary in Istanbul in a friendly. Due to the late announcement of the game only ten of us travelled. When we walked into our end that held 3,000 we were met by two of the lads from Tbilisi and yes we still had their flag. Last season when we played Everton at Anfield, one of the lads, Irakli from Tbilisi stood on the Kop for the first time. On his return he took the original flag they gave us

in Trabzon and we have had a replica made which has been to all of the aways with us.
PHIL ROOSE

Trabs on for Trabzon.

It was August now and we'd progressed through to the next play-off stage of the Europa League and in the draw we got Trabzonspor away. Sitting on facebook, probably perving at birds pics, Jack popped up and asked if I fancied going to Trabzon, so I thought, 'yep go on, why not?'. So Ian and Jack booked the trip and I was on my way to Trabzon via Berlin and Istanbul.

The countdown to Trabzon went fast and before you knew it the day arrived to go. My cousin Al owed me money for my 18th, so he said he'd take me the airport. He arrived and off we went to John Lennon airport. We got to the airport and met up with the lads Ian, Jack, Anto and Billy. I'd seen Billy at the matches before but didn't know him personally but for a week before the trip we just got chatting on facebook, so for a laugh I told him I had tourettes, so when Billy walked into the airport I started twitching and telling him to fuck off. He seemed a bit like 'oh fuckinell' so I dropped the act and told him I didn't have tourettes.

Our first flight was to Berlin and we had eight hours before the connecting flight to Istanbul, so we had time to go and take a look at Berlin. The flight over was good and we got into Berlin at about 5pm. After a quick discussion we decided to get a taxi down to the Olympic Stadium as you can get into the ground for four euro's and take a look around. It took us about forty minutes in a cab to get there. We paid to get into the stadium and I have to say it's one of the best grounds I've been to, quality. If we get them in the Europa or if a final is held there I'll deffo go. I had a little run on the track around the pitch and we got some photos on the pitch. After our little walk around the ground we just sat down and had whatever food we'd brought with us for the trip. I was a bit low on money but I was to be paid on the match day so I'd be alright. I got stuck into my home made ham butties, very nice as well. Anto had brought sausage rolls and passed them round. We then got a cab to Checkpoint Charlie and took a few pics and then found a decent bar and sat outside. Berlin is a nice city and everybody was friendly with us asking where we were heading off to.

The lads then wanted to go to McDonalds so we went there and me being on the money watch managed to get Billy to get me a Magnum McFlurry. It was time to get back to the Airport and that's when we met the most strangest of characters.

As we waited to board the flight a strange Turkish man who was now christened Voodoo Vinnie turned around and gave the five finger salute, he must be a Red we thought. The flight got underway and everyone was ready for a kip. I was sat next to Billy and after about an hour I woke up and Billy was already up. To the next aisle Voodoo Vinnie was wanting to get out of his seat so his ma got out the way and all of a sudden right on the plane Voodoo Vinnie was performing Voodoo. The air-hostesses where looking at him and tried to talk to him but he was having none of it. By now the rest of the lads got up so it was amusing to us but then he just walked off down to the bog. We noticed it had been a good fifteen minutes that Voodoo Vinnie had been away and the air-hostesses were trying to get him to come out of the toilet, he came out and seemed to be in pain. He sat down again next to his ma who seemed worried about him and we all just looked at each other and the air-hostesses asked if he was problem to us but we were sort of like 'No, it's alright'. Five minutes later he gets past his mum again and starts walking towards the pilots and you know when you're just thinking he's gonna do something, well he started performing Voodoo again and then the rest of the plane got onto it. He then had a walk down to the pilots area and everyone was sort of panicking that he'd break in and crash the plane. We were all a bit like 'Oh shit' and I started thinking of my life etc. Then the air-hostesses grabbed Voodoo Vinnie and we all gave a sigh of relief. Voodoo Vinnie was put back into his seat and that was it then, no funny business from him for the rest of the flight.

We arrived in Istanbul in the early hours of the morning and just went to the bar in the airport and sat in there until our flight was called up. The flight was quick and the good part was we got free sweets so being on a money saver I got a good handful.

Trabzon seemed alright from the window of the airport and as we got outside an army tank passed us by. We didn't have a clue where our hotel was but it turned out to be just five minutes down the road. It was supposed to be a luxury four-star hotel, it was alright like and would do us for the night. After we settled into our rooms we all headed off down to the beach which was the back garden of the hotel, we took a look at the pool but it was out of bounds as it was green and hadn't been touched for years. We had a quick dip in the sea and then I got a sun bed and fell asleep for about three hours. When I woke up I was all red and felt even more knackered, it was getting to about 4pm so we decided we'd go and take a look at Trabzon. We had a little sit down near the pool first and noticed a nice Turkish bird with her family on the beach and the bird was christened bird with the big tits. Ian seemed to be in love with the bird from a distance and the bird clocked onto the fact that she was being watched. Her family packed up and she went up the stairs at the top of the hill and turned round and gave a little cheeky smile, Ian was made up.

We got showered and changed then we ordered two cabs, one cab turned up and the driver just said we could all get in so with Jack being the smallest of us had to sit on Anto's knee as we all squashed up in the back of this dodgy Turkish cab. We got out of the cab and it was as if the whole of the town just stopped for a minute and took a look at us. I'm sure some Turkish lad said in his own language 'Who the fuck are they?'. With it being Ramadan the only places open were McDonalds and Burger King. None of the pubs were open so we had a little walk around and went into the Club shop in the town centre. We passed this five-star hotel and Tony Barrett was outside and let on to us so we had a quick chat about the team that was coming over. After the chat we decided it be best to head back to the hotel and hang around there so we went into a shop and got some drinks, crisps etc that would do us for the night. Anto got some Racki which is supposed to get you off your head after a couple of shots. Back at the hotel Anto got the shots out and everyone except me of course had a Racki, Jack felt sick straight away after his but the other seemed to be fine with it. For the rest of the night we just played black jack and chase the ace for hours listening to the Turkish music. It was getting late and we were knackered so called it a night. As me, Anto and Billy passed this room on the ground floor this forty plus aged brass was taking a client into her room and Billy considered knocking on the door but decided against it. Off to bed we went then.

The day of the match arrived and we went for what the hotel called breakfast, to be fair it was alright I just made myself some ham and cheese butties and had a bowl of their version of coco pops. Declan rang Anto as he'd arrived at his hotel, he'd gone with Pete and Helen his Southern mates as Pete had found a really cheap deal for the trip, so Dec jumped onboard with them. We agreed to meet at a bar near his hotel that was next to the beach but on the other side of town to our hotel. After breakfast we got another room for the night between us, just to keep our bags in for the day and if we wanted to have a shower after the match before we headed home. As we checked out of the rooms we'd stayed in they charged us for some items in the mini bars. Not our mini bars but the one everyone decided to take out of two doors down, I managed to get a can of coke but in the end had to pay for it.

We put the bags into the new room and I noticed my wallet was missing. I was nearly crying looking for it, I went down the beach and looked for it there and got back in the room and Anto had it ha ha, I'd left it on the desk in the reception when I was counting the money.

The taxi came and like before it was the same fella, Jack had to sit on Anto's knee but to be fair to Jack he never complained. We got to the bar and met up with Dec, Helen and Pete and pretty much stayed at the bar all day. Closer to kick off a group of Trabzon fans also came to the bar and we started talking to them etc and got a group photo with them with the banner the lads had brought with them.

It was time to head off to the ground and this Turkish fella sorted us a mini bus to take us to the ground. We got to the ground and all the bizzies had big packed lunches as they waited for the sun to go down so they could eat because of Ramadan. We got outside our end and Ian Kidd and his crew where there observing. Danny from Cheltenham was outside with the Bristol Branch so we let on to them. The kebab shop round the corner from our end opened up and we all got a kebab, I got a chicken kebab with rice and it was spot on. The gates opened and we were allowed in our end all 91 of us. Next minute the heavens opened and we were getting drenched so the Turks passed us waterproof jackets. With me being sensible, I put it on and got stick for it. Taggy's lot came in with little Mic and Anna (Liverbird otk). The atmosphere in the ground was nothing compared to Besiktas but for the size of the ground the Trabzon fans where decent. The game got underway and at half time with it being 1-0 to them, we all thought the European journey was over with how things were going, they were all over us.

A Trabzon fan decided to come to the match with an Everton shirt on and came up to our end to show us that he was wearing it. Little Mic got the Irregulars banner and climbed the fencing to get it high up, the Turks all thought he was mad. We managed to turn the game around and won 2-1. Our end went mad when both goals went in as it was a sort of celebration of we're all going on more European trips. As we got singing a Red got up and started a chorus of 'We're all on the Racki' and as he did, slipped and fell down about three seats knocking his head each time he fell down another level, it was funny but it must have hurt. The game finished and we clapped the team as they all came over to us. Turkish bizzies kept us in for a bit as the Trabzon fans chucked scarves and flowers into our end. Everyone pretty much gave the flowers to Anna and Helen. The bus took us back into the town centre and through the streets of Trabzon. We had a good singing session before diving into the same bar as earlier and staying there for the night. As it got late we headed back to our hotel but not before we got a decent kebab and then off to the hotel we went. Anto and Jack dived onto the bed so for four hours me, Ian and Billy headed downstairs and the three lads that were on our flight coming here were in the same hotel, so we just all talked in the lounge about the match and expectations for the new season. It got to the time we had to get to the airport so we went and got Anto and Jack up and made our way to the airport.

The flight to Istanbul went quick as we all slept. We all had a good chat about Istanbul 05 in the airport and the lads got gifts for their families.

Our next flight was to Munich (Germany) which again went pretty quickly as we all just slept on the flight again. We landed in Munich and we had another eight hours before our flight back to Manchester. They had this fifteen Euro group train pass on sale in the station at the airport so we got that and headed to Bayern's new ground. The new Stadium is right is in the middle of nowhere so there's nothing to see there except just the Stadium itself. Loads of people where going on the Stadium tour and we'd just missed the English speaking tour by half an hour, nobody was really keen on doing the tour so we went in both Club shops 1860's and Bayern's, I got some Bayern jellies for two Euro's. After the stadium we wanted to go to the Olympic stadium so we headed over to the other side of town and visited that ground. Before we went into the ground we sat in the park for a bit just sitting down on the grass. For the Olympic stadium Munich It's the same deal as the Olympic stadium in Berlin, four Euro's to get in and then you can pretty much do whatever you like. We got onto the pitch etc and to be honest it's not really that great, it's just the history of the place that makes it impressive. The Olympic village itself is impressive and nice. It was time to head back to the airport and on our way a couple from Stoke started speaking to us about our trip and what we'd done, the fella couldn't believe we'd done all the travelling just for the match.

Munich airport inside is great, everything you need and it's massive. As a farewell to Munich we went into the McDonalds and as ever I got the original Euro away meal of chicken nuggets and chips plus another Magnum McFlurry.

As flight time neared I think Billy got every single member of his family and the dogs a present. The flight was good and we arrived back in Manchester, with Billy living in Birkenhead his dad was picking him up but it's as if he'd been away to war, his whole family turned up for him taking his bag off him and everything, close family I guess.

The rest of us ordered a Delta and we were lucky it came after ten minutes and off home we went.

Trip over and about two weeks later the club sent us all a letter and a towel thanking us for going to the game.

DAVID WALTON

EUROPA LEAGUE GROUP STAGE
30TH SEPTEMBER 2010
STADION GALGENWAARD [23662]
UTRECHT. NETHERLANDS
F.C. UTRECHT 0 LIVERPOOL 0

We went to Utrecht but were doing the compulsory stay in Amsterdam. The day after the game we came out of the Hotel ready for a night out and noticed crowds of people coming up the road dressed in black with megaphones and music blaring. So we asked them what it was for and apparently they were marching for squatters rights.

By this time most of us were either stoned or pissed so we thought it would be a good idea to follow them.

As we marched up to the top of the street there was some sort of Mexican stand-off going on between the police and the squatters. A few 'Fuck the police' shouts came out and within a few minutes bricks and bottles were getting thrown. We thought it was a laugh and stayed with them.

The laugh soon ended though. The bizzies came steaming in on their horses, chasing and twatting everyone in sight, so the squatters and us scattered. We had three options as we ran down the roads, either find a stairway, get a few smacks or jump in a canal. I didn't fancy a few lumps on my head nor did I wanna get me trainees wet so we ended up getting cornered on some stairs by the police. It was then that we gave it the shit-bag, easy way out by yelling 'We're tourists'.

Moments later and the squatters are re-grouping. We'd just had a lucky escape but what did we decide to do? Yes, we stupidly decided to go with them again with some of us also acting like we were squatters. No names mentioned like but i think their hatred for the police shone through. Windows were getting smashed, cars were getting tipped up and the block paving was being ripped up for ammunition. Getting tear-gas fired at us soon put an end to that though.

There were a few disagreements between the lads with some wanting to carry on their freedom fighter movement and others having had enough of being involved in a mini war in Amsterdam, but after it had all settled it was something we all had a laugh over with plenty of picture opportunities to pose with the damage done.

ADAM KEARNS

EUROPA LEAGUE 2ND ROUND, 1ST LEG.
2ND DECEMBER 2010
GHENCEA STADION [20000]. BUCHAREST. ROMANIA.
STEAUA BUCHAREST 1 LIVERPOOL 1

We should have known at the beginning of this trip that it was not going to be plain sailing. A few weeks before Christmas and in the Europa League not many Reds were travelling over to Bucharest to watch Roy Hodgson's Red Men take on Steaua Bucharest, but seven of us decided we wanted to pay another visit to the Romanian capital after enjoying it a few years earlier.

The flights we had booked were from Luton, which posed the first obstacle of getting there from Liverpool. Our flight was at 7am on the Wednesday morning and after various people saying they would drive etc and then dropping out at the last minute the transport was arranged. One of the lads going with us said he could take four people, picking them up at Warrington. Me and my other mate arranged a lift from one of the lads we know from the game, we had to be at the Rocket at 3am in the morning!

Once six of us had met at my house at 1:45am, I phoned a taxi to take me and my mate to the Rocket to wait for our lift, and the others were getting a lift to Warrington by one of the lad's missus. First problem was the lad from Chester (Handbridge on the Dee) realised once he had got to our house that he had left his passport & match tickets on his bed! It was now a race against time for him to get back to Chester and meet the others up at Warrington. He had to phone his mate who took time out from work to bring him over to Liverpool in the first place, to come back pick him back up again and do another round trip.

Waiting at the Rocket at 2:30am in the morning when it was -8 degrees was not a pleasant experience, and when the others drove past us going to Warrington, they gave us the customary two finger salute and started taking the mick out of us. I was beginning to wonder if our lift would come at all. It did, five minutes later, so I could sort of relax then.

Well that's what I thought, after a quick phone call to make sure all the others were on their way including the passport-less fella from Chester, it was straight down to Luton Airport to catch our flight to Bucharest (the other lads who caught their lift in Warrington, informed us that the fella had taken his missus' 7-seater in the end, so we could have got a lift with them after all).

The weather for the previous two days had been snow and ice, so when the driver of our of 4x4 decided to start going into the icy outside lane doing 70mph I just closed my eyes and started to pray like the rest of us in the car, then ironically 'Life in the fast lane by The Eagles' came onto the radio. After a quick service stop we arrived at Luton Airport forty minutes after the others, who were already in the departure lounge waiting for us.

The lads who took us down in their 4x4 soon informed us that their flight had been cancelled (they were on a different airline than us) but the weather was clear down in

Luton, so we thought it was just their flight. Then about 10 minutes later our flight had been cancelled also, so when we contacted our other mates who were already through, waiting in departures for us, they knew nothing of the sort, and after a few minutes checking all this out our flight was actually going and we were allowed into the departures too.

The pre-flight drink at 6:30am in the morning was underway. Twenty minutes later we hear that our flight has actually been cancelled, but we were stuck in the departures lounge of the airport. We had to wait for ten minutes to be escorted back into the departures hall of the airport to sort out the situation. The queue for the Wizz Air desk was already huge when we got there, so we just had to queue up. We soon realised that we could do all this stuff over the phone. So six of us were on the phone to Wizz Air based in Bucharest (I think), while the other lad was plotting various routes we could take, eventually I got through to Wizz Air and there was only three seats available to Bucharest on the later flight. We decided we would all stick together. With no flight the following day, it was a question of where we can go (if anywhere). There were various options of places and then either train or drive. Sofia was mentioned then one of the lads said Cluj which is in Romania and there was seats left for a flight at 7:00am the following morning. So that was that. We all transferred our flights to the following day and the flight to Cluj. One of the lads said it was about a four hour drive from Bucharest according to the Internet. Wizz Air also confirmed this. So once that was sorted, we booked into the Holiday inn at the airport via a quick phone call to Barnes Travel back in Liverpool, who sorted this for us. As soon as we got there I needed to reprint all the boarding cards etc on the PC, while the others all enjoyed a couple of pints or two and decided how we would get from Cluj to Bucharest. I also emailed the hotel and said we would be a day late and explained we were still coming depending on the weather. When asking people at Luton airport and Wizz Air we were told that our flight had been cancelled due to bad weather in Bucharest – ice. But we soon found out that this was not true, the day we were flying was a national Bank Holiday in Romania and many people had not turned in for work, hence the reason behind many flights being cancelled/delayed.

The train looked like a no-go after seeing it took about nine hours and seemed to be a cattle train, so one of the lads said he would drive if we hired a car – great all sorted. We would hire a car once we landed in Cluj in case of any further bad weather. So we hit Luton for a day/night on the ale and taking in a local curry house too (which we would all regret the following morning). At about 6pm it started snowing in Luton. It was heavy and we were all thinking there is no way we are flying in the morning. We eventually made our bed at about 1:30am. Before being woken by the alarm at 5 and staggered down to reception to meet all the lads. The sight and smell of us was one you could not imagine – curry stains all over our clothes and smelling like a dead rat. All of a sudden one of the lads said – "The Tickets" they have gone, I soon remembered they fell from his pocket in the curry house the previous evening and one of the other lads picked them up and kept them (good job I remembered because it was panic stations, and the lad who had them even forgot he did actually have them until I reminded him)

So we staggered to the airport about a five minute walk away and the snow was still coming down very heavy, but when we got into the terminal we queued up for our flight – we could not believe it - it was actually going! Then it dawned on us, where are we actually going here?

After doing all the calculations we would arrive in Bucharest with two hours to spare. But as soon as we bordered the plane we were delayed thirty five minutes while they defrosted it. When we eventually landed in Romania we went to hire a car, the cheapest seven seater available. Which cost £120 (I think) including a sat nav.

When we got taken to the car, it must have been the smallest seven-seater ever invented, so we all somehow managed to get in with our bags all over the place. Petrol was purchased and we were off on our way to Bucharest. Well that was after driving around Cluj for forty five minutes trying to get out of the place and seeing the most bizarre funeral service imaginable (the coffin was in the back of a ford pick-up truck which had a brass band marching in front of it, most bizarre)

So eventually we left Cluj and we were on our way to Bucharest (we basically had no time to spare now, if we carried on it would get us there for Kick Off. The sat nav said it would take six to seven hours. We stopped after three hours of solid driving for some food and drinks at a local petrol station, which was littered with stray dogs (a common scene in Romania), so we grabbed some refreshments and set off again (the only soft person to volunteer to drive had to drive us the whole way, no-one else would take over especially after seeing the state of the roads we were driving on (it was single lane all the way, through every village and town in Romania)

Soon after leaving with no lights on the roads, the fog started to come down it really was starting to look like Transylvania. After a few nearer misses with articulated lorries on the way, it was finally declared we were going to miss the match. We had thirty minutes until kick off and we were still 200 miles away. We tried our best to get there, but it just wasn't meant to be. We were then on the lookout for a café/restaurant to watch the game. This was no easy feat as we were in the middle of Romania and we couldn't see any signs of life anywhere. We soon saw a log cabin with lights on and a TV. That will do us, five minutes until kick off we ventured into the little restaurant. As we entered it really did feel like we was on a different planet, the place really was a log cabin; it was full of stuffed animals and the most basic menu. I just ordered chips & bread there was no way I was having anything else to eat, some people ordered chicken (which was still raw when it came out and omelettes). The lager was ok though and only about 50p for a pint. The barking of the dogs in the back soon stopped once we ordered our food. I wonder who had that and thought it was chicken? After trying to talk to the owner, we showed him our match tickets. He seemed quite confused by this, but in the end I think he got the jist of it. On our way out he gave us a two litre bottle of homemade wine (it looked like piss and tasted like it, who knows what it really was)

Liverpool drew the game 1-1. It was the only away goal we scored in the competition that season and after attending every other away game we only saw it on a TV - typical.

Anyway we set off again all fed and watered, Bucharest was in sight now, but we soon ended up behind a police car, which wasn't the best, as the driver of our car had used one of the other lads driving licence to hire the car and used my credit card to pay for it, we didn't want to get pulled now, this would be all we needed, so after reducing our speed dramatically we stayed behind the police car for about 5 minutes, until he waved us on past him to a huge sigh of relief. We soon hit some motorway, the first bit of motorway on the whole trip, this was the road which would lead us into Bucharest. Finally we arrived, and got to our hotel at midnight. We made it, although we missed the game, we made it.

The bags were literary just thrown into the room, and we ventured out into Bucharest and to the Irish bar we had been the previous year. Upon our arrival we found some other lads who we know from the game in the Irish bar, one of them started to take the piss – It didn't go down well to say the least, no matter what anyone said we tried our best to get to this game, when most couldn't be bothered to make the effort or went home and got a full refund. So after an hour in there it shut, much to our disappointment. We had only just arrived and we deserved a good night out surely? The lad from Chester wandered off into the night and went back to the hotel because he was done in (well that is what he said anyway), so the rest of us, ventured about looking for somewhere to be open, we found one place but there wasn't one person in there and there was no ale – what is that all about? So we eventually found a bar about ten minutes from our hotel and it stayed open until we left the next morning at 6:30, we met two fella's in there who we know from the away games, and they had stayed in there the whole day and even missed the game. We went back to the hotel and sat and ate breakfast before going up to bed (for about three hours anyway). I was suddenly woken up saying that some fella is trying to drive off in the hire car. We had arranged for it to be picked up in Bucharest at our hotel and I had all the paperwork, which needed to be signed. After finding where we had left the car, it had indeed gone, so I started to jog around the streets, and there was the car with one of the fella's who was with us in it, everything was alright, we just needed the documents to be signed by the fella who was taking the car back, so we didn't get stung for anything, panic over.

So after getting up early again, I think I had about five hours sleep in the last seventy two hours now, we had the afternoon wandering around Bucharest, taking in the Steaua Bucharest stadium and various other locations. Our flight back to Luton wasn't until 19:00, so we had plenty of time. On our way back to the airport, we all looked and seemed absolutely done in, which was no surprise. We soon boarded our flight back to Luton and that was eventful too.

The flight back, again on Wizz Air we ended up sitting by some lunatic, who was so drunk it was unbelievable, how he managed to get on the flight is anyone's guess. We all tried to play dumb with him and pretend to be asleep when he would talk to us. But one of the lads regrettably started talking to him, he kept saying he was from 'two dogs' (Huyton), some of the things he was saying we would laugh at but after about twenty minutes it wore off. He kept pestering (in aggressive way) the cabin crew for drinks and was singing very loud. Eventually he bought all of us a drink and some other people (all mini vodkas) because he needed to get rid of all that monopoly money (Romanian Lei) he had. So when he got the bill, he didn't have enough, he ended up paying in English too. After annoying all of the people on the flight on the way back, we started to descend into Luton, and he went quiet for a bit, until about twenty seconds before we landed he stood up and started to get his bag, to which the cabin crew immediately shouted at him. The ground at Luton was covered with heavy snow and it was still falling. We were all thinking the police will be waiting when we get off to arrest this fella because he was just a complete nightmare. He was after a lift back to Liverpool as well, good job our car was full (even if it wasn't there was no way we was taking this nutter back).

Upon finding the car in the car park which was pre-booked the day before we left, we drove to the exit only for the automatic barrier not to rise. So after pressing the buzzer and giving all our information in, we were free to go. The roads were still horrendous in Luton, but it soon cleared when we started to hit the North West. Our driver dropped us off at Burtonwood services, so he could go back home more easily, we couldn't have asked no more as he had done all the driving in Romania nursing a very heavy hangover. So after phoning a taxi to pick us up, I was soon back home. What a journey, we may have missed the match, but this was a journey that will never be forgotten, the magnificent seven.

STE TRAYNOR

2012/13 EUROPA LEAGUE

2 August 2012 Third qualifying round
FC Gomel   0-1   Liverpool FC

9 August 2012 Third qualifying round
Liverpool FC   3-0   FC Gomel
Aggregate: 4-0

23 August 2012 Play-offs
Heart of Midlothian FC   0-1   Liverpool FC

30 August 2012 Play-offs
Liverpool FC   1-1   Heart of Midlothian FC
Aggregate: 2-1

20 September 2012 Group stage (Group A)
BSC Young Boys 3-5   Liverpool FC

4 October 2012 Group stage (Group A)
Liverpool FC   2-3   Udinese Calcio

25 October 2012 Group stage (Group A)
Liverpool FC   1-0   FC Anji Makhachkala

8 November 2012 Group stage (Group A)
FC Anji Makhachkala   1-0   Liverpool FC

22 November 2012 Group stage (Group A)
Liverpool FC   2-2   BSC Young Boys

6 December 2012 Group stage (Group A)
Udinese Calcio   0-1   Liverpool FC

14 February 2013 Round of 32
FC Zenit 2-0   Liverpool FC

21 February 2013 Round of 32
Liverpool FC   3-1   FC Zenit
Aggregate: 3-3
FC Zenit win on away goals

EUROPA LEAGUE GROUP STAGE.
20TH SEPTEMBER 2012
STADE DE SUISSE [31120]. BERN. SWITZERLAND
BSC YOUNG BOYS 3 LIVERPOOL 5

Planes, Trains and Automobiles: A Swiss Adventure.

There were sniggers all round, like a school playground, when Liverpool drew Young Boys in the Europa League to be played in the previously named Wankdorf Stadium. I'd not watched the Reds in Switzerland before, so a trip is quickly planned as there is not much time to think about going before the actual game comes round.

The journey begins:

Stage 1 of the trip was the automobiles portion with a pick up of 2am in the morning to enable us to drive the 165 miles South to Luton Airport from the North West for our 7.25am flight to Geneva. The number of times I've woken up at ungodly hours to watch the Reds in Europe is not worth thinking about. You just get on with it.

It wasn't my turn to drive so it enabled me to catch a valuable Thirty minutes shut eye. If anyone hasn't followed their team in Europe they probably won't understand it's a test of endurance, usually fuelled by strong continental lager, rubbish food (if any) and a distinct lack of sleep. Therefore, this bonus Thirty minutes in the land of nod could prove valuable in the day(s) ahead.

Breakfast beer:

6.30am in the airport bar and a nice cold pint of Becks slides down the neck for breakfast like a smooth Alonso pass, before we board the plane for our relatively short hop to the land of chocolates, watches and the Alps.

Easyjet bacon baguettes and a couple of cans of Heineken piss helps pass the flight and we are soon dropping into Geneva airport on the edge of the beautiful Lake Geneva, with the Alps protecting the area like a bus parked in front of Chelsea's goal in a Champions League semi-final.

A short train journey into Geneva centre followed before we killed an hour or so before our scenic train journey to Bern. A quick walk to the edge of the lake, a few pictures taken for good measure and time to grab a few cans for the two hour train trek through the beautiful Swiss countryside.

Now Geneva is an ultra expensive place but I've rarely seen brasses on the streets at 10am in the morning wherever I've travelled. Probably out and about touting for business from the business fraternity.

Scenic train:

Five minutes into the train journey and the cans are open and a card game is on the go between the seven of us. Broke just about even on the outward journey, the return will be so much better.

I'm no Michael Palin but this train journey from Geneva to Bern is the most stunning I've ever witnessed. On the edge of Lake Geneva for the first half and then through the countryside for the second. Think Steve McQueen for the countryside bit. I was just expecting him to fly over a hill on his TT Special 650 Triumph motorbike, with the German's in chase.

We arrived in the centre of Bern bang on time and due to the fact our hotel was five minutes walk from the Wankdorf, oh sorry Stade de Suisse, a plan was hatched to settle in an Irish bar for a couple of hours for a few sing songs, which stretched to four hours and an urgent dash for taxi's to drop our stuff off at the hotel. The local bar owner had generously (sarcasm) dropped the ale prices from 9CHK to 8CHK, which was still about £6 in real money!! That's how expensive Switzerland is. Funny how we always judge how expensive a European destination is by the price of the ale.

The local Liverpool fans were a strange lot if truth be told. They had organised some local 'fan club' gathering that included LFC chocolates amongst other things in the Irish bar.

Match time: One of our members was a little worse for wear (blaming the bitter in the Irish bar - that old excuse) but soon recovered as we made it into the ground about five minutes from kick-off after literally slinging our bags into our hotel rooms. Not as tight as the Braga away game when we were literally the last fans in the ground before kick-off but that's another story.

It turned into an exciting Euro away game, unlike some of the previous bore-fests we had encountered, with the 0-0 at a freezing Sparta Prague immediately springing to mind. That's the other thing about Euro away games, the game sometimes gets in the way of a good time. As we are losing, we bring on Jonjo Shelvey and eventually take all three points with a 5-3 victory. It was our young lads versus their Young Boys, with Gary Glitter nowhere to be seen.

A quick walk back to the hotel with hardly any trouble to be seen and we settle in the bar for a few hours for a natter and a chin wag about the game surrounded by fellow Liverpool supporters and a few from the Swiss Army for some reason. Never even knew they had an army with being neutral and all that!!

Homeward bound: It was an early start the morning after the night before and a taxi at 7.30am took four bleary eyed lads back to Bern train station for the return journey back to Geneva. The cards came out again and I had my most successful two hours of 'chase the ace' ever for a European away. I remember going three hours from Faro to Lisbon before our game against Benfica without winning a single hand. I think the card school cost me more than my flight in the end !!

A trouble free flight back to Luton before the car park of the M6 greeted us with a car journey that took us twice the time of the outgoing one, on a Friday evening when all I wanted to do was get home, throw bags in and get out on the lash again.

All in all, another super trip with good friends. Everything went smooth and we got the added bonus of a good result. If your team ever make it to Europe, make the effort and get across to support them with a few mates. There's nothing better when following a team but don't go on the official trip. Use planes, trains and automobiles if needed, it's much more fun.

NICK HARMAN

EUROPA LEAGUE GROUP STAGE.
8TH NOVEMBER 2012
STADION LOKOMOTIV [15000]. MOSCOW. RUSSIA
ANZI MAKHACHKALA 1 LIVERPOOL 0

So here we are again, Москва, Moscow, Russia, back in what used to be the USSR. I've been here before, some ten years ago, when a Michael Owen hat trick saw off a mediocre Spartak Moscow side in the tiny Dinamo ground. European glory was not to follow, a Valencia side managed by a certain Señor Benitez gave us a footballing lesson at the Mestalla and kept the ball for ninety minutes at Anfield – and we eventually fucked it up in Basel. Now we're here in Moscow because UEFA thinks a trip to Dagestan is too dangerous for us. How Grozny was a possible venue for this game is beyond me then, but anyway, here we are. And we've got a good chance of going through to the knockout stages if we can get a result here. Judging by Anzhi's performance at Anfield a couple of weeks ago, we've got every chance.

Going back 10 years, this is what I remembered of that previous Moscow trip:
it was cold
the heavy police/military presence everywhere in the city, and especially at the match
the Rossia Hotel with its many floors, uncountable number of corridors, rooms, bars and prossies
the fantastic underground system and magnificent architecture of the stations
didn't touch a drop of beer but stuck to the vodka for three days (with all necessary consequences)
and... not an awful lot of bars or pubs to be found to be honest
Now I'm curious how Russia's capital has evolved in those ten years, so it's with some excitement that I board the plane in Cologne. There's three of us: Marc, my best Belgian Liverpool mate, whom I've been going the match with since we went to Galatasaray together in 2002, and the other Marc, the baker, who happens to be the (Belgian!) president of ALSIN, known in our Gentlemen's Dining Club circles as "the other Dutch branch". We're flying with German Wings, and Lufthansa's cheap airline doesn't let us down. Punctual, friendly and classy from start till finish, so we arrive at Vnukovo airport in good spirits. Swiftly through immigration and another security check and then we make our way to the train station. The moment of leaving my house in Ekeren I had told myself, for the umpteenth time, "no, I'm not taking any tobacco or ciggies with me, I will NOT smoke for three days", so as soon as we enter the arrivals hall, I'm off to a kiosk, to buy a package of ciggies, 20 Russian Kent sets me back about 120 roubles, which is some £2.50 sterling I guess. And of course I have to buy another map. Got maps at home from every European city or town I've been to since following the Mighty Reds around the continent, but don't think I ever think of taking one with me when I leave to a place where I've been before... I buy one with the street names in Russian, so that should make the navigation a little bit easier.
A smooth one-hour train ride brings us to "Kiev" underground station, where we get

onto Moscow's version of the Circle line. Six stops later we are near our hotel, a short walk will bring us there. Or so we think. An hour and a half later we are still running through tiny little streets and dark alleys, we ask here and there, but no avail, the Basilica hotel is not to be found... "1000 rouble", says the taxi driver, when we finally stop one and ask to take us there. You just know you are being ripped off but it's nearly 8pm and we have lost quite a bit of valuable drinking time already. The cabbie does his best to give us the impression he is doing a couple of blocks, but in all honesty: he drops us right round the corner. Twenty quid wasted. Only to be met by a couple of Irregulars as we get out of the cab. "How much did that taxi cost you then, Nico?", is the sarcastic comment. And rightly so. Schoolboy error that.

Sod it. We drop our bags and head off to the nearest bar, which thankfully is just round the corner. No trouble finding that! "Three Russian beers please, and can we have a look at the menu as well?". Nice one, the menu's all in Russian, so I just point my finger at something and say: "I want that!". 'That' turns out to be a chicken skewer which comes with curly chips. Marc and Marc follow suit, as do John, Terry, Les and Chris, who have turned up a little bit later. More Russian beers follow and by midnight, when this bar shuts, we have several options. Follow Anna's directions, who has texted me saying she was trying every cocktail on a menu "in a bar somewhere near an underground station", try to get in touch with Mike again, no response from him yet, or follow Les who knows someone who told him that there is a bar somewhere near Red Square. So after about a good twenty minute walk we end up on Red Square where most of our group start taking pics. Fuck that for a game of soldiers, I think, been there done that ten years ago, let's go and find a place to drink. Priorities, you know. Thankfully Terry and I find a Chinese restaurant on one of the big boulevards off Red Square, where Marc and Marc join us for a final beer before going to bed. Terry and I look at each other and say "more beer". Believe it or not, we find another Chinese restaurant, again no need to have a meal, just have a beer sir, no problem. It can be a coincidence, but there seems to be more and more girls going out and they seem to get prettier and prettier as the evening progresses. We have a few more and start walking in the direction of where I think Mike will be hanging out. After trying one or two more Russian lagers in Che's bar, it's getting near 3am. "Shall we make our way back?", asks Terry, and he starts walking down the road, right past a bar called Coyote Ugly. "Hang on a minute, Terry, better go in here", I tell him, after seeing some scantily clad ladies dance wildly on the bar. "Two Russian beers", we say, in fluent Russian of course. "It's raining men, hallelujah", belts the jukebox, and the ladies behind the bar find it necessary to spray all and sundry with soda. "Do you want belly shot?", says the piece of paper that one of the barmaids passes me. A smooth, napkin-written conversation later I know what it is all about – and some girls have given us a demonstration as well. As the price for a belly shot turns out to be roughly the same as fifteen beers no need to say we opt for the latter... By 6am, after a private taxi ride which only costs 200 roubles for a fifteen minute dash. As the evening progressed, I had remembered what one of my mates in Belgium had told me, there's plenty of Moscovites who wait in their Ladas near bars

232

and restaurants and bring people home, just to make a bit of extra money. We are back at the Basilica hotel, where we are met by two very well-known and very sober Scousers who ask us where we've been. They've been looking for a bar all night and are surprised to see us turn up bladdered. Well, I don't think they were surprised to see me in that state but you know what I mean.

Next morning, I wake up to the smell of eggs and ham. Is right. I had ordered brekky in my room the night before. Five minutes later I'm back in bed and I get up about half one, I think. "We're in a restaurant just off Red Square", say the messages from the Belgian contingent. I really love these clear directions. On my way there I'm joined by a few more Irregulars who guide me to "that English bar near Red Square". Now knowing where the so-called general place to meet is, I leave immediately and go and find my Belgian mates. Marc and Marc have been joined by Marie, our Scouse friend who moved to Zeebrugge all them years ago, married a Belgian and opened a bar/restaurant that, amongst other local seafood dishes, serves the greatest shrimp croquettes known to mankind. Check out The Boat House whenever you get to Zeebrugge please (that'll earn me a pint). And Marie has brought Ringo with her, a West-Flemish drinker and good egg all around. With John and Terry we move back to that one pub, order a few beers and decide on ordering a meal as well. After waiting about an eternity I get served the Russian version of shepherd's pie, which is quite nice. The pub's filling up with well-known match-going faces, still no sign of Mike, and with some three hours to go, we decide to take the underground, then take another "private cab" to the Lokomotiv Stadium. All of a sudden, the match day atmosphere is there. We see plenty of Anzhi, green and yellow smoke bombs and nervous bizzies. We, that's just Terry and me, get rid of a few spares and team up with a Spartak Moscow fan who wants a ticket in our end. "Wait here for our mate Marc", we tell him. Not before going to some kiosk in a shopping centre where we buy some lukewarm cans of Russian lager.

"Did you Liverpool fans really have this friendship thing with the Anzhi fans today?", asks the Spartak lad.

"Apparently so, yes", is our reply. "Why would you do that?"

"Cos we are Liverpool, we'd do that with Spartak as well, or Galatasaray, doesn't matter." The Spartak fan shakes his head in disbelief. A bit later in the ground, after we've been searched half a dozen times and a translator had a thorough look at my banner (I've brought the old "PASS AND MOVE" banner with me and the double "S" in there makes him have a really close look), we understand why, when one of the stewards words it like this:

"They fuck our women, they fuck our religion, they fuck our traditions. They are NOT Russians.", pointing at the Anzhi fans in the main stand. I couldn't care less. To me, they are first and foremost football fans who've followed their team to what's supposed to be a home game for them, but they've probably travelled the same distance as us. Word has it that Suleyman Kerimov, Anzhi's billionaire owner, charters planes for the Anzhi fans to Moscow, but I really wonder if he has personally stepped in for the nearly 14,000 of them?

Anyway, the match is about to kick off and for the second time in this group stage (I had done Berne on a daytrip in the car with Marc (who else) and our great friend Bert to save some money.) I am quite sober. Stop press. Reread. Yes, I find that quite remarkable myself.

Still, quite sober or not, the game is not really that eventful and 0-0 would have been a logical half time score, only for Brad Jones coming out of his goal a bit early and a bit too far, so the giant Traore has quite an easy finish on his hands. 1-0 down at half-time and Mike, whom I finally met after about five minutes into the first half, gives me a rundown of all qualifying possibilities.

Suso comes on in the second half and gives the game and the Liverpool performance a welcome spark, but we fail to convert the few chances we get. Maybe I should stick to drinking…

Which is what we do. It's the usual wait after the game, with paranoid bizzies and soldiers guarding the exit, thankfully this time they are accompanied by nice female stewards who ask us for ciggies. I just knew these Kent would come in handy at some point. It's nice to see the girls wear Justice pins as well.

Some 45 minutes after the end of the game, we're on the metro, ready for some post match bevies. "Next stop Earl's Court," says the underground intercom and it comes as no surprise that Mike guides us (i.e. his mate Steve and me) to another "Che's bar" (where he spent most of last night while his text messages didn't reach me) without a hitch. A huge plate of nachos accompanies our beer, Terry joins up with us, as does one blonde stunner who seems to enjoy our company and intelligent conversations. As her boyfriend doesn't seem to like this, why else would he shove her off her chair so she ends up bang on her arse a couple of yards further. The penny drops that Russian standards haven't necessarily reached what we call civilisation these days. Poor girl, she looked so cute, sitting on my lap.

Anyway, Mike knows another "24 hour bar" and it doesn't take long for us to get stuck into the vodka (and coke). After a while Steve gets into this "I'm drunk and should go home, so Mike will you please help me across the road to our hotel, no I'll stay a bit longer, …" mood. So both of them are in and out and in out of the bar a few times. Meanwhile Terry has spotted a bottle of Hennessy brandy…

Next morning I wake up alone in my room, with a couple of text messages on my phone. "That underground station, 12.30pm". When I meet Terry later on, he tells me we had a few more Hennessy's in that bar, until I found out they had Becherovka as well… Apparently we became bessy mates with some Russian paratroopers, built like brick shithouses, who'd been to Iraq and tried to sell us an IPhone 5. The telly showed the Napoli v Dnipro Dnipropretovsk game and the barmaid said the way I pronounced the Ukrainian team's name was the best and most sexy she's ever heard. Guess who we can get in the next round if we get past Zenit…

NICO VAN DYCK

234

EUROPA LEAGUE LAST 32 1ST LEG.
14TH FEBRUARY 2013
STADION PETROVSKI [21000]. ST PETERSBURG. RUSSIA
ZENIT ST PETERSBURG 2 LIVERPOOL 0

Well that was an eventful trip!

I guess looking back we can say there was an element of 'fun' and we did have a good laugh but I think there was a huge slice of luck that a lot more of us didn't come unstuck over there and someone could have been seriously, seriously injured (or even worse!). Perhaps we should be thankful that they only used iron bars and knuckle-dusters rather than blades. I was genuinely shocked that they were happy to go 40 v 5 'cos I didn't think the Russians were like that. What happened to the 100 v 100 in the woods??

Mark looked horrific in the ground with his teeth missing. Can't believe he came in for the last fifteen minutes when two hours earlier he was unconscious outside the ground!! Spoke to Mark's mates last night and apparently he's a real mess now he's home. They think he's dislocated his shoulder with the beating from the iron bars.

We had a VERY lucky escape on the Metro after the game. There were those lads that piled on and booted me down the carriage, then they followed those others down the steps when we got off and gave them a tw@tting on the platform.

Personally I thought it was FAR worse than Napoli. At least over there you felt an element of control. Stick together, don't do anything stupid and they won't come at you, being the Italian sh#t-houses they are. The Russians however were up for anything and were obviously going round in big numbers just picking off smaller numbers. It was almost like sport for them.

We spoke to some Russians who actually bought us a few vodka's but laughed at suggestions of meeting up over here on Thursday for a few drinks. "No, we come to FIGHT" was the reply. They seemed shocked that we would even suggest that.

Anyway, I thought Saint Petersburg itself was a brilliant city and there was too much to see but I'm glad I made a genuine effort to get out of the hotel early (er, midday!) on each day and go sight-seeing. I was the first to bed each night (3am, 4:30am, 5:30am) so must have been 'slightly' sensible!!

The Church of Spilled Blood was stunning and I enjoyed my walk around the Fortress on Saturday (even if I did slip down a flight of stairs and end up upside down on the edge of the river with blood on my hands and covered in ice!!). Their Council have clearly never heard of grit, I lost count of the times everyone nearly went flying on the ice.

I know you all think I'm joking but I'm definitely not going back there again if we draw them another time. I've no qualms about going back to Napoli or Millwall 'cos there is still some element of control whereas over there it was just roll the dice and hope for the best. You were either lucky (us) or you were not (poor Nico!). When they think a lad with his girlfriend are fair game then you know it's not a nice place.

I've been there once and that's enough for me.
MICHAEL SMITH